Moving Beyond Boundaries

International Dimensions of Black Women's Writing

Companion volume
MOVING BEYOND BOUNDARIES
Volume 2
Black Women's Diaspora

Moving Beyond Boundaries

Volume 1: International Dimensions of Black Women's Writing

EDITED AND INTRODUCED BY
CAROLE BOYCE DAVIES
AND 'MOLARA OGUNDIPE-LESLIE

NEW YORK UNIVERSITY PRESS
Washington Square, New York

First published in the U.S.A. in 1995 by
NEW YORK UNIVERSITY PRESS
Washington Square
New York, N.Y.   10003

Library of Congress Cataloging-in-Publication Data
Moving beyond boundaries / edited and introduced by Carole Boyce
  Davies and 'Molara Ogundipe-Leslie.
    v.   cm.
    Includes bibliographical references and index.
    Summary: v. 1. International dimensions of Black women's writing –
  – .
    ISBN 0-8147-1237-1 (v. 1)
    1. Literature—Black authors. 2. Literature—Women authors.
  3. Literature, Modern—Translations into English. I. Davies,
  Carole Boyce. II. Ogundipe-Leslie, 'Molara.
  PN6068.M68   1994
  808.8'99287'08996—dc20   94-31075
                                  .   CIP

Printed in the EC.

For Aida Cartagena Portalatin 1918–1994

To my daughters Jonelle Ashaki Ayodele Davies and Dalia Abayomi Davies.
May they grow in beauty and strength as young black women.

To all the beautiful black women who have been students in my Black Women
Writers courses over the years and were committed to personal and political
transformations.

CBD

For all the women of the world
through the women of the African diasporas
wherever we are
that we may hold hands in action
across some necessary boundaries

and for all my male friends and brothers
whose faith in me remains steadfast.

'M O-L

Contents

Acknowledgements

A project of this size and breadth could not be completed without the support of a number of people. I would therefore like to identify the following:

Lisa Fegley of the Dean's Office, Arts and Sciences, SUNY-Binghamton, gave critical word-processing advice and assistance. Arlene Norwalk of the English Department, SUNY-Binghamton, helped with inputting some documents.

Celeste Mann provided contacts with Afro-Brazilian women writers, and the Portuguese versions of poems and translations.

Phillis Reisman Butler in particular and the NEH (National Endowment for the Humanities) fellowship to Brazil in 1992 helped in providing initial contact and knowledge of Brazilian culture.

A SUNY-Binghamton Faculty Development Grant allowed me to return to Brazil in summer 1993 where I met, interviewed or talked with Miriam Alves, Lia Vieira, Esmeralda Ribeiro, Sônia Fátima da Conceição, Conceição Evaristo and a number of writers of Quilhomboje in São Paulo.

Daisy Cocco de Filippis offered translations of and contributions from Aida Cartagena Portalatin.

Carol Beane provided translations of Chiriboga.

All the writers in this collection are thanked for their enthusiasm, interest in and patience with this project.

The staff at Pluto Press, particularly Anne Beech, are acknowledged for their initial interest in converting the *Matatu* special issue on 'Black Women's Writing. Crossing the Boundaries' into book form and their ongoing commitment to this ever-expanding project.

Artist Vanda Vaz Ferreira of Salvador-Bahia, Brazil for artistic interpretations of the meaning of these books represented in her cover design.

CBD

Editorial Assistants

The following Binghamton (State University of New York) University students are acknowledged for their time and interest at various stages of the production of this project. Some of them did tasks such as word-processing, handling correspondence, maintaining continuity and other support work which advanced the completion of this ever-mushrooming project.

Greg Thomas	Spring 1992
Siga Jagne	Spring 1992
Marie Soto	Fall 1992
Leo Wilton	Summer 1993
Joel Haynes	Summer 1993
Rhoda Basley	Fall 1993

The title for this two-volume collection comes from the closing lines of Grace Nichols' poem 'New Birth' from her prize-winning collection of poems, *i is a long memoried woman* (London: Karnak House, 1983, p. 67).

NEW BIRTH

Looking into the cascade
of foam
she saw that the hurricane
months had passed

that the air was quickened
with the taste of new birth
and the benediction of the sun

that the frogs were singing
from deep among the mangrove roots

The sun is singing
    the sky is singing
        I am singing into the day
            moving
beyond
      all   boundaries

Preface

'I think that an international network is absolutely essential, and I think it is in the process of being born...
We are brave and daring and we are looking ahead.'

'This is what Black feminism is all about; articulating ourselves, our needs and our resistances as women, and as women within our particular environments. We don't exist in abstract.'

'Our black women's vision has no horizon.'

'I really do like the idea of some day being able to take part in an international conference on Black feminism, a Black women's bookfair, womanist, feminist, whatever you want to call it. And I am planting that vision inside your heads and hopefully maybe you will take it up and help make it happen.'[1]

The quotations above are from Audre Lorde who, wherever she went, promoted the international dimensions of black women's existences; the various interconnections as well as the differences; the necessity of creating and articulating.

For black women, wherever we exist, one common imperative seems to be resistance, *in different ways* and *on different levels*, to a variety of oppressive situations in a variety of contexts as well as the on-going desire to speak for ourselves out of those same realities and indeed in spite of them. Audre Lorde was not able to be physically present to see projects such as this one become reality, but her vision and her own creativity live and continue to inspire. And indeed it is because of work such as hers that a collection such as this can have tangible existence.

I see this collection, *Moving Beyond Boundaries*, as one step towards the realization of that international network of black women. It is also a recognition of the myriad places where we exist and the variety of strategies we use as we speak to (sometimes against) each other across differences. The boundaries we propose to move beyond are those erected to impede our movements and activities, curtail our necessary growth, interfere with our realizing of freedom. These are boundaries of geographical location, national constructs, language, race, gender, sexuality, ability, ethnicity, history, class, politics, social and cultural locations, domination, aesthetics and standards and so on. Black women's writing, then, engages these boundaries at different points, and moves beyond them to reconnect at different levels in different understandings of what our worlds can be.

This two-volume creative and critical collection grew initially out of a special issue of *Matatu*, the journal of African writing edited by Holger Ehling in

Germany. Titled then 'Black Women's Writing. Crossing the Boundaries',[2] it contained critical and creative works by a number of writers from a variety of places. Pluto Press saw it and wanted to bring it out in book form with 'a few pieces' added. Those few pieces have turned into these two volumes, largely because of the tremendous interest from black women writers in many places.

The implications of the growth of this collection for me are many. I would like to identify only a couple: first of all, the necessity of leaving physically, conceptually or emotionally our own limited set of understandings and knowledges is central. This collection could not grow without that type of mental and physical journeying. My own possibilities for travel to a variety of places, of course, facilitated that process. I recognize that these opportunities are not afforded all of us, nor do they often come to many of us, so I am committed to using them to the greatest political advantage. In the summer of 1991, while visiting Toronto for Caribana, I met with 'Molara Ogundipẹ-Leslie who agreed to be co-editor of what at that time was a much smaller, one-volume undertaking and provided address contacts with writers such as Nawal el-Saadawi, who responded enthusiastically with two stories.

Since that time, this project has grown significantly. A six-month stay in London in spring 1992, as a professor in my university's London program, facilitated wider recognition of black women's writing communities in Europe. Then, my travel to Brazil, first as part of an NEH fellowship and subsequently on a university grant, allowed me to meet a variety of black women writers from that country. Many of them asked about black women's movements in the USA. All of these women have spoken of the desire to have an international movement or network which can at least provide knowledge of what others are doing. Attending the Caribbean Women Writers' Conference in Curaçao in the same year facilitated new meetings with Astrid Roemer, Daisy Cocco de Filippis, and Patricia Turnbull, and renewed interactions with people like Mayra Santos Febres. The African Literature Association conference in Guadeloupe allowed me to talk with Carol Beane concerning her work on Afro-Ecuadoran writer Chiriboga. The point I am making, though, is that having access to the material bases for travelling to different locations facilitated connections which in turn allowed work of this nature to advance, but at the same time it carried a responsibility. Still, that access itself can be critiqued and problematized in terms of unequal distribution of resources, even as it makes the point that if we are doing the kind of academic work that challenges the very boundaries of our existence, then we often have to find ways to make these practical connections as we allow the various voices of women to be heard.

In other words, we cannot be comfortable with subsuming definitions, when we ourselves have not bothered to discover the extent of these existences outside of our narrow set of identifications. We therefore cannot speak as black women with any definitiveness, for we do not know the range of our experiences and the dimensions of the various communities of black women who also feel excluded and want to be heard. Ours must be then a posture of constant learning. This of course relates to the ways in which, those who work in the academy, or struggle in communities as cultural workers, or barely manage to eke out a day-to-day living, underestimate the vastness of our existence as black women and get caught in narrow 'minoritizing' understandings of who we are. The black women's diaspora concept, then, is meant to identify black women in the same way that one can talk of the African diaspora in its dispersed and connected implications. Looked at from this particular point of view, one can clearly see a black woman's diaspora existing in a variety of communities in the Americas, Europe, Africa, etc, in communities wherever black women exist.

The mushrooming of this initially limited collection to two volumes is testament to the vastness of the output and speaks already to the need for more possibilities of work for the future. Indeed, there are more black women wanting to be heard than there exist avenues for that hearing. My commitment then is to use the resources at my disposal to make as many of those voices audible as is possible. Otherwise we have a very limited understanding of what constitutes black women's writing, of what we can do creatively and politically, and about the many faces of our realities. An understanding of the international dimensions of this writing, therefore, throws out a range of possibilities for intellectual and creative work.

In her editor's note to *Let It be Told: Black Women Writers in Britain*,[3] Lauretta Ngcobo says words which I want to echo here: 'We have been writing for a long time; it is now that these writings are beginning to come out into the open.' Clearly we are witnessing a rebirth as the Grace Nichols poem from which we get our title indicates. Joanne Braxton and Andrée Nicola McLaughlin, in *Wild Women in the Whirlwind: Afra-American Culture and the Contemporary Literary Renaissance*, would say that 'the current rebirth is the most extensive written exploration of that realm of shared language, reference and allusion within the Veil of our Blackness and our femaleness.'[4]

Moving Beyond Boundaries is expressed in two interrelated volumes. Some of the critical work in Volume II responds to creative writings which are in the first volume. The split between the two volumes developed practically when the decision was made to produce this as a two-volume project and is not meant to replay the creative writer/critic split. Indeed, deliberately beginning with assertions, we present a range of responses, personal and critical, to producing work. We also wanted to give the poetry space so that one can see some of the meanings carried by the poetic voices. Volume I is subtitled *International Dimensions of Black Women's Writing* in order to underscore precisely that in examining black women's writings, we are dealing with a trans-national project that moves beyond narrow national boundaries. Broken into the generic categories of narrative and poetry, the narrative section is titled 'Assertions: Stories, Reflections, Commentaries.' It contains short pieces from writers from a number of cultural sites, speaking reflectively and creatively on their existences. The second section 'Women Weaving Words: Raised Poetic Voices' includes poetry from women from a variety of writing communities. Subtitled *Black Women's Diasporas*, Volume II conceptualizes the need to do work relationally without reproducing the very terms and hierarchies of the institutions. It contains work. It also imagines other worlds of existence which act outside of the particular received geographies that we are forced to inhabit.

In terms of coverage, this collection is limited to written literature; however, it does not preclude knowledge of work on black women's oral culture.[5] Indeed, the writers themselves question issues such as orality and the scripto-centric in writing. The very demands of documenting our existence in this instance occupy the writing arena. We may want, therefore, to see oral strategies in writing, the separate aesthetics and ideologies of orality and writing as well as their interrelatedness. Geographical coverage is another area which needs to be identified and remapped. The intent was not to cover every area and every writing community of the world where black women create,[6] but, with the resources available, to work towards representativeness and to strive towards the possibility of full inclusiveness. Any shortcomings in this area are not for lack of trying but for the limitations of this particular project. Failures at full coverage, then, are not because of original intent or willful desire to exclude, as has historically been the lot of black women writers and critics, but stem from the availability of materials, access, and so on.

So, these volumes are not offered in any sense of definitiveness, but more as contributions to challenging conceptually the various invisibilities, erasures, marginalizations, silencings. Each new contribution does its work. It is our hope, therefore, that this will not be seen as an end. In fact, hidden here are the many processes of interconnection which went into the production of this volume.

Fawzziyah Abu Khalid wrote in August 1993: 'It's a warm and supportive feeling to know poetry from the heart of the desert is included in your collection.' So, even as it represents the culmination of work, *Moving Beyond Boundaries*, as its title suggests, represents simply another set of movements. We re-imagine, as we re-engage the task of 'writing new worlds' into existence.

Carole Boyce Davies
May 1994

Notes

1. Audre Lorde in interview with Pratibha Parmar and Jackie Kay in *Charting the Journey. Writing By Black and Third World Women* (London: Sheba Feminist Publishers, 1988), pp. 129–31.
2. 6:3 (Jahrgang 1989).
3. Lauretta Ngcobo (ed.), *Let It be Told: Black Women Writers in Britain* (London: Virago Press, 1988), p. ix.
4. Joanne Braxton and Andrée Nicola McLaughlin, *Wild Women in the Whirlwind: Afra-American Culture and the Contemporary Literary Renaissance* (New Brunswick, NJ: Rutgers University Press, 1990), p. xxii.
5. See the special issue on African women oral artists *Research in African Literatures* (forthcoming), edited by 'Molara Ogundipẹ-Leslie and Carole Boyce Davies. Indeed, our work tends to address orality and writing in different ways.
6. In this context we applaud Margaret Busby for her time and diligence in editing *Daughters of Africa. An International Anthology of Words and Writings by Women of African Descent from the Ancient Egyptian to the Present* (London: Jonathan Cape and New York: Pantheon Books, 1992).

Introductions: Crossings

Hearing Black Women's Voices: Transgressing Imposed Boundaries

Carole E. Boyce Davies

Hearing Black Women's Voices

I begin by asserting that it is not only the condition of silence and voicelessness that seems the most pressing at this historical moment but the function of *hearing* or *listening* on the part of those who wield oppressive power. In my view then, we need to foreground the need to HEAR WOMEN'S VOICES as well as MAKING WOMEN'S VOICES HEARD and therefore activate a conceptual challenge to selective hearing or mis-hearing. The appropriate critique of the inability of oppressors to HEAR allows for more resistance. Indeed, while some women have been silent or silenced, many black women have spoken incessantly without fully being heard and have often reached the point where they say nothing verbally and instead operate from a silence which often speaks eloquently.

The dual process of 'speaking anyhow' as well as critiquing 'strategic deafness' addresses some of the ways in which silencings have become entrenched.

Historically, for black women, physical and emotional brutality and various forms of epistemic violence often have been directed at curtailing articulations. The denial of black women's voices produces that emotional memory and stress which can implode or come out in explosive ways. This in turn produces another construction: that of the 'angry black woman.' Still it must be noted that it is not always anger that one sees in black women who have learned to speak, but passion. And in a culture where passion is negated, except in sexuality, a person who speaks passionately to issues is assigned to anger by the passionless.

Hearing, we know, is more than the function of attuning the ears to receiving sounds. Listening is not necessarily passive. Rather, both speech and hearing entail a series of developed responses which indicate meaning and understanding (or 'overstanding' as the Rastas would say). Just as in the transformation of silence into language and action, in Audre Lorde's words,[1] there also has to be a transformation which links hearing with action. Ideally, words should affect change, produce knowledge and create some material response. The critique that we can levy then is the kind of actions or non-actions which follow the denial of a 'hearing' in such a way that they consign black women's writing and thinking to the not spoken, not said, non-existent, the distorted, misunderstood or erased. Even in a time of great production of black women's writing, one still finds at the institutional levels, only cursory attention paid to this field: a course here and there in some department's curriculum; a book here and there in somebody's syllabus, often none. And at the level of government and media institutions, one still finds black women being denied a hearing or being defined as not credible speakers in their own right.[2]

The contemporary contexts for speaking about black women's literary voices are located in the larger framework of the ways in which black women's voices are heard or not heard in the various public and private arenas of discourse.[3] This introduction takes as its concern the necessity of locating black women's writing in these myriad contexts. This position comes out of the fact that historically there have been few avenues for the full hearing of black women's testimonies. Instead there have been systematic attempts to discredit us as credible representatives of ourselves. These attempts have ranged from the larger institutional structures where black women's voices are often absent to the local levels of women's communities where black women's voices are often dismissed as irrelevant. It may finally be that it is only within black communities that black women are assured some hearing. In churches, black women's testimonies are affirmed, supported. Still, in other contexts, we can sometimes experience situations in which there is no automatic support by black women of other black women's right to articulate themselves. And while this latter may point to the need within the general category of black women to identify the various sites of difference, there has to be some consideration, in each situation, of relationships to power and oppressive systems in a variety of societies and the ways in which many black women are distanced by or operate within these.

Public spaces for speech have been generally identified with paradigms of masculinity, rational discourse, absence or emotion, developed logical arguments, control of representations and so on. The senate, congress, courts, universities, media, pulpits, publishing houses, professional conferences are places of public speech. These sites of public speech have been historically barred to women. Instead, women were consigned to the domestic space or private sphere where a certain kind of talk was tolerated if it was about domestic issues, children, the home. Besides that, for a long time, there were certain issues which were considered private and therefore unspeakable: rape, date rape, marital rape, sexual harassment, incest, domestic violence, abortion, childbirth, and breastfeeding. And these are some of the subjects that some women who have spoken publicly have articulated. The shifting of privatized discourses to the public arena creates empowerment of women. But therein may also lie the accompanying repression and application of 'strategic deafness.'

Black women's position in a variety of societies can be apprehended by a series of analyses which take into consideration and interweave issues of race, class, gender, sexuality, national origin, ability and a variety of other conditions which produce a variety of subject positions. All of these are implicated in the ability to have access to public discourse. But, at the same time, we can be clear that all black women can be shuttered into the monolithic category of 'any black woman' by dominating systems with their various cultural inscriptions concerning that gendered/racialized identity. Issues of personal self-presentation as well as interpellation by dominant concepts of what any woman should be are implicated. Thus for black women, aspects of external representation consisting of phenotypic characteristics with their historical inscriptions (issues of hair, color, facial characteristics, physical features, and even clothing), are identified and immediately linked to competence, status, recognition.

We can therefore make distinctions between the condition of silence, being silenced, silencing, on the one hand, and what has been referred to by some as voicelessness and coming to voice or talking back on the other.[4] It is necessary to retrace a bit more of the discussion of voicelessness[5] which relates to the fact that, historically, black women were seen/are seen/have been seen as having nothing important to say. At the turn of the century, in the United States, records say, the following people who could not testify in court (i.e. have their voices heard publicly on issues): women, black people, children, the physically or mentally challenged. Black women during slavery and its aftermath had no protection from harassment, abuse, rape. Nobody listened to a black women when she said she was in pain, abused. Our bodies were for the taking. A black woman had no rights that anybody had to acknowledge. In all of the black female slave narratives, the history of sexual harassment of black women by both white and black men as well as by white women has been written. The reality is that the history of black women's experience under oppression was constructed as a lie, even in the face of evidence like a blue-eyed baby who looked just like master.

Thus, when a black woman gets up in a crowd to speak, (or presents herself publicly), she has to battle all the cultural and historical meanings about her even to begin to speak and then the content of her speaking is already framed as non-speech or not important.[6] The enforced dominant options have been:

1. be silent
2. speak only privately
3. speak only to your own community
4. speak out critically in the public arena and face the abusive consequences.

But it is also out of a recognition and understanding of that particular positionality that black women can express resistance. For, indeed, black women occupy a range of class positions in a variety of societies and have different access to hearing. So it becomes necessary, even as we provisionally use some of the language, to disrupt for ourselves the monolithic categories like 'community,' 'black,' 'women' and examine them in terms of a variety of writers and speakers and their relationships to these. And black women who recognize their access can use this to best advantage or become like the one woman juror in Audre Lorde's poem 'Power' who 'let go the first real power that she ever had,' in this case the power to speak against brutality by condemning its perpetrators.[7]

The larger question is, does any black woman have equal access to speech which is respected and really heard? While this may seem to be a moot question when we factor in the successes of some black women writers, the question still needs to addressed in various ways. It may be that because creative writing occupies the discursive field of the fictional, then it is easy for dominant culture to locate black women writers within the emotive, the expressive and not within the realm of the transformative and communicative. This is, it seems to me, radically oppositional to the way that black women readers relate to black women's texts at the level of necessary truths. For the social relations which produce black women's texts are often erased by the larger level of the economy of textual production: the academy, the larger community, the media.

Of significance in this discussion as well is the fact that while black women academics are witnessing and producing substantial research on black women, this has not yet had any major impact on the institutions, the state and their apparata, the masses of people. Indeed, the great deal of research and writing by black women on the conditions of black women's lives in the last decades does not seem to effect measurably how black women negotiate the rest of the society. A great deal of developing black feminist thought and revelation of the history of black women's roles in women's movements has taken place and now exists as a body of literature, but it circulates among the universities for the privileged who interact with some of these institutions and there are few mechanisms for community education and the utilization of these ideas. This, in part, explains why it is still possible to hear from black women themselves, as from the dominant culture, the most negative and uninformed representations of ideas concerning black women's history and women's empowerment.

It is very clear that we live in a climate where white men, in particular, feel that they are being/have been disenfranchised by the claims of many subordinated groups. Rather than find a way to negotiate and share power, many feel threatened and believe that it is their rightful legacy to maintain oppressive power. The issue of 'white male paranoia' entails, for example in the USA and Europe, the resurgence of organizations which have terrorized all groups and peoples defined by their societies as subordinate. In reality, however, white men still control between 90 and 95 per cent of all institutions – political systems, the business world, educational politics, the legal profession, construction industries, and the list goes on. The question we have to ask is the extent to which we take seriously the ones who are victimizing and claiming to be victimized all at the same time. The result is summarized in the pose of the complete paranoiac, a stock character in many films, who claims to be feeling threatened while all the while holding the devices that can destroy masses of people. The truth is that the most recent statistics on women and work indicate that the sexual division of labor in favor of men is still intact. And this means further that black women still remain historically distanced from sources of institutional power. So again, how do black women's literary voices exist in an empowering way in the midst of these realities? And what does it mean to produce another book on black women? Further, which black women can have access to the creation and production of literary texts?

In spite of all the negativities which can produce that enforced silence in many, I want still to assert some agency and the possibility of transformational politics and discourses which struggle for positive change. For black women's self-defining options for articulation are multiple even in the midst of censorship. Because we live in a time of complexity and contradiction, it is even more critical for black women to find multiple ways to raise their own voices and locate the sources of their power. Historical research is revealing the existing record of the insertion of the words of a variety of black women throughout history. Sojourner Truth, the famous women's rights' activist and anti-abolitionist had to battle these identified negative meanings and inscriptions whenever she rose to spoke. These included catcalls, eye-rolling, jeers, hooting, booing, and taunts which she had to silence and speak against. In effect, we can understand the assumption that black women are already silenced in the various authorities and power contexts in society.[8] But that does not mean we have to accept silencing. Like Sojourner, we speak and write anyhow. And the extent to which we are heard or listened to is directly related to the extent to which we challenge 'deafness,' 'blindness,' 'distortion,' and comprehension levels among those in power.

If we shift more deliberately some of the terms of current discourse away from silencing and speechlessness into other related questions (such as: When is black women's speech heard? When is black women's speech taken seriously? Who really listens to black women? What is the audience for black women's writing? Which black women are credible?), then those who practice selective hearing become the ones with the disability. Some of these questions have resided implicitly in the various discourses on speech and silence but tended to exist in submerged ways.[9]

The travesty of any oppression is when that same ideology is transferred to the oppressed and we begin to mouth the same language. Then we know that the oppression-of-self which is the final task of all oppression is in operation. For this reason, I affirm categorically the right of black women to speak out of their many realities and be heard out of the variety of their experiences and locations. And it is for me there that black women's writing attains its agency.

Within the terms of post-modernist discourse, according to Lyotard, silence can be taken as a text of speech. Still it is a non-speech in the sense of silence being equated with complicity (meaning you agree or give consent to what is happening) or silence equals silence death. Arguing that silence is not always a negative, especially when it is a voluntary act, Irene Assiba d'Almeida makes an interesting distinction between being silent and being silenced.[10] Thus, if a woman who is being raped at gunpoint is forced into silence, that does not mean she is complicitous in her own oppression. We may therefore want to stress 'being silenced' rather than the condition of 'silence' which in certain contexts can be more powerful than speech. If we were to ask the question how are women silenced, we can answer that the process of silencing takes place in many forms.[11] Everyone is born with some means of articulating or speech, but people can lose speech or their ability to communicate positively in society.

Maya Angelou in *I Know Why the Caged Bird Sings* describes being silenced by rape and sexual abuse and later of silencing herself for a number of years.[12] Still, this is the same person who in later years became an empowered speaker. In many cultures, bell hooks would assert that the right speech of womanhood is silence. In some cultures a beautiful woman is often defined as serene, silent, immobile. Women are often trained in silence. Little girls are cautioned and warned and sometimes beaten into silent submission for daring to question, or talk back, 'give lip' or otherwise speak. In addition, when women speak, their speech can be defined as or become gossip, small talk, baby talk, chattering, jabbering, fussing, prattling, and so on.

But women do talk, have historically spoken, do take the right to speak and do have the right to be heard. But there are different levels and contents of speech and different modes of expression ranging from mere articulation of a presence to significant/creative/informed speech. These also entail the ability positively to affect government policy, to change things, to affect the outcome of events, to alter situations, and thereby finally to be heard. This suggests knowledge, confidence, validation, affirmation and even recognizing lack of information or complete knowledge and knowing strategically when to speak. And whether we are heard or not at that point relates more deliberately to the ignorance of the audience or the disability in the intended receiver of these words.

Transgressive speech, bell hooks would assert, challenges situations of oppression, challenges power and talks back to authority when necessary, regardless of the consequences. Speech and speaking out and coming to voice are all forms of the search for modes of articulation by black women, locating places of authority, identifying the issues that are critical to our survival as a people and, above all, expressing the inner feelings, needs, and desires of black women in society. One may argue then that black women's writing occupies the position of transgressive speech because it transgresses the boundaries and locations for black women within the context of societal authorities and norms.

We may want to also identify women's communities where speech is validated and learn from them. It may also be necessary to recognize double messages or coded speech. The ability to speak in different ways at the same time (*Gumboyaya* of New Orleans)[13] as well as with a variety of reversals and double meanings also has relevance. In that context too it is necessary similarly to identify the pool of bad advice and negativity which women sometimes speak. Hearing ourselves speak also necessitates a certain literacy, critical analysis and cultural critique in the recognition of coded words as in the songs of slavery, testifying, speaking in tongues. It also may include the long reflective vision of life story as in *Having Our Say*.[14] It also demands different conceptual and theoretical strategies to locate black women's testimonies in different contexts historically.

Black Women's Writing: Transgressing Imposed Boundaries

The boundaries imposed to contain black women's full expression of their creativity include those of geography, nation, language, ideology, religion, sexuality, economic and social class, poverty, Eurocentric media, literary, historical, philosophical and other canons. Studying black women's writing in cross-cultural contexts must begin with the challenge to the assumption of North American/African-American identity as synonymous with Black women's writing in its entirety. This limitation works only to curtail our broader recognition of the many locations of our selves.

The contribution that this collection of writing makes is the expansion of the recognition of black women's writing. As an international category, with voices of black women from diverse places, generations, locations, expressing positions on a variety of issues, black women's writing has an existence beyond our limited imaginings. The issues of orality, non-scribal forms of writing have to be equally considered in any consideration of black women's speech and writing.[15] For if we operate completely out of the scriptocentric, we again institute a series of denials about the range and intensity of women's cultural production.

How do black women get heard? By assertively and bold-facedly transgressing the imposed boundaries; by being insistent, supportive; by speaking constantly directly or indirectly, though in multiple forms but always demanding hearing; by challenging the pretended disabilities of hearing; by constantly creating. This first volume of *Moving Beyond Boundaries. International Dimensions of Black Women's Writing* is divided into two parts. Part I, 'Assertions' contains stories, reflections, commentaries, essays. It is not limited to specific generic categories, shading the autobiographical reflection and the fictional story into the motivations and modes of writing. It contains contributions from women from a range of geographical locations, speaking out of their many experiences as black women in the world. They deal with questions of speech and creativity as do Atsango Chesoni, 'If I Speak I am Not Heard and if I Scream, I am "Hysterical"' and Opal Palmer Adisa's 'I Will Raise the Alarm: Contemporary Cross-cultural Sites of Racism and Sexism.' They articulate ways in which women find a writing path and creative mode as in Beryl Gilroy's 'Writing, Ancestry, Childhood and Self,' and Marion Bethel's 'Bringing Myself into Fiction,' and Marlene Nourbese Philip's 'Journal Entries Against Reaction: Damned if We Do and Damned if We Don't,' and Sheila Mysorekar, 'Pass the Word and Break the Silence – The Significance of African-

American and Third World Literature for Black Germans.' A number of pieces deal with writing, migration, gender and identity. These include Pat McFadden's 'Who Loves New York?' and Carole Boyce Davies' 'It's Cold Outside.' Specific questions of cultural experiences are identified in Nawal el-Saadawi's, 'The Price of Illusion' and Catherine Obianuju Acholonu's 'Mother was a Great Man,' and Eintou Pearl Springer's 'Man Peaba, Woman Peaba: Women and Folk Birthing in Trinidad and Tobago,' and the excerpt from Chiriboga's *Bajo la piel de los tambores* (Under the Skin of the Drums). Astrid Roemer's selection from her 'A Woman's Madness' speaks to the many struggles that women undergo in the process of finding sane relationships. This section closes with Ogundipe-Leslie's discourse on the poetic voice and language in an African and Diaspora context.

Part II, 'Women Weaving Words: Raised Poetic Voices' contains poetry from contemporary black women writers from as many language and geographical regions as we were able to receive work. I am particularly proud of the responses from the Black Brazilian women writers, Sônia Fátima da Conceição, Conceição Evaristo, Lia Vieira, Esmeralda Ribeiro, Miriam Alves, with whom I met and developed rapport. Black women writers from Britain, like Shanta Acharya, Sister Netifa, Maya Chowdhry, Dorothea Smartt, and Isha McKenzie-Mavinga, appear here as fitting representatives of the range of black women's poetic voices in Europe. In this particular context, the definitions of what constitutes a black woman's identity capture the complexity of that definition in Britain, including women of Indian and African descent. We made the attempt to include writers who are not normally canonical. In that context, as in any opening up of a discourse, the popularly identified writers have to be balanced by other voices. Many of these writers are getting their first exposure to a major audience in ways which a number of more established writers take for granted. For African-American writers in the USA, the work of black lesbian writer Jewelle Gomez, and other voices like Chezia Thompson-Cager, Gloria Wade Gayles, Rosemari Mealy are included with the more experienced writer Sonia Sanchez. We are pleased to have Nancy Morejón from Cuba contributing as well as work of Aida Cartagena Portalatin from Dominica and Mayra Santos Febres from Puerto Rico. In addition, newer voices such as Donna M. Weir, Lissette Norman, Joel Haynes, Gina Amaro, Jacqueline Brice-Finch. From the Anglophone Caribbean we are ably represented with poetry from Velma Pollard, Eintou Pearl Springer, Opal Palmer Adisa, Patricia Turnbull. The themes span the range of experiences, identities, locations, experiences, struggles, which black women face wherever they are. From Canada, Afua Cooper, Marlene Philip; from Francophone Caribbean and Africa, Yanick François and Irene Assiba d'Almeida; Amelia Blossom Pegram from South Africa; and Atsango Chesoni from East Africa and Abena Busia from Ghana.

One of the points to be identified in working on this collection or other related collections is the difficulty of full coverage. I see this collection as another step in a long process of building more visibility and audibility to the still developing picture and sound of the extent and range of black women's voices.

Addendum: On Speech, Silence, and Hearing

Questions of black women's voice were posed to a series of black women writers classes in collaborative learning processes. Some of their discussion is presented here in summary form.

I.   We can summarize silence and voicelessness as:

- not having anything to say
- the sense of always saying the wrong thing
- saying something which is ignored but which when said by others is taken as a serious point
- not being able to express a position
- words, arguments, and being intimidated into silence (Onwueme)[16]
- the death of words and so of action
- being forcibly silenced through external restraining devices in and over the mouth, as during slavery, and in contemporary times using social conditions, threats
- being removed from the centers of literary, public, discursive, or canonical authority.

II.   Women are silenced by:

- male dominance
- male control of language
- informal training at home
- training in school to be silent
- levels of education
- acceptance of the social value of woman's place in society
- other speakers (including other women)
- certain negative relationships
- public censorship
- self-censorship and self-doubt
- complacency
- fear of public speaking
- feeling one has nothing to say
- religious authority
- traditional values of community
- feeling the issue does not affect anyone
- fear of misinterpretation

- fear of being challenged
- fear of being hurt
- fear of being laughed at
- physical intimidation and threat
- deferring to authority
- economic position
- feeling they have no authority
- not having knowledge of subject
- discomfort with appearance (how one looks, is dressed, body size, etc.)
- fear of being construed as insane, evil or shrew-like
- fear of being characterized as difficult
- fear of not being liked by men
- violence, rape, physical abuse, and sexual harassment.

III. Women come to voice in writing or speaking or break through silencing by:

- recognizing the disempowering nature of silence when speech is demanded
- the examples of other women who speak
- learning from ourselves and each other
- cooperative/collaborative work and support
- developing self-assurance and confidence
- forming positive friendships and relationships
- forming positive groups
- training the next generation
- counseling and therapy
- expressing one's private thoughts in writing in diaries, journals
- raising one's voice (even yelling and screaming when not being heard)
- learning voice and tone control
- forgetting about self-censorship and control
- feeling more comfortable with oneself
- storytelling/singing
- finding ways to educate others
- moving from object to subject
- respecting other women's voices
- using body language and gestures which support other women when they speak
- referring to the speech and words of others who have been silenced
- working with modulation, pauses, techniques of articulation
- avoiding dumb (blonde) speech and/or baby talk
- avoiding preambles to speech that censor oneself (I may be wrong but...)
- locating one's sources of authority
- locating oneself in society and speaking from there

- giving others the right to speak
- watching interruptions and challenging those who would interrupt us
- interrupting, where necessary, discourses that are being framed to make us complicit or to distort or exclude us
- being conscious of the dangers of 'speaking for others'
- speaking anyhow
- practicing ways of speaking
- being boldfaced.

IV. Finding the source of our power in creative speech. One's personal creative power, personal passion, erotic, life energy or *ashe* can be obtained and developed in many ways. Some of the approaches which have worked have been through:

- seeking positive associations and organizations
- keeping away from negative energies and communities of negative circulated thought
- community involvement
- educating ourselves beyond what we think we know
- learning to think critically to do discourse analysis of all texts
- seeking modes of personal empowerment
- recognizing one's *ashe* through non-western traditions of spirituality as different from western conceptions of power
- affirming solidarity with other women's struggles
- being oneself involved in struggle for social change
- moving out of the debates of identity to actual practice
- living the transforming silence into speech and action (Lorde)
- speaking anyhow if not speaking proper (Merle Collins)[17]
- talking back (bell hooks)
- giving tongue (Marlene Philip,[18] Moraga and Anzaldua[19])
- finding modes of speaking out
- expressing oneself creatively for oneself
- reading/hearing the other women's words
- finding the ability to recognize creativity as self-healing.

Notes

1. Audre Lorde, 'The Transformation of Silence into Language and Action', in *Sister Outsider* (Freedom, Ca: The Crossing Press, 1984), pp. 36–39.
2. The public mishearing and/or denial of hearing of two black women lawyers, Anita Hill and Lani Guinier, in the US in the 1990s are cases in point.

3. bell hooks in *Talking Back. Thinking Feminist. Thinking Black* (Boston: South End Press, 1989) has pursued this issue in a variety of ways.
4. hooks, *Talking Back*. Ella Baker in the film *Fundi* speaks on various occasions of the principle of 'talking back' and how it related to her empowerment.
5. See for example the introduction to *Out of the Kumbla. Caribbean Women and Literature* (Trenton, NJ: Africa World Press, 1990).
6. See relatedly Gayatri Spivak's 'Can the Subaltern Speak?' in Cary Nelson and Martin Grossberg (eds), *Marxism and the Interpretation of Culture* (Urbana and Chicago, IL: University of Illinois Press, 1988), pp. 271-313.
7. Audre Lorde, 'Power', in her collection *The Black Unicorn* (New York: Norton, 1978), pp. 108-9.
8. See for example Spivak's discussion in 'Can the Subaltern Speak?'
9. See for example hooks, *Talking Back*, pp. 14-15.
10. In the introduction to her forthcoming work, *Francophone African Women Writers: Destroying the Emptiness of Silence* (University of Florida Press, 1994).
11. See Addendum for lists of avenues of silencings.
12. Maya Angelou, *I Know Why the Caged Bird Sings* (New York: Random House, 1969).
13. See Luisa Teish, *Jambalaya: The Natural Woman's Book of Personal Charms and Practical Rituals* (San Francisco: Harper and Row, 1985).
14. Sarah and A. Elizabeth Delany with Amy Hill Hearth, *Having Our Say. The Delany Sisters' First 100 Years* (New York: Kodansha International, 1993).
15. Widely cognizant of the importance of woman's role in orature 'Molara Ogundipe-Leslie and I are editing a special issue of *Research in African Literature* on the issue of women oral artists. This collection is limited to written work.
16. See Tess Onwueme, 'Bodies In Silence. The Missing Diaspora in African Literature'. *Drum Voices Revue* Fall-Winter, 1992/3 2:1/2, pp. 157-169.
17. Text of presentation at Caribbean Women Writers' Conference, Trinidad, 1990.
18. Marlene Nourbese Philip, *She Tries Her Tongue. Her Silence Softly Breaks* (Charlottetown, Prince Edward Island, Canada: Ragweed Press, 1989).
19. Moraga, *This Bridge Called My Back* and Gloria Anzaldua (ed.), *Making Face, Making Soul. Writings by Women of Color* (San Francisco, Calif.: Spinsters/Aunt Lute, 1990)

Women in Africa and Her Diaspora: From Marginality to Empowerment

'Mọlara Ogundipẹ-Leslie

Does the trajectory from marginality to empowerment apply only to the experience of African women and the African diaspora? Granted that all the terms of feminist and women's studies discourses need to be defined and re-defined in their contextual specificities and perspectives, African women, wherever they are, are not the most marginalized women on earth, contrary to the western social Darwinian habit of assuming that the African rests at the bottom of every scale. In some ways, African women had economic and social structures which gave them more social space and clout than their European sisters. Nonetheless, all women of the world are discriminated against and subordinated first as women and second as members of subordinate classes. In their biological subordination and exploitation lies a certain undeniable and binding global sisterhood.

If I am asked quickly to enumerate the common bonds of our global sisterhood, I would say:

1. biological oppression
2. patriarchy
3. exclusion from the material and mental resources of our societies
4. overwork: our double, triple, sometimes quadruple overload; physical hardship and suffering within production and reproduction
5. persecution for demanding equity and ending the silences used to entrap and divide us as women; persecution for organizing ourselves at last and for seeking to empower ourselves psychologically and structurally in society.

The UN Women's Decade brought the women of the world together to educate us about the differences that enrich our similarities. In Nairobi, Kenya (1985), we discussed our 'connections' and made our 'acknowledgements', Gloria T. Hull says. The women's movement discovered itself as women all over the world discovered each other, over and above the often specious and divisive confrontations between Western Feminism and Third World Womanism, actively promoted by enemies of the women's movement, particularly male sexists and reactionary women.

We could problematize the title of this essay: 'From marginality to empowerment?' When were women marginal? In their different societies and cultures? What were the natures of these marginalities? When did women's empowerment begin? What are power and powerlessness? In what time and space in their various societies were women powerless and empowered? How did marginality and empowerment work across the mediations of age, status, role, and variables within the kinship system; race, class, caste, and gender; ethnicity, geography, and nation; history, culture, and sexual orientation?

As African women of color who have been displaced into the United States of America, Canada, and the Caribbean, Latin America, Britain and the rest of Europe and the world; as displaced Africans, we have our own particular insertions into these problematics. At the risk of not having the time and space here for explicatory refinement, I suggest that women of Africa and her diaspora desire, within communitarian ideals, respect for and recognition of their contributions to their communities as individuals with collectively acknowledged identities. They do not wish to be worked to death productively and reproductively and they also wish to share and enjoy the world's resources. They wish to share in whatever there is to be learned and enjoyed in this wide, rich, and beautiful world, not to live and die only as somebody's pots of culture and suffering, the pots which receive the filtered water of other people's indigo dye of fulfillment; living vicariously only.

To these ends, African women in Africa and her diaspora, like other women of color around the world, are identifying their own issues (and not always antagonistically to other groups) while insisting that women of hegemonic societies and classes must eliminate their destructive patterns whether they be socially expressed or just internalized. Women of color across classes know that they have to struggle for physical and spiritual survival, as bell hooks once pointed out, in a racist cosmos where race has been a factor of historical and economic oppression.

Women of the African heritage know they must discover and affirm healthy and genuine versions of their various identities. They must discover class roles which will contribute to the positive development of women locally and globally. They must give voice to the historically harassed black women of African descent and empower them to subvert their self-crippling silences. They are coming together now as black women of African descent around their identities, as the great woman poet Audre Lorde says, in an impassioned essay (1986), questioning and redefining what that Africanness could mean within our particular communities, and upon the world stage; and not in the abstract, either, but concretely as in the lives of Afro-German or Afro-Dutch women, for example. We must discover 'diaspora literacy' and, through it, strengthen our similarities through our differences and our inalienable historical common origins and experiences. Not only does 'race through oppression' link us but also culture as filtered and burnished in the crucibles of captivity, displacement, and oppression. Throughout these excruciating processes, the resilience of our spirits and original cultures has come through.

We celebrate this resilience, the 'getting over', ourselves and our peoples, women and men, who evolved these cultures!

What does empowerment mean to us as black women of Africa and her diaspora? It means social recognition and dignity just as, most of all, it means space to speak, act, and live with joy and responsibility; as it has always meant for our ever-so responsible foremothers wherever they were in history. Our work, writings and exhortations as women in various forms and media show that we want to end our silences and speak our truths as we know them. We wish to have power which recognizes responsibility in dignified freedom; power which positively promotes Life in all its forms; power to remove from our path any thing, person, or structure which threatens to limit our potential for full human growth as the other half of life's gendered reality; power to collapse all screens that threaten to obscure our women's eyes from the beauties of the world.

Part I

Assertions:
Stories, Reflections, Commentaries

I Will Raise the Alarm: Contemporary Cross-cultural Sites of Racism and Sexism

Opal Palmer Adisa

'Wolf-crier! Wolf-crier!' they taunted. I held my ground because I saw the wolf, but they wanted to silence me. Something was not right. As far back as I can remember, I have been inquisitive. I have always sought to know the whys and whereofs of things. As a child, many adults said I was precocious, others claimed my mother indulged me too much, still others suggested that I needed a padlock placed on my mouth and blinders put over my eyes. Nonetheless, I persisted with my numerous questions, and always I sought more explanation. What was so wrong about asking questions and seeking answers for things that were puzzling? Why were silence and acquiescence demanded? I was told girls were prettier with their mouths closed, and blacks would get further by following the rules. 'But why?' I probed. 'That's the way things are,' was the reply. This response made no sense to me. The ocean was my favorite place, and it was fluid, constantly moving, sometimes calmly, but other times torrential. Why then, because I was female and black, must I be passive? Growing up in Jamaica, I had observed that the docile children in my neighborhood were always picked on and beaten up by the bolder, more daring ones. Boys were allowed aggression, and the lighter complexion children were allowed more errors, more freedom to be themselves. Something was wrong. I raised the alarm, and was dismissed as being jealous. The wolf wore many different faces, and established the rules for his benefit. So that when I, and those like me, protest this diabolic, unfair system, we are jeered and labeled wolf-criers.

It is this experience that leads me to reexamine the tale of the boy and the wolf. I wonder if the wolf was a stranger to the boy? Perhaps the boy was zoophobic. I remember being told about the little boy who cried wolf, and for his crime was abandoned when the wolf did attack. The lesson was clear: do not cry out until danger is imminent. But what does that mean? Wasn't the wolf lurking around all the while, waiting for the moment to strike? Why didn't a single person respond to the boy's continuous pleas? Aren't the people also to be blamed for the wolf's attack? I never understood, and still don't, why it was so bad for the little boy to cry wolf before the others saw the wolf. The wolf was there, and did strike. So why is silence being demanded? Who is benefiting? Who is being victimized? The boy and the wolf figure as a trope, a vehicle to warn those – women/people of color – who would speak out against their oppression. The warning is clear: to attempt such daring is futile; your own cries

21

will be used to make you seem like a troublemaker, a nuisance, even an imbecile. Do not cry out.

Likewise, I must not raise the alarm. Perhaps I shouldn't cry out at all. This certainly seems to be the message, in this the decade of the 1990s in the US. The liberals tell me that this is the era for black women, especially writers; look at the success and acclaim of Toni Morrison and Alice Walker. 'Only two!' I exclaimed. Yet there are so many, many more. Why aren't they heard from? Is there only room for one or two? The 'star' mentality or marginality? The liberals shake their heads in annoyance, move to a safer subject, insist that sexism is on the decline, and that the black woman is in vogue. The marxists, ensconced in academia, say I'm overreacting; the problem is class; race is not the issue. Once the whole political and economic order is transformed, race will fade into the background. I look at my black skin, examine the history of racism and conclude that race is an important and crucial factor. 'Misinterpretation of facts! Nationalism!' the marxists utter in dismay. And those with incomes above $50,000 and in secure government jobs call me a wolf-crier who, rather than face my deficiencies, shifts the blame, and looks for handouts. Haven't I heard about pulling myself up by the boot-straps? 'I am qualified,' I scream, but no one hears me. There is a mumble: 'Affirmative action, again.'

Why did the little boy cry wolf? Was he phobic? Did he see a wolf lurking near the sheep that retreated into the bushes whenever help came? Was the little boy a nuisance, simply seeking attention? The implication, in the telling of the tale, is that the little boy wanted attention. Maybe he was lonely. Yet the wolf appeared and devoured the sheep. How do I prove sexual harassment? Is it enough to say that my male boss makes sexual remarks, that every time he passes me he puts his hand on my shoulder, or that he tells me I am sexy and that he would really like to get to know me better, all the while his eyes roving my body like a wolf? Perhaps I should wait until he secludes me in his office, presses his body against mine and tries to force his tongue into my mouth? Am I a wolf-crier if the very first time he makes a sexual remark I report him?

How do I prove racism in the US when, as a black person, a black female in particular, it is assumed that I am an oversensitive bitch? Do I first investigate everyone's qualifications in the office, try to determine who is making more money than me even though they have less experience and qualification, wait to see how many times I am passed up for a promotion, try to mingle more with my co-workers, smile more, be more like them, and at all costs avoid mentioning my ethnicity? Then, and only then, if all this fails, provide a documented report of all my findings, beginning with the first day of my employment with the company? Never, never mention that offensive word – racism – before I can prove, without a shadow of a doubt, that such is the case. I am reminded that I/we tend to be hyper-sensitive on the subject. Strange, isn't it, that the onus is always on me/us, to prove that 'they' are who they are, and what we know them to be. The wolf knows the game, and the little boy falls prey to the rules over and over again. This sequence of events will only stop when the boy realizes that the rules only apply to him. I, a black woman, am that little boy.

The media and those sociologists who see African-Americans as an aberration say it's not politically correct these days to cry racism or sexism; these issues have been exploited (by whom I would like to know, and to whose advantage?) much too much in the past, and what those of us who profess to care about change need to do is to get ourselves qualified. (Always, the assumption is that we are not qualified.) Stop crying wolf; all the wolves have been killed. But the wolf is not dead. In fact, now the wolf stands in the open field for all who would observe to see. Look at the unemployment figures for African-Americans; note the cutbacks in grants and other educational funding; regard the gentrification of the Fillmore district in San Francisco and South End in Boston which necessitated the relocation of African-Americans and other people of color from these neighborhoods. The wolf is not dead; he's in disguise.

This is the reality that I have had to face, and women and people of color must come to recognize that the wolf no longer appears dangerous or threatening. The wolf no longer comes prowling out of the forest, teeth gleaming and bared. The wolf is a chameleon, a magician who often smiles with us, nods his head in agreement, applauds our effort, tells us what a long way we have come, then sets us up. The wolf is often a man, but not always; the wolf is the sociopolitical system that regulates and directs our life; the wolf is deadlier than ever, and much harder to smoke out. So why do I persist in declaring my blackness, my femaleness? I should have learned by now not to cry wolf, even when the wolf is stalking me. Don't cry until he attacks. Then, if I have the opportunity, scream for help, others will come to my aid, and applaud my bravery. But why should I wait? I know a proverb that says, 'Prevention is better than having to cure.' I do not want to be maimed anymore. I have too many scars that design my body. I want no more. I refuse to be the victim. Let someone else play that role. I am not the wolf, the culprit.

'There you go again, being a troublemaker.'

'You people don't appreciate anything.'

'You want everything now. Be patient, your time will come.'

Patience is a curse word for a slave. That is my history – slavery. I am made to feel ashamed of my past so I avoid talking about it because my enslavement reflects my deficiency, not my enslavers' inhumanity and greed. To bring it up, I am told, is to accuse, is to cast guilt where none should exist, is to create dissension.

Why am I a troublemaker because I refuse to be second-class – or is it third class? What have I been given that I should be thankful for? Wolf-crier! Me? One of the many things that African-Americans and other people of color – Chicanos, Asians, Native Americans – have been fighting for in this society is a voice. Many of us thought we found ours during the strident 1960s, and many of us did. However, just as we have witnessed the erosion of civil rights laws, we have also experienced our silencing; our tongues clipped, the microphones unplugged, the voices distorted. Others, like me, who refuse to be muzzled, who continue to make sounds from our larynx, guttural though they might be, who have abandoned the electronic microphones for the first long-distance telephone, the congo drums, we who have invented ways to decipher the interference on the line, are labeled wolf-criers. Yet no one has provided an appropriate or reasonable answer to my question. Why did the boy cry wolf in the first place? Each story teaches a lesson, but I reject the lesson I'm supposed to learn from this tale. If being a troublemaker means agitating for my rights as a black female, then I am committed to being a thorn in someone's side.

As an African-Jamaican I grew up in a society where both racism and sexism were operative and sanctioned by the society. Unfortunately, most of us in that society accepted the boy and the wolf tale as gospel. We did not probe or question. We were afraid to reinterpret it on our own because if we came to identify ourselves with the boy, rather than with the invisible authoritative voice that accused the boy of causing his own troubles, then we would have to act in a much more forceful manner than we had thus far, to dismantle the system that was oppressing us. Until I was a teenager, all the banks and other areas of commerce were owned and operated by whites (Europeans or Canadians), and even the bank-tellers were white or 'near white.' Women were restricted in their actions and were not allowed to go to movies, clubs, or soccer matches unescorted without gaining an unsavory reputation. The distinction was clearly made between a 'lady' – quietly spoken and submissive – and a 'woman,' who makes her own decisions, speaks her mind and so was termed 'loose.' That was the early 1960s, the era when I came of age. Racism and sexism were tabooed subjects among middle-class Jamaicans, but all that would begin to change by the late 1960s, early 1970s. In fact, many Jamaicans at home (and even some in the US) are still reluctant to talk about sexism or racism, choosing to regard these practices as foreign impositions, attempts to create rifts and divisions in the society. This attitude would be ludicrous if it wasn't so ironic, as the material preference of many Jamaicans is for foreign products which are held to be superior to local goods – part of our colonial legacy.

Racism is not manifested in the same manner in Jamaica as it is in the US; gone are the 'bacras' – white overseers/landowners – and most of the sugar estates, gone is the barbed wire which once fenced off the best beaches that were reserved for tourists, gone are most of the exclusive clubs – whites only – with exorbitant membership fees for which non-white Jamaicans needed a reference from one of its members, who were mostly white expatriates. Nonetheless, the 'brown-skin' person still reigns supreme, reflected in the features of all our Prime Ministers, past and present, save one – Hugh Shearer. The same race paradigm exists in Jamaica as in the US: to be white is to be privileged, is to be guaranteed a position in the society, while to be black means having to fight to earn a place. Government officials, some historians and scholars of marxist leanings insist that Jamaica's problem is merely a class issue. So that while attention is focused on class, the make-up of the society (95 per cent of African descent) and of those who are economically viable (whites, Syrian, Chinese and black, often in that order) will indicate that race plays an important role in class determination. Those who control the economy tend to prefer their own race and employ the majority population in a service capacity. Invariably, the majority of poor people are black, and the middle and upper classes are 'brown-skin' and white. One's color often determines one's mobility in the society. Black people are the sheep getting devoured, but who hears them? They are lazy, wolf-criers.

Sexism, however, is another matter; pervasive and entrenched in the very fiber of the society. Sexism cuts across all classes and color stratifications. You might say the unofficial motto of Jamaica is, 'Man is King.' Men are peacocks who strut about, flaunting their power. Jamaican men are allowed great sexual freedom, and it is often assumed that they will have sweethearts or outside women along with their wives. It is taken for granted that they will father as many children as they are inclined to, without providing support; they are not required to help with any domestic chores, but rather are to be waited on hand and foot; they spend long hours away from home with their 'buddies' – male friends – drinking rum, playing cricket or dominoes; they slap their wives and/or women whenever they believe they warrant it; in general, they are responsible to no one but themselves. Those women who object to this kind of behavior often find themselves divorced or without the companionship of a man, and are often referred to in a derogatory manner. They become objects of the widespread belief that something is wrong with such women: that's why they are incapable of 'holding' a man. Women in the society are still expected to cater to men. A man's value is seldom, if ever, questioned. I can hear the boos and exclamatory cries, 'Wolf-crier! Man-hater! Troublemaker!' For I have just committed blasphemy, high treason, for daring to put this in print. Inevitably, I will be accused of exaggeration. Even worse: I will be called an American propagandist, a lost sister, a communist, a lesbian. Name-calling becomes the weapon used to silence me, to keep me from examining and exposing those germs that keep all of us down. A smart wolf changes his tactic to suit the situation. Part of his strength lies in his ability to manipulate and create divisions where alliances should be a natural outcome.

When I first came to the US, my family were the ones who mistook some of their fellow sheep for wolves. An uncle who had been living in lower Manhattan for almost twenty years and who was about to retire and return to Jamaica warned me about associating with African-Americans. He said that they were lazy, they were not interested in school and were all into drugs, so I should steer clear of them. Although this sounded much like the argument some of my more prosperous relatives in Jamaica used against those people who lived in Back-

O-Walls, Trench Town, and other depressed areas of Kingston, I avoided making the connections. I took my uncle's advice out of fear and separated myself from African-Americans. Here, in the US, all of us from the various islands banded together, momentarily relinquishing our island rivalry, studied hard and avoided forming friendships with African-Americans. From what I saw in passing, my uncle's word held some truth. Then I met Theresa who was a diligent student, didn't talk loud, pop gum and wasn't into drugs. She was just like one of us West Indians (sic). Yet, she was African-American and different in many ways. Still we became friends and it is through that friendship, along with being introduced to the works of Langston Hughes, Jean Toomer, Charles Chesnutt, and other African-American writers, that I came to an understanding of the commonality, the shared history of African-Americans and people from the islands. We too in the islands have our so called lazy or 'wuthless' people who are not interested in improving their lot. The fallacy of this statement is too obvious and exhaustive to discuss here, except perhaps to say that we who have been slaves and colonial subjects have accepted unquestionably far too many stereotypes about us. Besides, it's easier to condemn one another than examine the sociopolitical structure that oppresses us all. For if we were to acknowledge our exploitation, then we would be required to do something to end it.

This was the attitude of the majority of West Indians in the tight-knit New York community that I was a part of in the early 1970s; we distrusted African-Americans, considered them lazy and felt they lacked ambition. We felt superior to them because we had our island homes to which we could return, so we snubbed our noses at them. African-Americans, resentful of this attitude which they identified as arrogance, resorted to calling us monkey-chasers. So that Marcus Garvey's tremendous success in this country in the 1920s, uniting African-Americans and West Indians, somehow got lost in this divisive game. Of course, West Indians are happy to cite Garvey and others like him who were and are leaders in the African-American community. I knew a young man from the islands whose preoccupation was to trace all the leaders, past and present, in the African-American community who were West Indians or of West Indian ancestry. This evidence, he felt, supported his claim of West Indian superiority. So in the early 1970s, in the New York area, I saw very little evidence of West Indians and African-Americans getting together. We were separated by a sea of distrust, and neither group seemed willing to ride the waves.

Looking back, I now see how the boy and the wolf tale gets reinscribed in the context of my experience as a West Indian in the US. The invisible, authoritative voice that accuses is removed, and the wolf and sheep become interchangeable. My objective then is to zoom in on the unidentified controlling voice that inserts itself and alters the entire outcome of the story. For if I am unable to identify this voice, this authority, then it remains at large and can and will create havoc elsewhere. What I am suggesting here is that the dynamic relationship that occurred between West Indians and African-Americans at various periods in our meeting needs to be reexamined. Even more importantly, I am suggesting that we reinspect that tale and locate the ownership of that voice which accuses the boy of being a wolf-crier. Who is the accuser in this tale? Who is being defended/protected? Because West Indians and African-Americans neglected to investigate this trope we erected a wall that separated us, rather than working to break our chains.

Perhaps it was my quiet rebellion against my parents and community which allowed me to form that friendship with Theresa which opened the road to other friendships, or maybe it was the result of an incident which occurred when I worked as a babysitter for a wealthy white woman on Park Avenue. I sat for Mrs P.'s two children for almost six months, and often listened to her say how delighted she was with me as well as her Jamaican maid. We were so polite and efficient, she said, and I am sure she never thought I would be anything else but someone's maid when I completed college. As it happened, the maid did not show up one day and my employer was going to have unexpected guests. She demanded that I vacuum her living-room, pick up the clothes scattered in her room and wash the sink full of dishes. I reminded Mrs P. that I was not a maid but a babysitter. I, moreover, informed her that I was not prepared to do any of the tasks she requested even for an extra dollar, her offering gesture. The maid, whom I knew, was a friend of a relative, and also a nurse's aid who was working three jobs to save to bring up her five children from Jamaica. When I began, she had warned me to refrain from doing any housework or such a request would become a habit; this apparently had happened with the previous babysitter so I was unequivocal in my refusal. Mrs P. became enraged that I should refuse her request – for wasn't my mother a maid? she screamed. We had never talked about my mother so Mrs P. did not know that she was an executive secretary. However, she had assumed that being less than two years from Jamaica my mother had to be a maid, after all weren't all Jamaican females somebody's servant? To Mrs P., all blacks were beneath her, in service capacities. Although she preferred Jamaicans, we were no better, just more docile and willing (no matter the reasons), not different from African-Americans, and often our alleged superiority was an excuse to exploit our labor. When I resigned from babysitting that afternoon I made the connection and understood clearly that I was not going to join those who accused the boy, nor would I allow them to silence me.

To some whites, all blacks, irrespective of where we're from, are the same. Some of us – African-Americans and Caribbeans – don't seem to understand this so we fight among ourselves. Some of our internal conflicts have to do with cultural differences and expectations. Some West Indians will and do work for less than African-Americans. This, I believe, is partly a result of wages in the West Indies that make any wage in the US seem reasonable, especially when one is accustomed to 'banding' one's belly. So knowingly or unknowingly island people surrender to greater exploitation, and rather than embrace African-Americans as allies we denounce them for demanding fairness and equality. Either way both groups lose, fighting among ourselves while the wolf roams freely. Mrs P. on Park Avenue was the first wolf I had to confront on my own. I was afraid. I hesitated. I didn't want to have anyone call me a wolf-crier again, but I also wasn't willing to remain invisible and voiceless. So I demanded payment and carved a path for myself. That was a victory, not just a private, personal victory, but a bridge, and there have been and continue to be other such bridges erected daily.

Sometimes, however, bridges take quite a while to build. It must not be assumed that African-Americans and West Indians have never worked together since the Garvey movement because this is not the case. While the general antagonism is widespread, there have always been members from both groups who have worked together and defended each other. My experience in New York in the early seventies is by no means the rule or the exception. Since that time I have become very intimate with African-Americans, especially living in California; they comprise the majority of my very dear and close friends. African-Americans and people of the Caribbean have come together on many issues in the past, Marcus Garvey's United Negro Improvement Association is but the most gleaming example. More recently, I have seen us work closely protesting the invasion of Grenada and fighting for economic sanctions against the repressive South Africa regime. Even more importantly, I am the mother of African-American children, their Jamaican ancestry notwithstanding, half of their roots and ancestry is here in this country. They are the great-great-granddaughter and son of slaves, rebels, share-croppers, janitors and maids, teachers and preachers, lawyers and doctors, and politicians. And I try to make my life an example for them. They will not face the dilemma I did. The fact of their birth is an indication that African-Americans and people from the Caribbean have much in common and must learn to work together and coexist. I believe we have come to realize that all of us are the boy, and he is not the enemy, but rather represents our sounding voice.

Reggae and calypso music and patties and roti have helped to bridge the gap between African-Americans and Caribbeans. My daughter is Californian, but she loves patties, talks about duppies (ghosts) like a Jamaican and dances to reggae music and has since she was three years old. African-Americans came to hear the music and sample the food and realized that the music ignited memories in them and the food was seasoned with some of the same spices that their southern grandmothers used. They came to party and eat and they ended up participating. Together, these siblings separated by the sea celebrated Labor Day on Eastern Parkway, Brooklyn, every September. Also, for the past two decades more African-Americans have been vacationing outside the US, and they often travel to the Caribbean. Once there, they are surprised, as are the islanders, to discover that they like each other, know each other's pain, and understand one another's frustration and anger. Both realize that they are among the few who know that the islands are much more than beaches and sunshine, but are the people, many of whom live nestled in the lush vegetation, and welcome all to their homes. The journeying back and forth is now both ways. African-Americans are going to the islands and falling in love with the people and the place. They have gone to establish businesses, to help their sisters and brothers develop their islands, to seek shelter, to be one with the people. And West Indians have established roots in the US, no longer working hard while deferring their dreams, saving to go home. For some of us, the US is now home. Caribbeans and African-Americans have discovered and are continuing to learn that sheep really like each other's company, especially when wolves in disguises are roaming.

The animosity that still lingers between African-Americans and West Indians has its roots in the colonial experience which has impacted all black people – on the Continent as well as in the diaspora. Each group feels it is superior to the other, consequently, we make much of our cultural differences which prevents us from embracing our similarities and our shared experience. As an African-Caribbean the effects of racism and sexism in the US are not different from the experience of my sisters, but I must admit that I find it comforting to say I have a little island to go back to, even though I know I probably won't go back. Because, irrespective of who controls the major commerce in Jamaica, or any island for that matter, I believe there is a feeling of belonging and sense of pride which comes from being the majority race in a society, and to know that you belong there – at least since slavery, after the demise of the Arawak and Carib Indians. Moreover, since Jamaica is always within reach for me (if only metaphorically), I am quick to raise the alarm on racial issues as opposed to biding my time. I am a black woman. That's how I am perceived and regarded, and although when I open my mouth to speak my accent is a telltale of my roots, I stand united with African-Americans. I know I am just another black face to the invisible accusing voice who is in charge.

The wolf as a symbol of all-consuming evil abounds in western tales for children: Little Red Ridinghood, the Three Little Pigs, and so on. In the chant, 'Who's afraid of the big bad wolf?' there is the invisible coercive voice that demands that we reply, 'I'm not.' This is both positive and negative. To assert that you are not is to summon up courage, but it could also mean disregarding the power of the wolf. However, there are other options; one of which might be to summon up courage, to acknowledge the threat of the wolf and work to establish strategies to capture and kill it. I would like to think I took this latter route which led me to embrace my African-American siblings.

Before moving to examine the manifestation of sexism, I want to suggest yet another way of looking at this tale. It is always assumed that the boy and the wolf are irreconcilable enemies, and that there is no room for their alliance. While this might be the case given the nature of the wolf as a predator, I want to recommend that we explore such a possibility because the more I examine the motif of this tale, the more problematic the invisible accusatory voice becomes. I believe many of us assumed that voice was the community which was outraged at the boy, but we must look closer and try to identify clearly that voice. Also, we need to ask ourselves, would the wolf attack if he were fed regularly? Moreover, we need to explore the spatial boundaries of this tale. Why does the wolf persist in venturing into the boy's spacial sphere? I am suggesting that this is a crucial link in the 'battle between the sexes.' This same tale is relevant, but the focus shifts. In this story, as in the Three Little Pigs, and Little Red Ridinghood, the devouring takes place when the lines of demarcation collapse. Perhaps that's why I am sometimes slow to denounce sexist acts. I am not sure who is venturing into whose spatial sphere. Also, I am acutely aware that the wolf has been left hungry for a long, long time. Blacks and other men of color are oppressed. I, as a woman in a patriarchal society, am oppressed. Blacks and other men of color have more authority than me, even in an oppressed, patriarchal society.

There are, however, other variables that I must factor into the interplay between women and men in Caribbean society. A West Indian friend refers to the male/female dynamics in discourse as 'playful-jestering.' In the Caribbean we are bombarded and seduced by derogatory and sexist lyrics common in calypso and reggae songs. Women in the Caribbean have been led to believe that sexist lyrics are a form of compliment, and therefore are flattered by the references to those specific areas of their bodies that are alluded to or openly sung about. Songs with sexual innuendo have long been a motif in reggae and calypso music, but some of the contemporary musicians, such as the soca artist Arrow with his 'Sexy Sexy' and the dancehall disc jockeys from Jamaica like Johnny P with his 'Panty Meat' and the calypsonian Devon 'Ruthven' George's *Bullpistile* album, have taken this element to the level of vulgarity. Nonetheless, this derogatory, sexist music gets dismissed by far too many as open flirtation, palaver. The absence of this consensual bantering in the US makes sexism easier to identify, and I find that I am less afraid to sound the alarm when the system or men are being chauvinistic. In the Caribbean, however, often the line of demarcation is blurred. I find that I must constantly ask myself how I should interpret a given behavior. Similarly, I am forced to reinterpret the meaning and question the relevance of the boy and the wolf tale for us today. I must always be alert for I am in open territory, and the attack on my womanhood is inevitable. As such, sexism, its manifestation, the perception of women, is not very different in the US than it is in the Caribbean. Perhaps the only difference is that, in the islands, men mask their sexual exploitation of women in the social area of entertainment, namely dance which traditionally has been an avenue of courtship. Consequently, women appear openly to welcome their defilement as a prize. Women trying to buy homes on their own or obtain passports for their children are faced with a demand for a man's signature, a man's presence, but Jamaican women are breaking down these barriers. They understand the threat that their presence poses when they venture into territories traditionally reserved for men. Thus they are all the more alert and prepared to challenge men to confront their sexism.

An interesting footnote to the boy and the wolf tale: most people in recalling the story remember that the boy raised false alarms and so is blamed for not having anyone come to his aid when the wolf attacked. As an immigrant, I am blamed for my isolation and dislocation. (I must note that I neither feel displaced nor exiled.) The position of the immigrant who, like myself, chooses exile is suspected not only by African-Americans as being an outsider, but also by my nation people who grumble that I have advantages they don't. My position is rendered more untenable when I criticize some aspect of their behavior that shows them in a not so favorable light. My understanding of my precarious position has made me visit Jamaica yearly. But to some I am a Ja-merican, an outsider. Still I will venture my observation that in the last five years I have observed significant changes, very few of which, from my point of view, are positive or supportive of the Jamaican culture. Americanization is firmly entrenched, and the people's desires are being satisfied by the availability of foreign goods; consumption in all forms is at an all-time high. The approximation of the Caribbean to North America, and the importation of American culture serve to sharpen the attitude towards race/color and gender division; racism/classism and sexism remain widespread. Friends in Jamaica have claimed that the former Prime Minister, Edward Seaga, had turned the clock back and that the popular commercial aimed at North Americans, 'Come back to Jamaica, Come back to the way it was ...' was an attempt to elevate and return 'brown-skin' and white people to a pedestal and reduce black Jamaicans to passive darkies who serve with a smile. Moreover, they say that during Seaga's reign, a noticeable number of North Americans and Europeans were invited into the country and placed in prominent positions that should have been occupied by qualified Jamaicans who were available. Yet there was very little outcry. Have Jamaicans internalized the warning implied in the boy and the wolf tale? Where are the wolf-criers?

Many Jamaicans insist that they do not have a color/race problem, even after the race riot in 1968 which closed down Kingston, the capital, for over three days while any white, Chinese or brown-skin person caught on the streets was subject to abuse because the black man said, 'We tired of de sufferation.' Shops, stores and other commercial businesses owned and operated by brown, white and Chinese people were looted and burned. This incident was much more than a class issue. The volatile sentiments were directed by African-Jamaicans towards all non-African-Jamaicans as well as those people who were considered to be members of the 'brown skin' group. During the riot which was sparked by the spirit of the Black Power movement and the lectures of the late Walter Rodney at the University of the West Indies, Mona campus (for which Rodney was deported and made persona non grata in Jamaica), the sheep – black people – stood together and demanded redress from the government which was considered to be an instrument of Britain, from Chinese and Syrian store-owners, and all white people who were considered to be exploiters of blacks. Not receiving any reparations, the African-Jamaican masses attacked those whom they identified as wolves, and probably for the first time since Paul Bogle's Morant Bay rebellion, 1865, or Bustamante Trade Union uprising, 1939, African-Jamaicans were acknowledged as a viable force to be reckoned with and their numbers counted.

In Jamaica, as in the rest of the Caribbean, the haves and the have-nots coexist in close proximity. The haves cannot avoid, or fail to see, the have-nots. The country is so small, and there are too many wolves who have not been fed for a long time. So not only do boundaries collapse, but the predator and the prey also become confused.

People who travel to Jamaica today and mingle with the black masses will hear the rage against oppression on the overpacked, stuffy busses, in the market-places, among the idle boys for whom there is no work or trade, at the riverside, in the dancehalls with the sound systems blaring. The grumble hisses like a hive of wasps trapped in a net, 'Is time black people get on top now; is well time.' This mass of forgotten people are wolf-criers whose voices are still muffled, but not for much longer. Aid was to have come to these people via the Caribbean Basin Initiative, but whatever aid there was has had very little to no impact on the economy nor has it improved the social conditions of the masses in Jamaica or any other island for that matter. Instead neo-colonialism is firmly entrenched, and the Americanization of Jamaica is in full swing. We see this not only in the fashion dictates, but more and more in the increase in number of food franchises such as Kentucky Fried Chicken and McDonald's; in the media, particularly television, as 90 per cent of all television programs are from and about North Americans; and in the frequent and large evangelist prayer meetings that are being held throughout the islands organized by American evangelists. Yet, the suffering of the black masses continues; their cry is not yet a thunder, but it is harsh. Many have turned their frustration and anger in, unto themselves, but that too is changing as the violence in Jamaica is more random and widespread. Like the little boy who was ignored, until it was too late, so too are the masses of Jamaicans.

As more women gain economic and political power, they and their young girls have recently been the victims of some of the most perverse crimes in Jamaica. Rape escalates daily, accompanied by the most blatant acts of misogyny. Women have not stood back and accepted their victimization. Not only are they screaming at the top of their voices, but they have gotten whatever they can get their hands on to defend themselves. The women's movement is viable because of the pivotal role that the working-class and poor women have taken; they are the most abused, sexually and economically by their mates as well as the men for whom they work who frequently impregnate them, leaving them more children than they can adequately provide for. Some fundamental changes have occurred with regard to women's roles, and women have gained a voice. Women have demanded that issues that impact them, such as domestic violence, child support, and the clothes-manufacturing industry for export, be placed on the political agenda. The first two issues are a direct result of the sexism prevalent in the society and the latter issue has to do with racism, or the exploitation of workers by American firms. North America has been and remains dependent on cheap labor from the Caribbean. In the early 1960s a large percentage of the Jamaican women who emigrated to North America did so in the capacity of domestic maids, as this was often the only way women could secure sponsorship to the US. This pattern began what remains an exploitation of Caribbean women as cheap labor. Nonetheless, mostly men and the conservative middle class, including women, have argued that these women are wolf-criers, emulating agendas set by American feminists. So they close their eyes to the demoralizing conditions that the women who work in the export processing zone are subject to, and they plug their ears to these women who scream out for help from the brutalization by their own compatriots.

Once we understand the subtext underlying the boy and the wolf tale, namely the will to silence people so they don't expose their oppression, we can then resist the urge to suppress our pain, and take a stand as the women in the Caribbean are doing. Notwithstanding the obstacles, working-class women have forged ahead and have made some triumphs. In Jamaica all children, irrespective of their parents' marital status, are afforded equal protection and rights under the law and basic schools have been established. Moreover, women can now get a modicum of assistance from the police in matters of domestic violence, and although still only available in the urban areas, a few sheltered homes are provided for women and children who must flee their homes to avoid physical and psychological abuse. Women have identified and are corralling the wolves. They are demanding safety and protection within specific boundaries.

Women of the Caribbean have rewritten the boy and the wolf tale. The boy is no longer isolated, and the entire society becomes responsible for its resources and the people who comprise that society. Formerly, throughout the Caribbean, working-class women have not had a voice. They were invisible and muted. The general belief was that these women could not and did not think about the socioeconomic conditions of their daily life, and that they were unable to formulate, much less articulate, ways to improve and change their existence. This is no longer the perception. In fact, working-class women throughout the Caribbean are showing middle-class and working-class men through the medium of theatre and workshops how to coalesce their energy to bring about change. Some of the leading groups are Red Thread in Guyana, Belize Rural Women's Association (BRAWA), Caribbean Association for Feminist Research and Action (CAFRA) based in

Trinidad, and Women and Development Unit (WAND) in Barbados. However, the most formidable women's working-class organization, with an international reputation, is Sistren of Jamaica. This group which began as a small experimental theater workshop has grown not only to a leading educational theater performance group but has purchased property, produces textiles, leads educational workshops, and continues to be the mouth-organ for working-class women to come up with solutions to their exploitation. Further, Sistren brings to the attention of women throughout the Caribbean, as well as the isolated groups of women scattered throughout the rural areas, those issues that demean their existence by exploiting their labor and abusing them as women. Sistren's 'grass roots' theater collective has been instrumental in educating working-class women about alternate ways to circumvent as well as dismantle the system that oppresses them economically, sexually, and politically. Sistren's very existence challenges the government and the men of the society as these women demand to be heard. And they are being heard and taken seriously not only by women of their class, but by the society at large, including those men who are ready for change.

Sistren's strivings mean an improvement for the entire society as the betterment of women's condition affects the children, and women and children are the majority of the population. Of equal importance are the strong cultural links and pride in the indigenous culture that this group advocates. Sistren speaks the language of the masses and incorporates the folklore and songs of the islands into its theater productions. The incorporation of folk culture is an important factor when the government is doing everything to increase tourism sometimes at the expense and often demise of the local culture. Sistren and its other sister groups throughout the Caribbean challenge the Americanization of the Caribbean and alert the people to the changing face of colonialism. I am glad that these wolf-criers are around, and I hope their voices gain strength so that they continue to cry and gather all the people to band together collectively to keep their society safe from harm, and free from outside domination.

Ironically, while the struggle to eradicate sexism is in full force, and women from different class and ethnic backgrounds are working together to this end, the struggle for an independent – not only in name – Caribbean has been squashed with the support of many of the people. While it is true that the population was split over the invasion of Grenada and America's stance ('No more Cuba in the Caribbean,' hence its vicious assault), the people's ignorance and paranoia about communism allowed them to sanction America's invasion. The Caribbean is not America's backyard. People of the Caribbean have the right to choose the kind of government and political system under which they wish to live. It is America's historically racist attitude toward people of color that informs their dealings with the Caribbean. We the people of the Caribbean are the little boys left alone with a wolf on the prowl. Yet Caribbean people fail to see or refuse to acknowledge that America's paternal attitude is rooted in racism, and that the Caribbean is still being treated as a base for raw material with its people supplying ready and cheap labor. This attitude and the unequal relationship that currently exists between the Caribbean and America contribute to the eroding of the indigenous culture and the material preference for and aesthetic surrendering to American's goods. The relationship is unfortunately a case of the sheep welcoming the wolf into their pen, mindless of their pending danger.

This action also reflects on the racial situation in the US today. Many of us believed that all we had to do was get civil rights laws passed, remove those signs which advertised segregation, and the interaction between the different races would resolve itself. Well deep, instilled beliefs die a very slow death, and sheep can be put in wolves' clothing; evidence of this abounds. Racism in the US is as prevalent as before, only more subtle; it has, in fact, gone underground, hence it is more lethal, harder to detect and smoke out. This does not mean that spontaneous demonstrations of racism like the Howard Beach incident in New York and the burning of Vietnamese homes in San Leandro, California, are examples of a general increase in racist assaults. To the contrary, racism manifests itself and has far greater impact in policy areas: more stringent requirements for college entrance, the rezoning of cities, and the relaxing of affirmative action laws. In Berkeley, California, the allegedly liberal city where I live, far too many young students of all races, between the ages of 19 and 21, believe racism is a thing of the past. Only recently, a young, privileged, African-American male student of mine said there was no racism in California because he has never been the victim of a racist attack. He considered himself the rule, rather than the exception; he insisted on walking around with blinders in the very community where racism lives and breathes. He said I was a wolf-crier, that my attitude was rooted in the sixties, that black people have 'overcome.' What, I ask? The back door, the segregated counters, the obese Aunt Jemima image, the bulging-eyes, shuffling darkie, the Sapphire, loud, mouth, slut, the shifty buck with dice in one hand and a knife in the other? What have we overcome, as a group, not as a few selected individuals? And if we have overcome, does it mean we no longer have any need to cry out? Have conditions improved significantly for the majority of Americans, irrespective of their race? The high unemployment rates of the 1980s and 1990s suggest otherwise.

How do I make these young people understand when they don't even know what the sit-ins and demonstrations were about, when they don't know anything about Brown versus Board of Education, 1954, Little Rock and school desegregation? How do I get them to understand that I am not 'tripping,' that racism is as odious as ever, except that now it's dressed better, and will smile at you and pretend to like you until the dagger is too deep, and too close to your heart to be removed without sure death? How do I help those other young adults who are at the other end of the spectrum, those who believe that in order to be 'black' and love themselves they must hate white people? How do I help them to understand that self-love has nothing to do with hating others, and that racism wears many hats? How do I tell them so they hear, that they cannot say they hate racism, then declare that they hate all white people? Nor can they decry racism but practice sexism. They cannot have it both ways. Who is the wolf? Who are the sheep? Is the little boy still crying for help? I must make them understand that disguises are easy to come by, and rhetoric is not a defense, nor is ignorance or assumed superiority. I have learned that I must speak with these young people on an individual basis, I must help them to reason, to gather data and evaluate their findings. It is crucial that I show them how to establish links with others, to embrace difference rather than negate that which is least like them, not to be afraid to learn, to listen to each other and to know when to defer and accept changes.

All tales are instructive, and there is much to be learned about the values of our society by studying the story of the little boy and the wolf. Such an exercise can be fruitful if we carefully deconstruct the tale, identify the symbols and the trope upon which the tale is established. Moreover, we can begin to see how we are coerced into accepting our own silence. Racism and sexism are linked parts of the same political structure. Both issues impact me as a black woman and in some instances I cannot separate one from the other. Once I could not get the word feminism out of my mouth; it was trapped somewhere in my throat. Now it spews out, sometimes even when I don't intend for it to.

I am a feminist, a black feminist in the tradition of Mary Prince, Granny Nanny, Harriet Tubman, Sojourner Truth and Nzinga. I want for women, what I want for all people: equality, the right to be whoever and whatever they aspire to be. I am not a man-hater, but I will not put black men's needs above black women's. Both our needs are valid. It is not a contradiction for black women to fight racism and sexism at the same time; their struggle is essential, although many people will disagree. And it does appear as if there is a campaign to separate both issues.

Political correctness is now the buzz word in the political arena, and on college campuses these days it seems to be 'sexism.' The gender dichotomy resounds in all spheres: academia, media, politics. Sexism is the most discussed topic, so I am led to believe. 'You've come a long way, baby ...' Sure. Now we women can smoke and help to hasten our deaths as quickly as men; we can wear pants, even to business meetings; we can make the first move, initiate sex and die from AIDS; we can be executives, the boss who has balls? Oops! tits; we can even go to the moon as the first black and explode into a million bits becoming heroes; we have arrived. Yet, the national figures tell another, not so optimistic, story. Women's salaries are still computed along a whitened scale – still meaning white – and remain far below those accorded to men. The scale of measure is white again and mine, as a black female who has not yet been advanced to the level of womanhood, is far below 'the generic white woman's.' How long a way have I come from the kitchen or the cane or cotton fields?

I am the daughter of slaves, cane-cutters, banana men, domestic workers, nursemaids, secretaries and chemists – hard-working women and men who decided that life was more valuable than death, even if slavery was the price. I am proud of my ancestors, and I cherish the strides we have made, and that I believe I am continuing to make. But I am mindful of the errors: our willingness to forgive, turn the other cheek, withstand, our fear of rocking the moving boat, our indecision, our waiting for some unknown messiah to save us. Perhaps that is why I've been told so often that I am too outspoken, too aggressive, that I want too much too quickly because I see the wolf outside, but I also see the wolf is sometimes us, or in us. Black on black violence is generally the inability to embrace others.

To want a life that is better for my daughter and son is not to want too much. To want to be paid the same for doing the same job as any man, white, black or other, is not to be too aggressive; to expect that my mate will share fully in the rearing of our children and in all domestic chores is not to want change too quickly; to want a better life for all people, all genders, is not to be too idealistic. I am a wolf-crier, but note: I am not raising a false alarm. The wolf is there lurking; there are no safe boundaries anymore. I see him and he sees me; it is a game that he plays. He knows that I will sound the alarm and others will come to my aid, but if they see no threat, and I repeatedly raise the alarm, after a while they will dismiss my interventions. They will say that I am wasting their time, that I am seeking attention, that I am crazy. The wolf will strike when I am defenseless, and I will be blamed for having being victimized.

I am a wolf-crier, and each day I gargle so that my voice gets stronger and clearer so that it can ride on the wind. I will keep crying. I refuse to allow the sheep to be eaten. I refuse to become paranoid, afraid of my own voice. I refuse to be discredited. Long ago, I refused to be silenced. I will continue to raise the alarm until the wolf is caged or becomes my ally. Time.

If I Speak I am Not Heard
and if I Scream I am 'Hysterical'

Atsango Chesoni

I wanted to kill a man and yet I had never learned to make a fist. I wanted to kill a man because my sister does not sleep. My sister does not sleep because she cannot sleep, because a man stole her night and so she rages to the dawn yearning to close her eyes but knowing she must keep a vigil.

My sister has kept a vigil since the night her stomach shook. Her stomach shook and she could not stop it. She could not stop her stomach from shaking because it was not her stomach anymore. Her stomach was not her stomach anymore because her thighs were not hers anymore. Her thighs were not hers anymore because her womb had become a tomb. Her womb has become a tomb because a man who can make a fist and knows how to kill, a man who knew how to seal his fingers into a knife and switch his penis to steel, slashed his way into my sister's womb.

Passing water for my sister became scar stripping, the wound between her thighs burnt afresh by water become acid. Nobody believed her.

'Oh, were you cut?' they said. 'We do not see the redness of your flesh. Bring us a saw, let us scrape the scar, we do not believe this is a knife wound. We do not like to hear of the toilet,' they shouted, 'even when the sewer is full.' My sister retched her body raw and still they asked: 'Does your stomach hurt? Why do you smell so bad? Go away, you are spoiling the air.'

The man who knows how to make a fist, who knows how to kill, came and said: 'I say this girl eat poison yesterday, she said it was her food.'

My sister – whose tongue was so swollen she could not speak, thighs so weak she could not walk – lifted her finger and pointed at him and gathered her fingers into the center of her palm. I heard the people laugh and say: 'We do not speak of the toilet even when the sewer is full.' Gagged and gloved they rolled my sister to a ridge and as they neared the edge of the ridge they began to fall one by one. The smell from the edge of the ridge – the air so thick they could not see – only the flies were at home there. In the rift lay the decaying bodies of women and underneath their bodies were the bones of women.

One of the people, wearing a white skirt, white blouse, white headscarf, white shoes – the woman in white – but a woman like me, said to my sister: 'Why did it take you so long to vomit? A girl who allows her thighs to be forced open allows her thighs to be forced open by men with knives and deserves to be ill. I do not believe you are ill anyway, it took you too long to vomit.'

'You are making all these things up,' another person said, 'so that the man with the knife can give you some money.' The people threw my sister over the ridge and into the rift that is filling up with the bodies of women decayed from carrying others' stench.

'I believe you,' said the woman in white to the man who knows how to kill.

'I believe you,' a man said.

'We believe you, man who knows how to kill,' the people chanted.

My sister will never sleep, she rages the night. I, a woman – a woman like the women whose bodies decay once were – cannot sleep until I learn to make a fist.

The Price of Illusion

Nawal el-Saadawi

Translated by Ali Azeriah

He was sitting by the electric fan, his big head in a reclining position. Apart from the wisps of gray hair behind each ear, he was bald. His ears were big and delicate, the hairs of which wavered at the touch of air from the fan. His small eyes had lost all their eyelashes. His fingers, the bones of which bore testimony to old age, appeared even bigger in the dim light of a small lamp that trembled on contact with the electric current amidst four burnt lamps, the insides of which had turned swarthy as time passed. His voice had a hoarseness to it. The 70 years he had lived had been gnawing at the vocal cords since the day he uttered the first word in the cradle. He gave free rein to his tongue as he stood on a wooden platform, and was still speaking till the very last minute when he shot up, believing the whole world was listening; and that she, being part of this world, was listening, too. Every time she interrupted him to answer a question, he would go on speaking, lending no ear to what she was saying. He would talk and talk, raising his right hand in the air in disapproval, as if to bring the air to a halt: 'Please, Fatiha, don't interrupt me!' he would say to her. 'Let me finish, then you'll have *mutlaq* (absolute) freedom to talk.'

When uttered, the four consonants of the word *mutlaq*, particularly /t/ and /q/,[1] leave behind them a dignified echo, one that is imbued with the dignity of the letters of a pristine Arabic alphabet, like a pure-bred stallion. And an even

1. A pun is intended here: the words *mutlaq* (absolute) and *mutallaq* (divorced), both of which contain two consonants proper to Arabic, an emphatic /t/ and a velarized /q/.

purer larynx, such as his, is certainly capable of velarizing and amplifying, age notwithstanding.

She was sitting in front of him, clad in home garments. She was not wearing any make-up or any color that might add a bit of life to a pale cheek. Nor did she apply any lotion on the skin of her face to hide the swelling veins under the epidermis, or the wrinkles, or the black spots advancing like freckles.

That he saw her in that sort of appearance did not bother her in the least. Nothing made her feel embarrassed about her age, except the three teeth which she would pull off at night. In the morning, she would wear them above the large aperture right under the upper lip. When she smiled or laughed, she made sure not to open her mouth too much so as not to display the braces.

He was sitting in front of her. Nothing would embarrass him as he opened his jaws to the last notch, exhibiting a maxilla furnished with three pitch-black, decaying teeth that were hanging loosely above a naked mandible.

His voice is still strong and presumptuous. He is a man! In spite of his being bald, toothless, and shortsighted, nothing would defile his manliness, except his pocket. Although he is ten years older than she, he looks at her as if she were living the last days of her life; as if there were no other role for her to play in life, except to listen to him. He is still a man. His heart never ceases to throb at the sight of young girls. Isn't it a right of his to enjoy life until the very last minute? Isn't it a right of his to wed himself to a young woman who will protect him from harlots and the AIDS virus? She will wash his clothes, shoulder his concerns and be all ears during the long lonely nights as he reminisces about his youth.

'Please, Fatiha, don't interrupt me. I feel an urgent need to enjoy myself; I cannot afford to waste the very little time I have left, now that the mask has fallen off the illusion of my life!'

'And what was the illusion of your life, Mohammed?' She doesn't know exactly, for he does not give the illusion a name.

But what's in a name, Fatiha, now that the mask has fallen? I could have fallen with it, had it not been for the fact that I had realized, ten years before Gorbachev did, that there was a mistake in practice, and perhaps in theory, too. And why not, Fatiha? After all, this theory is nothing other than the work of human beings. Its major flaw is that it runs against the course of history and against this nature of ours which has been bequeathed to us over thousands of years. Can people stand equal like the teeth of a comb? Can the difference between people be overcome? A case in point is these dissimilarities which Allah has created between man and woman, can we redress them, Fatiha?

At this point, the ghost of his deceased wife visits him. They had lived together for 40 years. During all this time her voice had never risen above his. She passed away as silently as she lived. But his young bride's voice raises high. 'I wish it were only a matter of voice raising, Fatiha! Do you know what she told me when I proposed to her?'

Fatiha does not ask him what the bride said. She heard the story from him yesterday when he paid her a visit after sunset. After Fatiha's husband had passed away, no one visited her, except him. He was an old friend. They were friends since childhood. He used to eye her in the presence of her husband. And she knew exactly what his look meant, thanks to her female sense.

She would shun him in loyalty to her husband present. Following her husband's departure, and after she was a lonely woman without a husband, his eyes were robbed of their glow; as if the reason for which he desired her was only because she belonged to another man. He wanted to own her, not because he yearned for her; but because of a burning desire to break the other man, to triumph over him.

'Do you know what this girl told me, Fatiha?'

He does not refrain from repeating the question to himself. His hoarse voice cracks up as if his vocal cords had been severed with a knife. He does not refrain from inflicting pain on himself, like someone who hurts himself by rubbing his finger into a wound on his body and, in so doing, finds great pleasure in the suffering. The greater the pain, the sweeter the pleasure.

She knows the story from A to Z, and she does not feel inclined to know more. Her mind was on something that happened yesterday at sunset when, after many long years of house confinement, she went out into the street to smell fresh air and to watch people. But no one looked at her. She was dragging her feet, like the old man she used to see trudging along the street when she was a young girl. As a young woman, she would be walking along the street and all the eyes would stare fixedly at her. They were filled with a glow. Her female sense informed her that she was desired, wanted, and yearned for. She felt great elation inside. The whole world desired her. And all she wanted was a man, a husband, whom she would marry in accordance with the precepts of Allah and the teachings of His Messenger.

As she was listening to him, her eyes spoke, 'But, Mohammed, the mask has fallen off the illusion of my life, and I do not have much time to waste. As for you, you're like me, a worthless chunk of meat, old and tottery. You and I stand equal in senility as we did in childhood.'

Mohammed cannot stand the word 'equality.' His eyes respond to hers, 'Yes, Fatiha, I have lived my life deceived by this illusion called "equality". Look at your fingers which Allah has created, are they equal? By no means, they are not! Equality, Fatiha, is against nature and against the Will of Allah. But the minds of today's girls cannot think straight. This spoilt girl wants to be equal to me, can you believe that? I am 40 years older than she is. I have raised generations of young people like her, and she still wants us to be equal. Can you imagine that, Fatiha?'

He was addressing the questions to himself incessantly and providing all the answers. He heard his voice repeating time and again that he had raised one generation after another, teaching them such values as justice and equality. But he soon became aware of the fact that he had contradicted himself just now. He spoke without restraint, believing that she had not discovered what he discovered.

She is sitting in front of him, nodding in agreement. Her face is marred by a sad smile which he cannot see clearly as he is lying down on the bed at sunset, alone and deserted. He tries to stand up, but he feels weighed down under the load of a heavy body and a heart full of sand. Then he walks towards her and talks to her, discharging the sand of his heart on her so that she, too, will shoulder part of the burden, just as his deceased wife once did. And like all the deceased wives, Fatiha remains silent. Nothing on her part can hurt him more than when she diverts her eyes away from him and, thus, loses some of his words; or so it seems to him.

'Do you know what this spoilt girl told me, Fatiha?'

But she is not a spoilt girl. She is a young woman in her thirties, who has just graduated from the school of medicine. Having had no luck with employment in her profession, she was hired as a stewardess with Gulf Air. She got herself a husband from the Gulf who pressured her into giving up her job and becoming a housewife, which she did. In the first month, she lost her job and, in the second, her husband was reunited with his first wife. She went back to live at her father's in the half-meter space which was reserved for her in front of the sink in the dark kitchen. From there she could see the apartment in which she once lived with her husband and which commanded a view of the Nile. He was so enamored of her before marriage.

'What are your wishes, ma belle?' the rich husband from the Gulf would say.

Her lips would not part to put her wishes into words: 'I want an apartment in my name or such a sum of money or any other material request.' How could she? Her father had inculcated in her spiritual values that filled her soul with that noble feeling of disdain for anything material. She bowed her head in bashfulness, such as is seen on the face of the virgins, and said, 'Nothing, darling! I want you, that's all.'

He knew a woman's worth only in terms of the price he paid, in terms of a property, a piece of land, a precious stone or a piece of diamond. What comes his way at no cost leaves him without a price. That was why, when a second husband came to ask for her hand, her bedridden father said to her, 'Once bitten twice shy! A righteous woman would never give herself up without a price or an apartment of at least three rooms.'

'What's wrong with today's girls, Fatiha? I offer her myself as a husband who's made himself a name and who has a history, and all she is interested in is the material price. Can you imagine that, Fatiha? In her I saw the pure angel from the paradise of love soaring over me. But the veil has fallen, as did the illusion. Has love ceased to exist in the hearts of women in these wicked times? In our days, we loved and we were loved; we would throw ourselves in fire for the sake of justice. Was all that an illusion? Doesn't man need illusion to live, Fatiha?'

Fatiha tries to reply, but in vain. And what can she possibly say? Can she say, 'Yes, Mohammed, we cannot live without illusion'? Can she say, 'The harshest thing about the passage of time is that it removes the veil from the face of illusion in a harsh and merciless manner'? Can she say, 'Life without illusion is like this old face of yours before me, like that shattered voice of yours which never knows a moment of repose, like those eyes of yours which have been robbed of their glow. Desire, there is not; lust is gone; passion does not exist; and the shiver which accompanies the touch has died'?

'I cannot get my mind off this girl, even though she has humiliated me. Can you believe it, Fatiha? All my achievements are worth nothing for her, so long as I am unable to buy her an apartment in her name. What sort of humiliation is this, Fatiha, that a woman should lay her conditions on the table before the marriage has been consummated, and that this condition should be an apartment, for example? Is she selling herself to me, or is it I? If only I could afford to buy her that apartment!'

His voice becomes even more hoarse as he repeats, 'If only I could afford to buy her that apartment; if only I could ... ' As he enunciates the two letters of the conditional particle 'if,' a gloomy expression pervades his eyes, such as may be seen on the face of a defeated man whose only worth is measured by his pocket. But the latter cannot afford the price requested by a woman who wants him only after he has paid the price. He badly wants her even though she has made her conditions clear. And the higher the price, which he does not have, soars, the more he wants her. There is no way he can afford that price, even if he steals or sells himself at the marketplace.

'I have never felt so humiliated in my life, Fatiha!'

Sitting in front of him, Fatiha is gazing at him with the compassion of a mother. He is ten years older than she, and much more important in status. He has made himself a name; she hasn't. He has a past and a history to back him up; she has neither. She has nothing to her name, except the illusion that he would look at her in the same way he did when she was another man's property; when his eyes glowed with lust for her; when he wished her to offer herself to him uncon-ditionally and at no cost, except for mutual love on the basis of justice and in accordance with the precepts of Allah and the teachings of His Messenger.

He is sitting in front of her, speaking with the voice of a heavy-hearted son who pours his worries into the heart of a mother, placing upon her shoulders a burden she cannot bear, one burden after another. He purges himself from filth which he leaves for her to clean without a charge, like a mother who gives freely and without anything in return, but love.

He leaves her. Heavy-hearted, she remains in her seat. She vainly tries to shake off the heavy burden or to leave the filth unwashed. She loathes the pungent smell of filth, the waning of a senile man in his last days, unwearily and listlessly seeking the favors of a young bride in the prime of life. And all the bride can see of him is his pocket. Nothing can hurt him more than an empty pocket.

She goes out into the street for fresh air and to watch people. Things become blurred before her eyes. She cannot see the pavement as clearly as she used to, the names of the streets, the ads, the moving pictures. Is it because of senility? Or is it because of life without a veil, now that the illusion has fallen?

The glow in the eyes of a passing young man, as old as her emigrant son, riveted her attention. Their eyes met, which rejoiced her heart. She followed him in slow steps. She quickened her pace. She felt great, rejuvenated. It rekindled in her the fire to become as she once was, before the illusion fell. As she quickened her pace, she felt as though she were racing time of which very little was left. She felt she could put her life on the line so that Life would return to what it was like before Time laid it bare.

Man Peaba, Woman Peaba: Women and Folk Birthing in Trinidad and Tobago

Eintou Pearl Springer

Man Peaba, Woman Peaba, Tan Tan fowl back ... the words of the calypsonian have faded into obscurest depths of memory, loath to be recalled to function now when needed. They serenade the wealth of herbs that we use for medicinal purposes.

Call to mind the rural Afro-Trinidadian woman, far away from the availability of modern medicine; call to mind as well the gravid female scion of such a woman, to whom modern obstetric practice is available, but who nonetheless holds fast to a measure of what she has learned.

The time is approaching for a new soul to enter the world and the home must be prepared; made clean physically and spiritually. Kojo root and sweet broom are mixed in a bucket of water with disinfectant, washing soda, and sour orange. The house is thoroughly scrubbed with the mixture. Then, the spiritual cleansing out: the old condensed milk tin, or some other utensil, is pressed into service. Solid bits of asafoetida are mixed with different kinds of incense and dried orange peel. The lighted match is dropped into the container and cheeks billow out as air is blown on to make the substances come well alight. Now held by the makeshift handle, the receptacle is taken around for a careful 'smoking out' of the inner and outer environs. Then lots of old newspapers and clean disused clothing are collected.

Now it's time for the midwife to be called. It is late at night and a female relative or husband walks the long dark road. The walker goes nervously, but in returning walks confidently and quickly alongside the midwife, for the spirits of the night dare not trouble her who buries the navel strings of her people.

The mother waits and prays. Her time is upon her. She hopes that things will go well, for she has faithfully followed the advice of the midwife in preparing herself for this moment. Religiously, she has eaten of ochroes to make her passage moist and slimy so that her baby will slip through easily. She has drunk lots of ice water and eaten of much ice so that the child will be plump and round. She has eaten lots of green leafy vegetables, green figs and porridges to make herself and her baby strong. Shining bush and water grass have been boiled and the extract drunk in lieu of water. She has drunk water too, in which pumpkin has been left so her baby, when born, should have unblemished skin.

Now it is left in the hands of the Almighty. 'It eh easy to make child,' the old women had said, 'when you belly big is one foot in (the grave) and one foot out.' This baby, unlike the others, has given her a lot of problems. Early in pregnancy she had often felt on the verge of miscarriage, but the midwife had tied underneath her belly tightly and firmly with a piece of brown cotton. This, she felt, had helped her to keep the baby and had made carrying all that extra weight a little easier.

At last, the quick purposeful steps of the midwife are heard. She comes briskly into the room calling out over her shoulder, 'Put on some water to boil.'

Most births tend to go to the normal safe way that nature intended. The skilled midwife easily handles the breached baby, putting the baby back into the correct position. When, however, an episiotomy is necessary, the midwife uses a long fingernail, kept specially for such an eventuality. She would make it as sterile as possible in the situation and then use the fingernail to make the slit. Of course, the midwife cannot stitch up the cut, and so it never heals very well. Since the woman would most likely have several more children, prolapse of the uterus may occur. Many of our older women must now have surgery to repair the pelvic floor, damaged after an improperly healed episiotomy. Some midwives are helpless to deal with a retained placenta and some women have died of hemorrhage. Some, however, specialize in helping the childless woman become pregnant. The combination of herbs and oils almost always seem to work and save the woman from the dreaded stigma of infertility; of being termed 'mule.' It is strange, though, that still people almost never think of the man as being infertile! It is always the woman who carries the blame for a childless union.

Now, however, the midwife is caught up in the trauma of a birth. She prays as she gently massages the woman's belly. Occasionally she would bring the candle near to the writhing figure on the bed so she could see more clearly the progress of The Stranger.

At last the baby comes. The cord cut, baby is handed over to the elderly female relative to be bathed in warm water and dressed. The baby is carefully fed with tea made from the young leaves of the lime tree. This is lime bud tea, to clean out the baby's stomach and promote sound sleep. The prepared sachet of indigo blue and asafoetida is pinned on to the little vest and baby is placed on the bed on which is an open Bible with a pair of scissors across it. These things combine to give protection against the dreaded *mal d'yeux*. With such a mixture of traditional and Christian ritual, what can go wrong! The mother's afterbirth is expelled now, and she has her stomach bound up with brown cotton. This 'belly band' will ensure that she is not left with a large stomach after giving birth. She is given a meal: broth made from a young home-grown chicken. Then she is brought a mug of brew from the leaves of the vervain shrub. This is to stimulate her mammary glands and ensure her a good supply of milk. She has, however, been drinking this all through her pregnancy and carefully been hardening her nipples by regularly passing the teeth of a comb over them. They should now not hurt and crack when exposed to the sucking of her infant.

The midwife comes every morning to tend mother and baby. By the third morning, mother is up and around but not doing very much. On this day, she is given a heavy dose of castor oil to clean out her insides. She must also nurse her baby so that the insides also are purged by the oil. The mother has her regime to follow. She drinks her vervain, porridges, and soups. She drinks a brew made from leaves of the *Carile* bush to help expel any retained clots of blood. Boiling water is poured on to the leaves of the hog plum bush and the root of the wild coffee shrub, then the mother sits over the steaming brew for as long as she is able to bear the heat. This water is then replaced by clean warm water which she uses to wash her inner vaginal areas carefully. She knows that this effusion will help her heal quickly and draw down any unwanted matter that still clogs her womb. She carefully preserves herself and her baby from drafts, chills, the evening dew, and cold water. In these early days, visitors, apart from relatives and close friends are not welcome. All first-time visitors must give the baby a silver coin. If the baby particularly resembles any member of the family, that person must pay the baby while it is being breastfed. Breast milk is also used to wash baby's eyes if they seem weak or if they seem to have a cold in them.

The bit of umbilical cord that remains is carefully powdered with boric powder and banded down to ensure quick healing and to prevent the development of an umbilical hernia. When, at last, this bit of cord falls off, it is buried in the yard of the house, a ritual rooting the child to country and family and preventing this part of the infant from falling into the wrong hands where it could be used to inflict spiritual harm.

If the woman's children are born in another country, when they come home there is of course no navel string to bury to tie them to their true homeland. The relatives would then take some earth from the yard and boil it into a brew for the child or children to drink. Often, the children are not told what they're drinking.

To absorb the blood loss after her baby's birth, the woman uses large homemade sanitary towels. These are given to a female relative to be washed, but this person must always be paid with a silver coin, or her eyes will go bad and she may even become blind. On the ninth day, the mother has her first bath since parturition. In some districts the oil is drunk on the ninth day and coincides with the bath. The ninth day is a very important one for it marks the end of the official 'lying in' period. The bath is given on this day. It is a bush bath. *Carile Congo-la-la, malomae*, Sweet Broom, St John Bush, Ruction Bush, Black Sage, and the panacea *geritout* are some of the most popular bushes used.

The water is put to stand in the sun until it is quite warm. If there is insufficient sunshine, then the water is heated on the stove or fireside. The leaves of all these bushes are crushed up in the water and left for a while. The water now has a reddish tinge given it by the St John Bush. The woman is then bathed and she makes sure to hold some water in her mouth to prevent her from 'taking cold'. It is the first time her entire body is being exposed since the baby's birth and so the bath is taken as quickly as possible. Right after her bath, she is given a mixture of red lavender and liquid asafoetida to drink. This is spiritual protection for her. On that day, too, the house is again carefully smoked.

In the period immediately after childbirth, a woman's greatest fear is not to contract a 'lining cold.' This cold is so termed because it is believed that a woman's pores are open, and her entire person, but particularly her womb, is vulnerable to a cold at this time. It is believed that this cold can kill her or render her infertile. It is only a very skilled midwife or someone with great knowledge of bush medicine who can cure such a cold; hence, the elaborate precautions against chills and exposure of any kind.

The mole of the baby's head (fontanelle) is also very vulnerable. The infant can contract a very dangerous head cold if the mole is not carefully protected. Mothers, therefore, no matter how hot the day, will not venture beyond their front porch with their young infant if the head is uncovered. For at least three months, the mother is felt to be in a delicate position – but after the first six weeks most restrictions are lifted. She may then expose herself to a little night air and bathe with tap water; she can now sweep, but not sew; for as long as she breastfeeds there are certain foods that are proscribed from her diet, for they can give her baby gripe. Among these are coconut, split peas, dry pigeon peas, curry powder, and pepper; anything too highly seasoned or acid is also banned from the diet. The young baby's eyes are protected from any strong light. If there happens to be electricity in the home, it is not turned on in the room where the baby sleeps. A candle or lamp is used instead. Even the mother is advised against strong light either of sun or electricity; and against sewing, reading, or writing in any but negligible proportions before the baby is three months old.

A jet, a bracelet of black beads, is bought as quickly as possible. This is worn on the baby's hand and adds its strength to the power of the indigo blue sachet in preventing *mal d' yeux*. When the baby has a fit of hiccoughs, a thread is taken from its clothing and stuck on the forehead with the mother's saliva. If the baby has difficulty in sleeping, lime bud tea or tea made from the young leaves of the sour sop tree is administered. The baby is not supposed to be taken out before being christened and consecrated to God. The parents dare not take the chance of exposing an unblemished soul to the machinations of the devil. In the house which has been spiritually cleansed before the birth, and also nine days after, and where no one whose good will is suspect is allowed, the baby is reasonably safe.

The mother who has her baby in hospital cleans her home before going and immediately she returns to the home. Many mothers pin their sachet of indigo blue on their babies born in hospital and suffer the scorn and contempt of the nurses. Mothers, too, refuse to stay in hospitals and are glad to be discharged as early as possible to go home to the treatment they think is right. 'Dem nurses and dem want to kill people – imagine dem telling me to go in dat cold bathroom and I now make chile.' This is a comment regularly heard in the clinics. Mothers are not now advised to sit over hog plum bush and wild coffee root, but over warm salted water; they are not told to use a comb on their breasts but a spatula.

Postscript

The 'untrained' midwife is still an important person, especially in rural districts. She has many years of experience and handed-down knowledge at her fingertips. There must be some way in which traditional skills and practices could be married with modern obstetric medicine, especially in the light of the worldwide recognition of the intrinsic value of many indigenous medical beliefs; indeed, the reality is that the practices here described still exist to a large extent, in varying degrees, in different districts of Trinidad and Tobago.

My thanks to Public Health Nurse/Midwife Maelena Green for valuable information supplied for the purpose of this article. The above information has been culled from the practice of folk medicine by three generations of both sides of my immediate and extended family. This paper is specially dedicated to the memory of Daniel 'Gimpie' Arttley, my paternal grandfather who died aged 105 years in 1972, a highly respected practitioner of folk medicine in the village of Santa Cruz, Trinidad.

Who Loves New York?

Patricia McFadden

Our flight was delayed by two hours and consequently we arrived at Newark airport later than expected. It happened to be rush-hour, so the shuttle bus from the airport to the bus-depot took even longer than usual, and we missed the last bus to Ithaca by 15 minutes. After a long flight across the Atlantic with a young child who had been extremely tolerant of my impatience, I decided that there was nothing to do but wait for the next bus which would leave New York at 1.30 A.M. It was just 6.45 P.M.

For the last ten years or so, I have managed to get around wherever I have lived without the luxury of a car. I say luxury, because in most of Africa and the so-called third world, at least 90 per cent of people do not even have regular and reliable transportation, let alone private vehicles. I have learned to get around as a 'strand-looper' as the saying goes in Southern Africa, because I have been able to pay for the use of whatever public transportation does exist, notwithstanding the inconvenience, which includes waiting.

As soon as we had gotten off the bus, I realized that I would have to keep my wits about me, because it became clear that, as in any other part of New York and of the US for that matter, it was survival of the fittest. This important survival instinct was to reach almost ridiculous levels in the course of the evening's wait, with a three-and-a-half-year-old child and several pieces of luggage.

Let me say at this point that the Port Authority, as this particular New York bus station is called, is a mean and cold place. I say that in both a literal and figurative sense, and anyone who has had to spend even just a few minutes there will know that it is typical of most of the backyards and dumps to which poor, mainly black, people in the US have been relegated.

So there I was, jostling with the luggage, when I realized that the ticket office was on the floor below. I cast a few forlorn looks about in the hope of eliciting some help, because there just was no way I could get down either the stairs or the escalator with a child on my arm and three pieces of luggage. And I couldn't leave my bags unattended because the desperadoes had already begun to move in our direction. So I stood at the top of the stairs and tried to be calm. I looked down at my son, who was quietly taking in the scene with the calm of a child who is secure in the presence of an adult whom she/he trusts.

Quicker than a wink, a tall black man, whom I had noticed from the corner of my eye, was at my side, bowing slightly, offering me his willing hands. I said, 'No, thank you, I can manage,' although it was obvious to all that I could not. He smiled a small, mean, smile and moved on. The other 'hunters' – most of whom were black males, by the way – seemed to slow down in their tracks, watching with anticipation while I tried to find my way out of what is an everyday situation for so many women at bus and railway stations.

As I tried to figure out what best to do, another, older, black man came to my side. He looked at me knowingly and asked, 'Why don't you take the lift?' Relief flooded through me as I thanked him profusely, and it was only later that I realized he had been laughing at me and my fear. I felt guilty at having been afraid of my own people, perceiving them as a threat rather than as a safety cordon. But my better judgement prevailed, because never in my life had the link between racial identification and safety been further apart. Those men did not see me as a sister or as a racial ally; to them I was a 'greenhorn,' 'a Jill come to town,' 'an easy take,' and if I gave them the slightest chance, they would take whatever they could off me. Maybe, in the midst of that mess of miserable humanity, there were some who were relatively less 'hungry,' but to me, stranded in that unknown place with a small child they all looked and smelled like hyenas.

We dragged our bags to the corner of a large, dirty lobby, bought some greasy-looking pizza which must have been at least three days old and tasted even older, and sat down to assess our next move. One young man who had approached me earlier, when we were looking for the Greyhound Bus ticket counter, returned to try his luck. He asked me where we were, and when I told him that he was a busy-body, he burst out laughing and exclaimed, 'Ha, no one has called me that before. You are cute, lady,' and strolled off with the loping walk that reminded me so much of the young, unemployed black youth back home in Southern Africa. Dressed in expensive, 'liberated' (i.e. stolen) clothes, they stroll around the townships and city streets with a limping crab-like walk (bumping, as we call it), exuding their budding 'manhood,' and imposing their sexist nonsense on any woman who happens by. The difference in this case was that most of the men in the Port Authority bus station were dirty and shabbily dressed, although they still retained their male arrogance.

After a short while sitting at the corner cafe, a young worker came up to us and politely informed us that they were closing and that we would have to leave. Reluctantly, we headed for the waiting-room. Mandla, my son, had decided to retrieve some of the toys we had bought during our transatlantic flight, so he quietly sat down on the filthy waiting-room floor and proceeded to play with his miniature planes and cars. At any other time, I would probably have screamed at him to stand up immediately, as he was getting himself dirty, but fatigue and resignation enabled me to ignore the dirty floor while I used my remaining strength to keep awake. As the sociologist in me came to the fore, I settled down on the hard, unfriendly wooden bench, and took a good look at the women and men around me.

Several things struck me at once. The most frightening was the way in which we were immediately perceived as an easy target. As soon as we got off the bus and entered the Port Authority, we entered the world of the underprivileged. And it is a mean and dangerous world. A woman on her own anywhere is open to a multitude of threats, but in a society like the US, where 'dog eats dog' is the norm, one of the last places a black woman with a young child wants to be at night is the Port Authority. Although I never once let my guard down, and never smiled or looked sympathetically at any of the miserable people around us, I knew that given the slightest chance, they would pounce on us. No one threatened us, nor did anyone even come close enough to us for me to feel in any physical danger, but my fear hung like a nasty smell above us for most of the evening.

One middle-aged black man, who was unusually clean and chirpy for someone who had lived most of his adult life on the street, came over to us several times that evening, and with a friendly yet serious warning told me to watch out, because I was in the midst of 'mean niggars.' The irony of it was that while he was just as disadvantaged as all those around him, he felt above them in some way. Maybe he had been on the streets so long that he had acquired a higher status than the more recently arrived desparadoes. Whatever the reason, he said something to me later that evening as he passed by us in the waiting-room which struck me as amazing, to say the least. He warned me again about all these 'niggars' who were waiting for a chance to rip me off, and then he turned to my young son and said 'Now, you take care of your mother, because you are a big man, and she needs your protection in this place.'

The smile on my face slowly vanished as the real meaning of what he had just said dawned on me. Here, in the midst of all the dirt, the destitution, and the degradation of homelessness and poverty; here, in a place unfit to be used even as a waiting-room, this man, who had nowhere to live, no job, probably no family, and certainly no acknowledged status in the wider white racist society, was articulating one of the most sexist and patriarchal expressions I had come across since coming to the US a few months earlier. He was telling my three-and-a-half-year-old son to take care of me. I could not believe my ears. But then I remembered that patriarchy does not require that one be clean and employed or well-fed in order to articulate and perpetuate it. Patriarchy as a male ideology thrives in all situations of inequality.

Logically, what he was saying made no sense. How could a little boy protect me, his mother, his actual protector in reality? But what he had said was not unusual. In fact, one often hears older men especially, but sometimes even women, saying to little boys such things as, 'You take care of your mummy now, you hear.' It is meant as part of the process of the socialization of male children into the role of 'protector of women,' and it is a socialization which goes on throughout the man's life. Then, when a woman says, 'No thank you, I can take care of myself,' the man is baffled, and takes her refusal of his offer of assistance as either 'playing hard to get,' or as a rebuff. He can actually feel hurt by such a refusal, because to be a 'man' around women is what he has been taught all his life. The significance of what the man had just said slowly sank in as I watched him continue his rounds of that wretched-looking community of drug addicts, prostitutes, and other victims of the US capitalist system.

There were all sort of people in that dirty, cold, and smelly room, most of whom lived there all year round. They wander about that part of New York City during the day, especially in the summertime, and maybe even sleep in the parks at night when the weather is warm. But as the fall creeps into the city, they make their way back to the bus stations and whatever relatively warm public places they are still allowed to huddle in during the night.

The characters I saw that night had several things in common. All of them were destitute, they had no place to go. There were mainly black men of various ages, ranging from early twenties to middle age, and they were in various stages of collapse. The younger black men seemed to be in the worst shape, with such dejection on their faces and in their entire beings, that it made me want to weep. My feelings swung from anger and a deep-seated hatred of that destructive system which consumes young people, sapping their strength and destroying their future through poverty, drug-addiction, unemployment, prostitution, ignorance, and violence, to the urge to do something to help those women and men in such desperate need. Then I quickly reminded myself that missionary feelings would only get me into trouble, and would never solve the problems facing poor people anywhere in the world, least of all in the US.

Most depressing was to see women in those conditions. I have seen thousands of women living on the streets in Africa, with babies dying in their arms. So this was not new. Africa, however, has been pillaged of almost everything and people are homeless and poor largely because of a combination of stolen resources and corrupt, irresponsible petty-bourgeois regimes, but when one looks around at a society like the US where there is simply too much wealth accumulated in too few hands, the plight of the homeless hits one even more deeply. The women were more pathetic than the men, because being homeless not only makes them 'less of a woman' in a sexist/patriarchal and racist society, but there is also the implied accusation that such a woman, more than any man, is a failure. Women are supposed to be the custodians of 'morality' and the 'family,' of 'virtue and womanhood,' etc. How can they be sleeping on the streets? It must be their fault that they are frequently the victims of repeated rape, physical and psychological abuse, assault and manipulation by pimps, etc. Those women who are addicted to drugs live wretched, wasted lives, and often die young, never having known any dignity and self-worth.

After a while, I could no longer bear the smell and the depressing sights in that waiting-room. We still had an hour to go but we took our belongings, which had become an embarrassment rather than an unconsidered necessity, and went to the boarding area. We were first on the bus that left for Ithaca that early morning, and I stayed awake throughout that long journey, with the faces and smells of that waiting-room whirling in my mind. It had been the kind of political 'shock' I had needed because, like most petty-bourgeois elements coming from the 'third world' to the US, I had been living in a clean, comfortable neighborhood where it's easy to buy the myth of the American Dream.

Writing, Ancestry, Childhood and Self

Beryl Gilroy

My Approach to Writing Fiction/Faction and Prose Poetry

I write about the under-class which is a familiar phenomenon, since not one of us is secure at every point along the continuum of Life. I write about the old and the infirm, of people struggling to find an identity, but identity, to me, is not strands of effectiveness, group-belongingness or economic stability. Rather, it is the fear of being forgotten, of failing to resist the anguish of indifference, rejection and betrayal; and of being unable to fuse all the expressive moments of life into a panorama of reality that could be called authentic. Identity is having the strength of will to love deeply, and this struggle to love is an intriguing part of the human existence.

Following the search for identity, however false or fragile, allows me as an author to explore the key themes of existentialism and to build characters around them. The existentialist approach to writing about culture and identity engages, in my opinion, such concepts as subjectivity, choice, free-will and individuality, thus counterbalancing the belief that society, its structure and its laws should bear all responsibility for the outcomes of individual lives. The ability to choose and to act freely and judge from the centre of self does not only affect existence, it also enhances human effort in the struggle for existence.

In the stories I write there is no need to reach beyond man's attempt to deal with his own darkness, as that is part of the chaos of life itself; only later can we take charge and make what we can of the life that has been given to us. Most black people are in that position.

I try to offer interior experience with its insights, mystery and moments, and its urgencies of intuition and anxiety. My work is filtered through my knowledge of psychology.

Frangipani House was my first published novella and the book through which I became known, although I had already published *Black Teacher*, an autobiographical account of my time as a teacher in Britain, as well as many other language books used in British schools during the 1960s, 1970s, and 1980s. It is therefore *Frangipani House* that I will first address, although the same form of discussion will support other works I have written.

The story revolves round an elderly widow in a low socioeconomic environment in which the bonds of the extended family have become eroded through emigration and changed memory. Cultural change brings with it a certain blurring of insight and deadening of feeling, and the cords of seminal relationships are worn away under the circularity of work, and the efforts to sustain work. In fact 'work', as the telling heritage of women, is central to the lives of all the women in the story.

Mama King is to be spared work, her helplessness enhanced and her dependency extended as her daughter's concern for her forces them to consider a 'Home' for her. Relations, who cannot comprehend the often accrescent life of an emigre, exploit the opportunity to care, and in so doing neglect Mama King. The relatives themselves have been placed through their own existential struggle in a moral vacuum, and the old lady becomes a lucrative source of income for them.

The 'Home' then is a foreign country for both mother and daughters, providing boundaries for the former and boundary situations for all of them. The 'safety' of the Home makes it impossible for the old woman to give herself to the creation of new meanings in her life. In the world outside she is known and well-regarded. Inside the home she becomes psychologically if not actually anonymous. She is deprived of psychological movement. Her physical movement is also circumscribed and this kind of control increases her irritability; yet she remains intuitive, resourceful, impetuous and restless. In flashes of memory she recalls her identities, for through her past roles, life had reconstituted her many times, and she can link the facts of her present existence to her past states of being.

Her reflexive speech, repetitive and even primitive in content, recaptures her past life, and she is able to establish contact with other inmates. There is little activity in the Home and she is almost conquered by dread and despair. In the grip of isolation she observes the coming death of Miss Mason, and places it against her own ontological death. Miss Mason, who is symbolic of the 'Old Maid' fossilized by parental indoctrination and sexual sublimation, keeps in touch with her deepest needs through fantasy and poetry. Except for her 'past work' as a teacher she is in darkness, for her youth, limited by her intellectualism, has spawned an old age circumscribed by a frozen environment.

'How old am I?' Miss Mason asked like a sheepish child. 'Am I a hundred yet?'

'No ninety. You quite active for your age. And you inquisitive too.'

'Why is it my birthday?' Miss Mason asked. 'I don't want birthdays. I want to die. But I can't, I only sleep ...'

Miss Mason slipped her comforter into her mouth, cuddled her doll and climbed into her bed.

Subsequently Mama King escapes into the underclass, into her own muscular interior life. Her daughters arrive, carrying their moral vacuum with them, so that they can 'save' her. The young women are concerned with absolutes: right, wrong, good, bad, clean, dirty. To sustain these feelings they must further compress and distort reality. Respectability becomes paramount. The old woman must be returned to the Home! She must be saved! In their efforts to save her the two women develop deeper anxieties, deeper guilt, more comprehensive nausea of the conditions they have created. Mama King is rendered more helpless and is deprived of her last link with reality and choice – work, affirmation of self and the 'I' of personality.

Mama King's granddaughter, who throughout the book represents disquietude and solicitude, carries life within her. This germ of life demarcates her personal center and she feels able to answer the question, 'When I am not, where shall I be?' She becomes rescuer and comforter. She is 'process' and that will continue through the child she bears. She will 'be' in her child.

The matron, queen of the world of dependency and infirmity, stands apart as negation and the pleasure of condemnation. She too has moments of reflection, isolation and insecurity which show in conflicts and in situational anxieties. There is no emotional tranquillity for her, no feeling of ultimacy except in the recounting of her personal history with urgency and shame.

Le Cage, who left for the US as a young man and has now returned to visit, is also a part of the urgent re-creation of history, but in an alternative mode. He has made what he could of his existence. But by his visit his life coalesces in a moment of confrontation with Mama King for whom Time has become the absurd and the past once more re-creates the present.

Mama Ginchi and her 'son,' and also the Grandson Markey are all bench marks on the passing of time, friendship and kinship. Nothing is certain except death, and friendship is an interlude, a respite along life's road.

Every life needs a hero, and for Mama King her hero is the ideal husband – not husband as known but husband as desired. A husband who could re-create, transform or simply rearrange reality. Existential writing with the power of its key themes gives me the ability to confront the issues of 'black' life in process. The crux of this is anxiety, which ranges around interpretation, causality, order and disorder and the pressure of values in which priorities could become lost, and people are left incomprehensible even to themselves.

My Grandmother Sally Louis James (1868–1967)

She was my maternal grandmother and a woman of elemental energies that showed in an animated face. She must have been a beauty in her youth with her grey-brown eyes and well-marked features. Small and slight of stature, her ankle-length long-sleeved dresses made her appear taller than the five feet she was. Whatever the fabric of which her dresses were made, however important the occasion on which she wore them, or however much the color varied, each had a mandatory pocket in the gathered skirt where she housed her clay pipe, leaf tobacco and money bag. She always wore a headscarf to hide her salt-and-pepper braids but she took care to place a felt hat, set at a jaunty angle, over the scarf as if to say. 'Hey, I am an individual.'

She had borne my grandfather 15 children, 10 growing to adulthood to produce 34 grandchildren. She combined several races and was indeed a very petite and lively woman. When I discovered her and attached myself to her, she lived in a large thatched cottage with an arbour where cockscombs, bachelor buttons ferns and poinsettias grew in profusion near the door. Though I did not then know, it was she who had brought me to her home, an ailing two-year-old, and restored me to full health. She was sure I was born for something. Present at my birth, she had saved me from suffocation by the caul with which I was born. It must have been a severely frightening experience, for to this day I am disconcerted by having my face covered.

My grandmother understood freedom, which to her meant being able to organize and take account of those moments when intention became action. I later understood how the way she raised me shifted the limits of my childhood from being owned and manipulated by older family members, to questioning and debating the content of whatever was offered as edicts or laws or certainties.

My grandmother believed in 'personhood.' She took me everywhere she went so that I could learn the importance of commitment and responsibility. She involved all her younger grandchildren in the management of her poultry, which she farmed commercially. My special job was to douse her pigs when the sun was overhead and there was no question of forgetting to do it.

She had a formidable reputation as a herbalist. If she was unsure of a herb she scrutinized it through the magnifying glass which was her treasure. Sometimes she let me use it to examine tiny plants and animals, which gave me a keen interest in biology. She commanded one of my cousins who went to school to teach me to read. As he had no suitable book, he taught me from his book, a primer in the Royal Reader series, but when she saw him thumping me she taught me herself. I was surprised at the extent of her literacy, when I grew old enough to understand our colonial inheritance. She encouraged me to read whatever was in the house, regardless of difficulty or suitability. In a short time I had read well-known works by the literary stalwarts of that time.

When I was seven my grandmother held a party attended by a few of her friends and we sang a duet, 'Just a Song at Twilight.' Afterwards I recited the Twenty-third Psalm and the Lord's Prayer without a mistake. She was proud of me. I kept on bowing until she plonked me on a chair. 'Don't over do,' she whispered.

I can remember being punished by her for using a catapult. By sheer accident, I hit 'a nice girl' in the face and she arrived with her mother to complain. After that my grandmother decided that I should get a taste of schooling by attending the little private school run by one of her sons-in-law. I was in a state of panic. But the die was cast, and I went for a short time on those days when they sang, drew things and did problems from the Chamber's arithmetic books.

Then boredom set in. I despised all the sitting down when there was so much going on outside. Each morning as 'school time' grew nearer, I would begin the most enormous sobbing, and after about ten minutes or so my grandmother would say 'my eyes were too red' to go to school. In next to no time we'd be off fishing or just weeding the crops. It was interesting just to watch the creatures in the water or the interplay of light and shade from the overhanging branches, or gaze up at the clouds scudding high above me. At that time, I felt most blissful – so far away from the dust and noise of our single village street. I would improvise little poems, and recite them to her and tell her the longest words I had found in my Collins Gem dictionary as we fished and cooked or drank our coconut water.

My grandmother was not fanatical about religion. We were members of the Anglo-Catholic Church which was then in the care of a Barbadian priest, the Rev Griffiths, a coal-black man with a scholarly way of preaching. He used to test me on the meanings of words and concluded, 'She will do well, school or no school.' So I continued walking on the sand, collecting shells and being a child of nature until, suddenly, my grandparents decided that, at the age of eleven, the time had come to think of my confirmation. To be confirmed I had to go to the church school; I was to be a chorister.

When I think of what I endured in that place, a cold shiver even now runs through my body. The best person there was the new priest, Rev Headman, who taught the catechism. He relied on me to know the answers to his questions. The work was much too simple for me and it was only when they put me in Standard Six that I began to accept the inevitability of going to that place. It was crowded and the headmaster had his favorites. I was not one of them.

The teacher taught me much of what I'd taught myself. For the first time my grandmother proved impervious to my stories and rantings against the school, but as a sop bought me some books at the plantation sale. One turned out to be Palgrave's Golden Treasury Book Four. I was not particularly mindful of it until the day I found, among the 'additional poems,' 'The Forsaken Merman' by Matthew Arnold. It was the first poem I was to read about the sea that meant something to me.

The Merman married a mortal and took her to his kingdom in the sea, where they lived in amity and love and raised a family of children. One day, however, they wandered up to the surface from where they heard the church bells ringing. That reminded the maiden of her past life.

> She sighed, she looked up through the clear green sea.
> She said, 'I must go, for my kinsfolk pray
> In the little grey church on the shore today
> Twill be Easter time in the world – ah me!
> And I lose my poor soul, Merman, here with thee.'
> I said, 'Go up, dear heart, through the waves.
> Say thy prayer and come back to the kind sea caves!'
> She smiled. She swam up through the surf in the bay.
> Children dear, was it yesterday.

As I read the poem, its sentiments turned on the lights of reality at full voltage. I lived near the sea, heard all its voices, watched the sunlight glinting like scattered glass between the ripples, and heard the music of the rollers heading shorewards. I had been familiar with all that legend could invent. Mermaids sang to lure sailors to their deaths; Massa Kruman, the giant of the sea, seized the largest cutters in a single hand; the Chick Charnies fooled Pirates and Brigands with their lamp-sized glowing eyes. I had even 'seen' them on calm days. Sometimes the sea yielded other flotsam of the most disquieting kind. That day nothing mattered except my imagination and the despairing voice of the Merman.

> 'Come away children. Come away, come down.
> She will not hear though you call all day …
> Come, dear children, let us away.'

It was very hot. Nevertheless, I wanted to share the most poignant moments of the Merman's grief with someone, anyone, who had a heart.

We were a large family. Surely I would be able to persuade someone to enter into that labyrinth of fantasy and feeling with me. But alas, no one would consent to listen even for a moment! I was very hurt by a combination of rejection and frustration and it showed on my face. I set out to find my grandmother who had gone visiting. Subsequently I ran into a confabulation of women, my grandmother in full flood on the subject of icing wedding cakes, a skill for which she was renowned.

I blurted out my problem and she replied, 'Tell me! I want to hear about this man who had a tail where his legs should be!' I laughed and sat down. She listened to every word and then I read bits to her friends.

The poem released in her buried memories of the myths of my country, for my grandmother was born a mere generation away from that dreadful time of slavery.

She talked of the 'Long Bubbies', the ghosts of dead field-slaves who nursed their children as they worked and so stretched their breasts to incredible lengths. They served when the women returned as spirits after death as implements of pain to beat their masters into hell. She told me of the Cabresses, the mulatto courtesans who were hired out to earn money 'in bad ways' for their masters and mistresses. Of Long Lady, who rode the moonbeams, of Adopi, who roamed the woods. She acted out each of these creatures. To her, life was a great dance over pebbles, stones, thorns and grass and in remembering another age, she transformed the invisible into the tangible.

She was a storehouse of colloquial proverbs and came out with such gems as, 'Stone a seabead doan feel hot sun,' or 'Rice got motion a pot but meek and mild a plate,' and 'If you eye deep, start to cry early day dawn.' Unconstrained or unconstricted by conventional prejudice, she found the courage to thrust into life each and every day, and emerge carrying in her hands the appropriate responses. When she took me to see the Folk Theater from Union in a rendition of 'Samson and Delilah' or 'David and Goliath,' or to the Palladium, our local theater, to see what life-truth 'Sam Chase' performed, she giggled like a child beside me.

I was leaving what was then British Guiana and went to say goodbye to her. 'I'm going away,' I said, 'to university. In England and perhaps to America.' She was silent for some time and then said, 'You won't be here to bury me, but follow your luck. You remember the four-eye fish that use to come a back door?' I nodded. 'They keep two eye to find food and two to see danger. Be like-a dem. Remember, you got you caul.'

'Tell me something about this time, this moment,' I replied.

She touched my hand slightly and said, 'Oh Lord, thou has searched me and known men, and there is not a word in my tongue, Lord, but thou knowest it.'

'Yes,' I said. 'God knows where I will be in a few year's time. Perhaps with a family of my own to take care of.'

She died before I returned with my children for a visit after 18 years. She was nearly 100 years old. She will always be an evergreen memory in my life. A staunch supporter, she respected all my youthful endeavors and taught me the life-skills I have taught my own successful children. She showed me tremendous kindness and warmth. She made me distrustful of mediocrity and victim-mindedness, and helped me at all times to face situations, so as to avoid what she called 'spirit poorness.' As the echo of the healthy voices of my childhood, she said 'gratefulness' rather than 'gratitude' bonded a gift to a giver, and also left room for surprise and reciprocity. To be able to feel, she said, was to combine all the human senses in a single act, like 'opening an umbrella over everything.' Her own motherhood had taught her how to be a grandmother slowly and gently, for her skills to mother, she was sure, grew old along with her. She controlled us by insight which kept her ahead of us in thinking about problems, and in the belief in the essential goodness of mankind.

> Gentle as a breeze her love. Its power all enduring.
> It touched which every spot was sore and instant was the curing.
> There dwelt in her a little child who always showed resilience,
> And understood that success came through hard work and persistence.
> Thoroughness was her delight, it made for sure survival,
> To act in anger was a blight that hindered joy's survival,
> Yes, soft and gentle was her love yet strong and heart-enriching
> As certain as a raindrop's touch and equally life-giving.

When I am feeling tired or happy I think of my grandmother, of the places she took me, and of the days we spent together, and recall her commonsense and her kindnesses. She was a practical, hard-headed woman, who cut and thrust to the tunes of the time. Everyone respected her. I'm glad I knew her. She was a friend of my childhood in particular, and saw childhood as a time that children should enjoy.

It's Cold Outside

Carole Boyce Davies

Delphine stepped briskly through the swirling pieces of debris and garbage. The closed, shuttered and barricaded stores which she passed made the usually busy shopping area seem like a ghost town or a war zone now in the early morning hours. The street was empty. She maintained her pace, fighting back a feeling of dread and loneliness. She avoided the shiny black surfaces which she knew meant a sure fall. And she hated to fall. It meant looking around to see who was looking, getting up quickly, ignoring the pain so as not to look like it was serious. Falls were too painful and humiliating. She concentrated on her strides remembering the last time she fell, the blue-black mark that stayed on her thigh for weeks. Thoughts and bits of memory swirled around in her head and presented themselves from time to time.

With all these falls, in this snow, I sure to get old before my time. I must buy some nice boots with fur inside and a nice sole to grip the ice.

She looked down at her feet, at the worn black shoes with the little heel and the pointed toes which she had picked out because they could be worn both to work and if she had somewhere interesting to go. She decided that as soon as she got her next salary she would do something to improve her appearance and her chances in the winter.

Her friend Pat, who lived in the room across from her, had shown her a new pair of shoes that she said she had paid only twenty dollars for.

I'm sure I could get something a little cheaper. Twenty dollars is plenty for one shoes when you have responsibilities. I have my two children back home to mind. I can't study she and she showing off and the weekly fashion show. Every Sunday is a different thing some man buy for she. She get a stereo just so for her birthday. And imagine, a whole new-fashioned bedroom set with mirrors and thing last Christmas and look at me here with nothing.

She remembered Patsy's words, from yesterday. 'Chile, I here in America and I am going to use what I have to get what I want. Back home I live in a little two-room shack in Laventille, me and my five sisters and their children and my mother work so hard, veins was standing up on she hands. Her legs was bulging with varicose veins and she never had a good day where she could sit down. To even bathe she had to walk down the street to get water. I look on at she and my sisters getting pregnant for these useless men and I say that ent happening to me.'

She wished she could be as tough as Patsy but she hated asking men for things. Thinking about that: I have to send something home when I get paid next week.

Delphine hugged her second-hand coat closer to her slim body and counted. Only two more blocks to get to the subway. Then she thought of how cold the wait would be for the train that would take her all the way to work. God, she hated that long ride. And at this time in the morning, those old drunken bums are still around to harass a lone woman. She remembered that day on the train, however, when a nice-looking, middle-aged man in a suit sat next to her. It was in the middle of the day and she was going to the employment agency. He was the business-like type, reading his newspaper. Carelessly, it seemed the paper spread over on to her legs. She could not move because the train was crowded. Suddenly she felt his hand working its way under the paper to the V of her lap. She had jumped up, glared at him and stood for the rest of the trip.

'What a place! You can't trust nobody. Oh God, it's so cold!'

She could never take the clinging coldness. One more block to go. The clock at the corner said 5.30. A few people were coming from the adjoining street. The coffee-shop owner was just beginning to cut through the piles of newspapers which had been left out front. She waited for a car to pass and then she crossed the street.

Leaving Brooklyn early Monday is better though than staying in Far Rockaway on Sunday night. She always had to leave the kitchenette early on Monday mornings after her Sunday off in order to make it to work by 7.00. Otherwise, she would have to sleep there and that meant being on call for free even when it was still her day off. She thought of the week ahead. Mrs Lefko's daughter, Ada, would leave as soon as she got there. First she had to change the sheets and wash all the urine-soaked linen and bedclothes. Day and night she had to listen to the voice of the complaining old woman whom she worked for. She was always calling her, demanding something, chastising her for being too slow, fussing about the lazy help nowadays.

'I had a woman from the islands who worked for me before,' she told her one day. 'She could move a whole wardrobe by herself and clean behind it. I never had to tell her anything. She knew what to do.'

She even tried to slap me one day but I looked at her so hard she didn't bother. I would have hit her back like my mother's friend, Miss Esme, said she did to hers. She is so weak yet she is so ungrateful and so stingy, always checking to see that I don't eat too much. Some days when she piling on the pressure, I wish she would just go ahead and die instead of making everybody so miserable in the process.

'But if the bitch dies I am out of work,' she said out loud and caught herself.

A cold gust of wind blew as she turned the corner and entered the subway station, descending the grimy, littered flight of stairs. Life is hell in this New York, oui. If only I could make my way back home, there is no way I would be here. I miss the warmth. People are friendly. But money is slow. Yes, I'm better off here. She bought a token, entered the turnstile, found a dingy green bench and sat. Her mind trailed off in the early morning dampness as she waited.

Sundays are nice. It's the only time I can be myself. She thought of Stanley. She smiled briefly to herself. Even though she saw him once a week in the little room they shared, the memories lingered all week. Stanley was good enough to her. He had turned sleepily when she woke up and his arm on her leg told her that he wanted her. She wanted him but knew she didn't have the time. He had massaged her nipples briefly then ran his fingers through her pubic hair and, finding her wet, entered quickly. She looked over his shoulder at the clock and realized that she had to get up and catch the train. He would sleep and get up later. She moved her hips frantically, knowing this would climax the encounter. She got up, ran to the bathroom, sponged her vagina and got ready quickly. A sense of incompletion hovered over her. No wonder somebody was always after him. She frowned briefly but smiled again.

Patsy had told her all the stories, that she should leave this good-for-nothing man and find somebody who could give her something. 'I would never pay any rent so a man could lay about with his women while I am away working,' Patsy had said. But Stanley is from back home and where will I find somebody else? She sighed and looked down the tracks.

The station was deserted except for three or four people scattered at different points. Each person seemed determined to maintain his own space. One man in gray overalls peeping out of a worn brown coat, a lunch-pail in his hand, leaned to one side. A nurse in her off-whites seemed deep in her thoughts. A woman with a baby wrapped up in several blankets huddled in a corner with a large plastic shopping bag on the bench next to her. Delphine felt the cold blow through the station and it seemed to go right through her bones. Old disinfectant mixed with urine assailed her nostrils from the nearby toilet. She felt a rising nausea. She fished a mint out of her pocket and put it in her mouth and the nausea subsided as fast as it came. A cleaner on the other side of the platform worked his way through the surface filth with a big blackened mop which only wet the tiles. She looked up and down the tracks. No train yet. The turnstile creaked and a big beefy man with a tool-box in his hand came in. His nose was red and running into the mustache under it, she noticed as he drew closer. He looked at her and smiled.

'It's cold enough for you, baby?'

'Man, it ent start to get too cold for me yet. I young and strong and I could take it,' she responded bravely, hoping that would halt any other attempt at conversation. She looked for the train as she hugged herself. Ignoring her sarcasm, he continued.

'I would give anything to be in the islands now – the rum, the beach, a nice island girl and me. I know you Jamaicans are used to the sun. I always wonder why you all leave the islands and come up here.'

She was saved from answering by the sudden aggressive arrival of the train. She purposely sought a different car so as not to continue the conversation. The futility of having to explain that she was not a Jamaican and what she was doing in New York infuriated her. The darkness whizzed by as she looked out the window. She was only 31 but she suddenly felt like a tired 65. This was not what she had in mind for herself. This was not how she had pictured herself in New York when she was back home.

This hard work, the cold and this woman is killing me, she thought. The woman acts like I am her slave. I wish I could do something else with my life. But until I get my green card from them, everything has to wait. Then I can take some courses, get a diploma and a better job.

These dreams seemed far away now. She had to give Stanley some money to pay the rent. She had to send some money home. One hundred dollars a week seemed like a lot of money, but it really can't reach far here.

A stream of people began to move in and out of the train at each stop. Their faces were vacant as they stared in all directions, deliberately avoiding the eyes of anybody else. Bodies weighed down with boots, hats, scarves, coats. Anguished looks. Furtive looks. No smiles. Now there were hardly any seats in the car. Her eyes fell on the advertisements on the walls of the train. One was for a religious birth-counselling place. She thought about her difficult pregnancies, the nausea and swollen feet, the perpetual hunger only filled by green mangoes and plums, the long, hilly climb to the house on the hill after working all day cooking at the cafe. The yard children would run to see what she had brought home in her bag.

She watched the people come and go, feeling the icy wind from outside as the door opened and closed. Still a long way to go. Far Rockaway! The name suited the distance you had to go to reach it. Once Stanley had come with her for company. It was nice having somebody to talk to on the long ride. But he had grumbled all the way: 'Oh God! This place too far boy! Not me again! Is me alone to ride back to Brooklyn.' Still she was grateful. I don't blame him. If not for my children, I wouldn't bother to do this either. I want my children to go to high school at least, especially the girl. She is bright they say. She writes well. She learns her lessons fast. She searched quickly in her bag and fished out a frayed-looking letter.

Dear Del,

I want to come to America with you. Please send for me soon. I tell my teachers I going to America soon. In the mean time, please send me a dolly with gold hair. I want one that can walk and talk. Granny is not too well these days. I learning to cook and help her out. She lets me hang out the clothes for her. Please send me a dolly for my birthday. And send a bicycle. Benny only want cowboy boots. His father does give him money to spend but he only buys caps for his gun. I miss sleeping by you in the night but I know you will send for me soon. Tantie Joan sleeps here now too and she combs my hair in the morning.

Your daughter,

Sharlene

Delphine smiled wistfully. Children don't always understand. Everybody thinks that when you in America you have plenty money. Next time I get pay I must send her the doll. But maybe a nice brown-skin one. I tired of golden hair.

Two more stops to go. She examined her fingers slowly, feeling the growing roughness in some areas. She looked at her watch, five minutes to seven. Finally her stop. She got off briskly. The cold air whipped around her ears and across her face and tried to go down her neck and into her bosom and up her coat and in between her legs. She braced herself, turned up the collar of her coat, wrapped her scarf more securely and walked through the cold. Several cars went in the direction of the parkway. The sidewalks were not very icy. Neat blocks of frosted grass fronted each house. The sidewalks were clean. Big green trash containers lined the street. She cleared her mind and prepared herself for the week as she walked. A few more long blocks and she was there. Her toes felt numb in her shoes. The soles of her feet tingled.

As Delphine turned the corner she noticed two cars parked in front. She mounted the side steps and rang the bell with some urgency. Mrs Lefko's daughter-in-law, a pale, trembling woman let her in.

'Who is it, Reby? We want no visitors.'

'It's a black woman. You're the maid, right?' she caught herself and asked Delphine with a little gesture of embarrassment. 'Come right in out of the cold.'

'It's mother's help,' she relayed to the other voice.

'Well, tell her what happened,' the voice said coming closer. 'Mother passed away last night at eleven. So, we won't need you anymore. But now that you are here, please come in. I paid you on Saturday so we don't owe you anything, right. But if you stay today and help us sort out her things, I will pay you for the day's work. You can help me clean up this place before you go. And you can take anything that you want because all this stuff is going to the Salvation Army.'

Delphine looked through the window at the trees with the frosted leaves. Pine trees in the distance with clumps of snow casually decorating them made the landscape seem just like those Christmas cards people still sent back home. She wondered if she should leave but it was cold outside and she needed to catch her breath.

Mother was a Great Man

Catherine Obianuju Acholonu

It was a dry harmattan evening. The leaves were already falling from the trees and the wind blew them this way and that. But for the rustling whisper of trees bending to the wind, a big hush pervaded the village square as Oyidiya and her two daughters, Mmema and Ikonne, moved past and into the family compound. Neither of the three women spoke. Their heads were bowed low. Their minds were occupied by the same nagging feeling of guilt. They had gone too far. They had tried to rearrange the destiny imposed on Oyidiya by her *chi*[1] and now they were learning the hard way.

Mmema and Ikonne were both married to prosperous and well-to-do husbands. Their husbands were both in the beer business. They were agents of several beer and mineral drink manufacturers and this yielded much money. Oyidiya was lucky with her daughters; they were rich and easily came to her assistance whenever she needed them. Mmema had been given to her husband Kaka 20 years earlier. Kaka was about 30 when he paid her bride-price.

Oyidiya still remembered the day she and Mmema went to the big Orlu[2] market to sell palm kernels. Orlu people live on top of the hill about seven miles away from Mmema's people of Umuma who live in the valley. In those days if one wanted to get to Orie, the big Orlu market, early enough, one set out at the first cock-crow. Then one would be sure to arrive there before the sun was overhead. Now the motor car has made everything easy, Oyidiya thought. The Orlu people were queer people. The people of Umuma did not trust them; they regarded them as semi-strangers who could not be trusted because they had opened up to the white man without reserve. Why, they would even sell off the wares on your head while they talked and drank with you. The Orlu people on the other hand regarded the Umuma people as enemies of progress. Umuma people were timid and hateful; they hated to see progress and happiness in others. If an Umuma man saw that his neighbor's or brother's children were doing well in trade, he would quickly ask the witchdoctor to prepare some poisonous concoctions to kill them with. In Umuma, if you made progress, you would keep it secret; an Umuma man who owned a car would never drive it home or that would be the last day his eyes would glimpse the sun.

These notwithstanding, Oyidiya had given her first daughter, Mmema, a young girl of barely 14 years, in marriage to Kaka. Many said it was because of Kaka's wealth, others said it was witchcraft. But Kaka had been spellbound by the beauty of this little tender thing whose skin was as smooth as a water pebble and as light as a ripe banana fruit, and whose eyes twinkled as they told countless exciting stories. He had quickly paid the bride-price and Mmema had been escorted to his home with Ikonne to keep her company. Then they had sealed the relationship by being wedded in the church. Ikonne grew into a very attractive young girl resembling Mmema as she grew, only she was taller and stronger-looking. Kaka wanted to make sure that this little girl who had been almost a daughter to him would not get into wrong hands, so he got her attached to his bosom friend Odili, from a neighboring village, who was also in the beer business. Now, both men were rich and their wives wielded economic power in their respective homes. Oyidiya was proud of her daughters and grateful that their high financial standing made it possible for her to realize her plans; and even though she had no son of her own, people respected her because of the prosperity of her daughters which was always felt around her. She had even taken the titles which were reserved only for rich women of high social standing.[3]

As Oyidiya remembered the events of the past years, it struck her that she and her husband had almost exchanged roles. Nekwe, her husband, was a man who surpassed every woman in beauty. He was tall and skinny, with a skin as light as ripe udala fruits; and, as if to crown his beauty, Nekwe even had *mbibi* patterns on his face and arms (*mbibi* were elaborate sketches carved into the skin and darkened with some black substance to enhance beauty). These scarification marks were often associated with vanity. Now, as the thought occurred to her, Oyidiya wondered why her husband, who was now dead, did not instead go for the *ichi* facial marks that were emblems of manhood, valor and productivity. But it would hardly have become him, she thought. Nekwe was not the manly type. Was it not she, Oyidiya, who had to stand on her feet and defend her family whenever another family challenged it? How often did she have to defend her husband against his fellow men? Yes, the gods knew what they were doing. They always joined together in marriage people of opposing qualities and thus ensured harmony.

Oyidiya did not want to admit it, but now as she went through her life in her mind, she saw clearly that she had been the man of the house while her husband, Nekwe, had been the woman. Yes. She had even indulged in excesses, for which she was now paying. She felt a strong pang of guilt and remorse. She, Oyidiya, had gone too far. She had not accepted her lot. She had forced the hand of her *chi*. And now this was the result.

Oyidiya walked faster. She thought her own guilt feeling surpassed those of her two daughters, who, in fact, had no hand in the decision that was now costing her her peace of mind, except perhaps in so far as they had given her the financial support with which she had realized her plans. Oyidiya walked faster still, then she stopped and turned round to face her two daughters.

'But I did the only thing any woman would have done under the circumstances. You are not blaming me, are you?' she burst out.

'Nne,[4] nobody is blaming you. Humphrey will come back. We shall do all in our power to see that they release him soon.' Mmema did not even believe herself. Humphrey, she was sure, was going to face the firing squad for armed robbery.

'Kompin will die in that place, my spirit tells me he will not come out of it alive. And it is all my fault. If I had heeded to my *chi*.'

Humphrey was Oyidiya's last child and only son. As the old woman could not pronounce the complicated white man's name, she called him Kompin. The tears were now running down her cheeks. Oyidiya was now very old, and she had suffered a lot, chasing after a male issue which always eluded her. She had had the misfortune of bearing exceptionally beautiful children, for the understanding was that such children were water spirits and never lived long. Oyidiya knew this, but what she could not understand was why it was only the male issues that turned out to be water spirits while her female issues all lived and bustled with excessive vitality. No, something else was responsible for the early deaths of all her male children. She was sure her husband's second wife, Njido, was responsible. Njido was a witch and was clearly eating off all her boys, hoping to lay claim to their husband's property. Even now the cold war had begun. Njido and her wretched boys were claiming everything, and they had ensured that her only son Kompin was safely behind bars. They had bewitched him, she was sure of it. Why did I not think of this before? she questioned her mind. My *chi* has definitely fashioned me for great things, but Njido is bent on foiling it. Yes. My *chi* has fashioned me for greatness …

Oyidiya remembered, as she took the last steps towards her family compound, that she was a woman of no ordinary birth. Her parents had been rich and very prosperous. But what made her more proud was the fact that she was of royal birth. She was from a family of chieftains, and her father, Uloka, had earnestly desired her birth. In her village, no prospective chief would ever attain his royal stool unless he begot a daughter. A man's first daughter was his constant companion and bosom friend. When his wives quarreled, his first daughter would be called in to descend sternly on them and sort out the quarrel. The first daughter of every Igbo family commanded a high position and pride of place, she was her father's 'two legs' while the first son was his 'right hand.' In many parts of Igboland it was the first daughter who ate the best part of the meat whenever an animal was slaughtered in her father's compound. Oyidiya remembered the story her mother had told her of how her father had had to marry her as a second wife in the bid to get a daughter to complete the requirements of his chieftaincy coronation.

'Your father was rich, he had a large yam barn, a hard-working wife, four able-bodied sons and, above all, the royal blood of his ancestors flowed through his veins. But the elders were adamant. They would not hear of a chieftain without a daughter. "That is the custom of Ikeduru", they insisted, "and nobody will change it."'

Ada still remembered how she shook with fear as she stood by her father while he made his pledge to the elders; how she, a mere child of six, had had to put up with the discomfort of the heavy jigida[5] strings on her hips and the ivory armlets and anklets that had darkened with age; she remembered, too, the discomfort of having to pronounce the difficult words that would give credence to her father's solemn pledge to the people of Ikeduru.

'But why a daughter?' Oyidiya had asked her mother. 'Surely a son would have been of greater importance. Our people only want sons.'

'Yes, they want sons, but they always say that to beget a daughter first is a blessing to the family. A daughter caters for the well-being of her parents in their old age; sons only care for their immediate families. They care little for their ageing parents. A son caters for continuity of the family name and external image, but a daughter caters for love, understanding and unity within the family circle. She brings the brethren together and sorts out their differences. Our people believe that it is a curse to beget only sons and no daughter. They will not put up with a chieftain who has no daughter. They say that his homestead is standing on spikes and sooner or later will be razed to the dust.'

So, whereas other girls of her age felt inferior to the boys, Oyidiya was treated with special preference. She did not have to put up with the absurdities that forbade women to whistle, or to climb trees, and because none of these sanctions was placed on her, she grew up with the exuberance and freedom that was allowed only to boys. She did not realize the difference in the sexes until the day she bled between her legs. She had gone on a cricket-hunting session with her friends, most of whom were boys. Oyidiya sighted an ube[6] tree full of ripe fruits, and made straight for it climbing with youthful abandon. Then somebody, one of the boys, shouted:

'Oyidiya is bleeding. Oyidiya is bleeding between her legs.'

She could not remember how she got down from that tree. The boys jeered at her all the way home. That was how she parted ways with her male companions, especially after she discovered from her mother that that awful experience would be repeating itself every seven market weeks.

That was many many years ago. Looking back, Oyidiya thought what an irony of fate it was that she who had been a highly desired daughter should afterwards hang in the balance because she had no male issue.

Oyidiya was left with no choice but to do what in Igboland was reserved for women of high social and financial standing, to which class she rightly belonged: she must have her own son, and if he would not come from her own womb then some other woman would do so in her name and on her behalf. She summoned her husband's kinsmen and told them she was going to take a wife. The men said they were surprised she had waited so long to take that inevitable step. And so after a series of visits with kegs of palm wine and presents to the Umuado village, Nekwe's kinsmen brought home to Oyidiya a young girl of 16, looking so ripe and full that one would have expected from her only male issues. But that was not to be, or maybe she did not stay long enough to find out. When her first two issues turned out to be girls, Oyidiya got impatient and sent her home to her parents. Then Oyidiya married again, but this time the young woman was having difficulty in conceiving. Oyidiya invited a witchdoctor to administer treatment to her, but, to her dismay and shame, the healer eloped with the young bride.

Oyidiya was not one to brood over a shameless woman when she could marry as many as she wanted. So she quickly married again, but this time, there was no Nekwe to supply the male seed. Nekwe was bitten by a snake on his way to the farm and died soon afterwards. But the new development did not dissuade Oyidiya from keeping the new wife. After all, what were a husband's male relations for, if not to see to it that their dead brother's name was not buried with him? So the new wife bore her first issue which turned out to be twin girls; but she and her new babies did not outstay the night. They were quickly bundled back to the girl's parents. It was a pity the white man had put his nose into everything, otherwise mother and daughters would have been killed and thrown into the bad bush, Oyidiya had fumed.

Oyidiya was now quite old and physically weak, but her heart was strong. She was bent on leaving behind her, after her death, a son to claim her own share of her husband's property and to retain her homestead. She, Oyidiya, daughter of Uloka, would not leave this world without a son to repair and breed life into her hut. It was a pity that girls had to marry and leave their fathers' houses to breed life into other men's homes. If she did not have a son before her death, her hut would be demolished and soon the children of the other wife of her husband would begin to farm on it. That was not to be. She, Oyidiya, was going to prevent that. After all, was her name not Oyidiya – the one that resembled her husband? Or, rather, the woman that resembled a man, she quickly corrected herself.

She had long forgotten about her second wife, who had escaped with the witch-doctor, and was recovering from the ill luck of the twin girls when, one day, a distant relative of her husband, who lived almost buried and forgotten in the far-away town of Asaba across the great river of which she had heard only in stories of adventure, came home with the story that changed everything. Oyidiya's forgotten wife, Chitu, was living there and had long given birth to a baby boy by her witchdoctor lover. Oyidiya smiled to herself. The gods had blessed her at last, for the son was hers. In fact, all Chitu's children were hers, but she was not interested in the girls; all she wanted was the boy. In spite of his questionable breeding and heritage, Oyidiya wanted to hold him in her arms, to feel his young muscles, to smell his boyhood. Gradually the feeling grew into an ache, a longing. Oyidiya summoned the kindred of her husband and told them of the new development. Some thought it was not wise to bring in a son from the lineage of wizards, it would not go well, they argued. But there were many others who thought that the gods had finally heard Oyidiya's prayers. It was therefore agreed that the boy should be brought home; if necessary, he would be abducted.

Oyidiya sent word to her daughters, inviting them to give her financial support. She had to pay a lot of money to the young men who undertook the journey. And so Humphrey was abducted and brought home to Oyidiya, who performed several sacrifices of appreciation to her *chi* and to *Oguugwu*, the god of the village that catered for justice and fair play. Oyidiya remembered it all so vividly, now, as she pushed open the carved wooden door that led into the compound. Yes, she now had a son, but she had something else in addition; she had misery, frustration, even more – anxiety, for Kompin was an embodiment of all vices. He was a cheat, a liar, a thief, a glutton. Right from the first day he was brought into Oyidiya's home, the little boy, who was then barely four years old, had been caught eating the fish from the soup-pot, and since that day he had never ceased to be in trouble. Now he was locked up in the white man's prison at Orlu.

As soon as she heard the news, Oyidiya had sent for her daughters, and though they had tried to bribe him out, it was all to no avail. Oyidiya was sure this was going to be the end of the boy and of the dream that had spurred her on and filled her with hope even at the most trying periods. He was going to be shot by the soldiers who now ruled the country. She too was tired, she had lost interest in living, but she would not give up the fight. She was going to retaliate from the grave against her husband's second wife who had taken the ground from under her feet. Oyidiya pushed at the carved wooden gate of the dwarf mud-wall which creaked open to allow them in. As she took the last few steps and disappeared into the cold dark interior of her thatched, mud-walled hut, she was oblivious to everything around her; she did not see her dog, Logbo, whimpering its welcome, she did not hear her two daughters calling her from behind, she was only conscious of a dry ache somewhere inside her head. Then she swooned and was about to fall when Ikonne caught her, and, tenderly, the two women laid their aged mother on to her bamboo bed. Oyidiya the fighter, the husband of three wives, the manly woman, was no more. But before she breathed her last, Oyidiya gave her last instructions to her daughters.

'I have fought a good fight. You two should not give up now. Before they shoot him, be sure to keep a wife here in his name. Then my life shall not have been in vain. The gods and my *chi* have fashioned me for great things.'

The two women exchanged glances. 'Mother was a great man,' they both agreed. 'We must prepare for her a befitting burial.'

Notes

1. *Chi*: God, personalized; destiny in Igbo world-view.
2. Orlu: a small town in the Igbo heartland.
3. In Igboland, women who wielded much influence and power in their communities were rewarded with titles, especially if such women commanded respect and high regard.
4. Nne: an Igbo appellation for 'Mother.'
5. Jigida: a string of disc-like beads worn round the hips by young maidens.
6. Ube tree: the native pear, the fruits of which ripen by becoming darker on the surface.

Bringing Myself into Fiction

Marion Bethel

I Was Fixed: the Primary Years

I wish that I could say to myself and to you that it was Obeah that fixed me because it really was the only fixing that I knew as a child growing up in the Bahamas. No, it isn't the Obeah man or woman whom I charge with my fixing or even with my country's fixing. Yes, there are many Bahamians who have a healthy respect for the powers of Obeah. I'm even aware that the setting of our general election dates are fixed by the power of Obeah. But no, it isn't the Obeah fixing that nearly had me trounced.

For I was undoubtedly fixed at about the age of four by a six by three feet painting, vibrant and colorful in the 1950s and 1960s, now faded and yellowed, that stood then and still stands on the wall of the Nassau International Airport. Whether I was sliding down the bannister railing or tripping lightly down the stairs above which this painting loomed, I used to eye that scene carefully each and every time. I never seemed to tire of experiencing this painting and its message nor the many other versions of it in school books.

And I liked that scene a lot in whichever way it was presented – the peace and holiness of it held me every time. For certain there was no evidence of strife or turmoil and there was, in bold relief, the cross on the sails of the ships and in the hands of the man. I didn't miss a thing through those primary years. The discovery of the Bahamas and the new world as taught to me was the most important event for the Bahamas and the world.

I didn't have to revisit that painting because I can conjure up in an instant an accurate mental picture of the landing of Columbus and his crew on Guanahani. But I was driven to see if it still stood. And I suppose I ought to have known the answer. We have crisp new 1992 one dollar bills with his head instead of Elizabeth's, quincentennial stamps, telephone directories and other insignia all glorifying the event everywhere. We have a freshly painted Columbus standing dead centre of the city. Why not let stand an old painting by one Mr D. Cavill, painted in 1957? Why not?! What surprised me when I revisited the painting was this: it had not been retouched, not embellished, not called upon to participate in this celebration.

You too may have been fixed by this painting. Or your school curriculum, your church, family or community. Maybe all of the above! Come on now, bare your soul and be a witness! Sing with me this frequently sung childhood ditty:

In 1492 Columbus sailed the ocean blue
In three fine ships and eastward bound
He found the world so big and round.

A harmless song, maybe! In any case we calypsoed to it, junkanooed to it, we even cussed with it, but the fact remained it was an ever-present song and game. And, for me, Columbus reached the level of god. After all, he did found the new world; he did not fall off the edge of the earth. In the beginning there was Columbus ... he was a good, courageous Christian explorer and so must we be in his image. And his arrival, indeed, was our genesis.

Genesis, Exodus, Leviticus, Numbers, Deuteronomy, Joshua, Judges, Ruth ... How many books are in the Bible?

If you've been fixed too, I trust you will understand my preoccupation; or, on the other hand, you may think I am plain mad. Anyway, I need to share with you that it's taken a long long time for me to understand for myself the meaning of the Columbian legacy – to make the necessary and painful connections between my life process and this legacy.

When I used to look at this painting of the landing of Columbus on Guanahani and read about this courageous man, I was always glad Columbus made it to Guanahani after such a long and gruelling voyage, glad he met such friendly natives, glad they exchanged gifts and glad that he happily went on his way to discover more Caribbean islands. Most of all I was glad about the 12 October holiday every year.

You ask whether I cared about the inhuman treatment of the Lucayans and later the African slaves. Well, teacher didn't present it that way, so the answer is no! I was pulling for Columbus all the way through primary school, thrilled he made it to Guanahani.

And I'll never forget two important sentences in my history book: 'He fell upon his knees and gave thanks to God.' I tell you, I was completely sold on this godly man. And: 'He took possession of the island in the name of King Ferdinand and Queen Isabella of Spain.'

I was unashamedly hooked on the Queen Mother, Elizabeth, Philip, Margaret and all their children, so how could I, a colonized colored child, feel anything but royal admiration for the royalty of Spain? Columbus did all the right things, used all the right symbols. Church, Crown and Columbus! I was Columbus's girl!

And I must say that this fix didn't cause no pain; none that I couldn't bear anyway or at least redirect to another child more powerless than myself. Oh, and I was quick to hurt the feelings of a Haitian child or pick on someone whose skin was darker than mine, nose flatter and broader, hair shorter and tighter, lips fuller than mine. And I was too quick to want as friends girls and boys who had light skin, good hair and straight noses. Where was the pain?

Yes, like every other colored colonial child I thoroughly enjoyed Tarzan movies. Cheetah, the chimpanzee, was far more articulate and human than those natives. I loved Tarzan and Jane, and was as loyal to them as Cheetah and the good natives.

I knew the natives were from the dark continent of Africa but they and I had no relationship to each other. Reading about little Black Sambo and seeing him in his loincloth was truly a delight. Tarbaby stories were so, so funny. And the pain!

Watching cowboys and Indians slaughter each other and the cowboys winning at the ordained time was a Saturday afternoon well spent at the Capitol cinema.

I learned many of the psalms, collects and stories of the Bible by heart and could recite the names of all the books of the Bible without blinking or breathing. I read the Royal Reader six days a week and the Bible on Sunday. I thought the words British Imperialism were nearly as sacred as the words Jesus Christ.

Everything was bright and beautiful! Or was it?

No. When at nine years old I first discovered the word 'African' written on my birth certificate I was devastated. Why not 'Mixed'? Or even 'Colored'? I was humiliated. Why African? Why!

It was in the late 1960s when I of the 15 summers began to wrestle with this fix. I had no name for it then, this condition. As I sweated through the Civil Rights and the Black Power movements, I still didn't call this condition the 'Columbian legacy.' And I of the 15 summers cut and washed my processed hair into an afro and promised never to put a fix on my hair again. And so began my resistance to the fix.

Bringing Myself into Fiction

Initially, I had set out to explore the concept of a national literature of the Bahamas. This issue first rooted in my mind about ten years ago when I became fully aware of the body of literature called 'West Indian Literature.' I had then asked the question in this manner: What accounts for the relative dearth of literary production in the Bahamas as compared to that found in Jamaica, Trinidad, Barbados and Guyana? Through this exploration I had hoped to pull together my thoughts on this question, to begin to understand and appreciate the forces (historical, political, economic and social) that have influenced and continue to influence our relatively slow literary growth. Further, I had hoped thereby to continue the development of my own literary voice and to take up the challenge to make a small contribution to what I call 'Bringing the Bahamas into Fiction.'

While laboring over this task for months, reading history and sociology, literary criticism, books on West Indian literature, I found this exercise leading to its natural conclusion: a very academic approach, relevant and productive in its own right. Nonetheless, it was stifling my need to engage my emotional intelligence in the development of a voice. The competing inner voice thus persuaded me to write in the 'personal essay' genre. I have heeded that voice and would like to share with you some of my journey as an emerging writer. Even though artistic production is essentially individual, the writer is definitively a social being, a product of her or his community. At one level, then, I am speaking of 'Bringing Myself into Fiction.'

I first discovered the phrase 'Bringing the West Indies into Fiction' in a critique by Stuart Hall of Edgar Mittelholzer's novel *Morning at the Office*.[1] Apparently, this Guyanese writer in the 1940s consciously set himself the task of 'Bringing the West Indies into Fiction,' adapting the phrase 'Bringing America into fiction' which had acted as a catalyst for the growth of a national American literature in the nineteenth century, in writers such as Walt Whitman, Herman Melville and Mark Twain. I wondered about the magic of these words and the possibility of invoking them on behalf of my own community. However, I was not certain as to what had prompted Mittelholzer to commission himself this task when clearly the 1930s had produced significant writers in the Caribbean, such as Claude McKay, C.L.R. James, Alfred Mendes, Albert Gomes, C.A. Thomasos, de Boissiere, to name a few, who dealt convincingly with the 'peasant' and 'barrackyard' themes in West Indian life.

Michael Gilkes, in a chapter on Mittelholzer in *West Indian Literature* edited by Bruce King, sheds some light on Mittelholzer's mission and its significance in the development of West Indian literature. He states:

> But the real importance of Mittelholzer's work in the development of West Indian fiction lies in another direction: in its pioneering concern with the problem of identity, what Denis Williams called more accurately 'the lack of assurance of the indwelling racial ancestor'.
>
> For although the attempt, in the novel, to identify and proclaim clearly the uniqueness of a West Indian society and way of life began with earlier writers like Claude McKay, C.L.R. James and Alfred Mendes in the 1930s, it was Mittelholzer who first raised the question of psychic imbalance and the resultant 'angst' of identity which is the most central and urgent theme of West Indian literature.[2]

What do I say in defence of my invocation of this phrase at the individual or the national level? In neither case am I ignoring or discounting the many Bahamian writers, published or unpublished, visible or invisible, who labor in the service of their gifts. I am grateful that these writers exist. Their work matters to me. On many occasions my spirit has been revived, my courage strengthened as I listened or read and received their gifts. Nonetheless, as an emerging Bahamian writer I am painfully aware of the lack of a national artistic tradition, of the need to seek out our/my identity and claim a literary heritage, a national consciousness. The lack of assurance of the indwelling racial ancestor, the lack of assurance of a developing national identity, a national consciousness, for me means a certain death. And so, when I speak of bringing the Bahamas and myself into fiction, I speak first of the writer's need for a national audience under whose vigilance the Bahamian imagination can continue to develop; under whose care the writer's confidence can grow and under whose responses a failure means simply the need to reconsider. It is *then* that I feel many more Bahamian writers will begin to address questions such as: Who am I? What am I? How did I come to be? What does Bahamian society mean to me? What do I embrace? What do I reject? And that age-old question: What does Africa mean to me? And, indeed, for the Bahamian, an important question: Am I a West Indian?

In an article entitled 'The Political System and Its Constraints on Cultural Sovereignty,' Khafra Kambon of Trinidad and Tobago states:

> If we examine the societies culturally, we find that despite the complex influences which have gone into shaping the Caribbean, the values and lifestyles are dominated by imitation of Europe. These realities are not just effects of cross-cultural influences which are to be expected in the close international contacts of the modern world. Our cultural crisis goes much deeper. The Caribbean has not been able to form an image of itself by which it can deal with the rest of the world. The inner cultural consciousness is too underdeveloped for effective qualitative judgements to be made about what to accept and how or what to reject. Too underdeveloped for authentic values to govern the way of life.[3]

Here I make my stance very clear concerning the cultural and identity crises created in the wake of slavery and colonialism and re-created in the wake of neo-colonialism in the Bahamas. It was the Bahamian artists, musicians, writers, dramatists, who more than anyone else struggled with the issue of a national identity, an artistic tradition, a national consciousness. In the 1970s we saw a proliferation of artistic production by Bahamian writers who were trying to create an art that could be identified as authentically Bahamian. They attempted to anchor their work in what they believed were the roots, the source of our culture. Rex Nettleford, in the Introduction to the *Bahamian Anthology*, says this of Bahamian writers and our search for identity:

> Out of the belly of the beast of colonisation and slavery and the consequences of dehumanisation and suffering have come the art of survival, the skill of struggle and manifestations of human courage. The celebration of much of this – in an indigenous literature with the lexicon of Europe, the tonal texture of Africa and the syntax of special peculiarities of the Caribbean and the Americas – is a Bahamian acknowledgement of a rich heritage which challenges us all to explorations and to a creativity that bears the mark of revolutionary integrity.[4]

It is my sense that this exploration and this creativity barely became airborne before they apparently waned due to a lack of assurance of the continuing development of a national consciousness to sustain the energy, the spirit. In *The*

Wretched of the Earth, Frantz Fanon makes a precise connection between the development of a national consciousness and the development of a national literature. He states:

> The progress of national consciousness among the people modifies and gives precision to the literary utterance of the native intellectual. The continued cohesion of the people constitutes for the intellectual an invitation to go further than his cry of protest. The lament first makes the indictment; and then it makes an appeal. In the period that follows, the words of command are heard. The crystallization of the national consciousness will both disrupt literary styles and themes, and also create a completely new public. While at the beginning the native intellectual used to produce his work to be read exclusively by the oppressor, whether with the intention of charming him or of denouncing him through ethnic or subjective means, now the native writer progressively takes on the habit of addressing his own people.
>
> It is only from that moment that we can speak of a national literature. Here there is, at the level of literary creation, the taking up and clarification of themes which are typically nationalist. This may be properly called a literature of combat, in the sense that it calls on the whole people to fight for their existence as a nation. It is a literature of combat, because it molds the national consciousness, giving it form and contours and flinging open before it new and boundless horizons; it is a literature of combat because it assumes responsibility, and because it is the will to liberty expressed in terms of time and space.[5]

It is within this historical context that I began my journey as an emerging writer – a journey I must make in order to possess the meaning of my total experience. When I began writing seriously a year and a half ago, I was compelled to relate myself consciously and imaginatively to my background as a descendant of African slaves, a woman, a Bahamian, an Antillean and the offspring of a colonial and neo-colonial entrepreneurial class. For me this effort was crucial, as I felt the need to identify the areas of life and human experience which would claim my spirit beyond the limitations seemingly imposed by the various indentifiers of race, class, sex and nation. Integral to this effort was the task of determining my relationship to the existing literature of the Bahamas, the literatures of Africa, the Caribbean, Afro-America, Latin America and the literatures of Europe and Euro-America.

This effort began approximately ten years ago. It was not one of immediate revelation or insight, but a slow, painful, stumbling and sometimes blind journey towards a discovery of the self; the cohering of a personal identity, a personal integrity with a social reality. Even as I was witness to the complexity of life, an active participant in the complexity of life, I still had to battle with the security, the comfort of interpreting reality in one-dimensional terms such as race or class or sex. It is through the acts of engaging life and reading that I have come to know other possible selves, other identities. And yet as I move towards these other possibilities, I carry the original particulars of race, class, sex, nation, with me. And so be it! Ralph Ellison, (author of *The Invisible Man*) in his introduction to *Shadow and Act* speaks of a similar search thus:

> This was no matter of sudden insight but of slow and blundering discovery, of a struggle to stare down the deadly and hypnotic temptation to interpret the world and all its devices in terms of race. To void this was very important to me, and in light of my background far from simple.[6]

For Bahamian writers, and at this moment for women writers in particular, there is the challenge and promise of a whole, new, psychic, spiritual, mental and moral landscape to be explored. It is exhilarating to be writing at this time in what feels like a resurgence of artistic productions, a reawakening of consciousness. It is also a disorienting and confusing time. There are tensions in the seam of the social and cultural structure but the tensions also contain the seed for our cultural emancipation and spiritual growth. Frantz Fanon defines the task of the writer in this context thus:

> It is not enough to get back to the people in that past out of which they have already emerged; rather we must join them in that fluctuating movement which they are just giving a shape to, and which, as soon as it has started, will be the signal for everything to be called in question ... it is to this zone of occult instability where the people dwell that we must come, and it is there that our souls are crystallised and that our perceptions and our lives are transfused with light. (p. 229)

I think that says it all.

For me, then, the act of writing is an act of survival, an act of resistance, a drive towards self-knowledge as I locate my voice in relationship to my community, the Caribbean, Africa and the world. As a woman, writing is part of my refusal to be completely trounced by a male-dominated culture; as a black person it is part of my active resistance to being fascinated and tyrannised by the brute power of European and Euro-American cultural philistinism; as a Bahamian who has benefited tremendously from the emergence of a local black bourgeoisie, I write in the service of those who remain at one level powerless and voiceless and who prepare to claim our power and voice. You may wonder why I have fragmented my unity, my wholeness in this way. Unfortunately, or maybe fortunately, that fragmentation, that disjointedness, mirrors accurately my movement into writing.

Where is the support for this kind of writing that is an act of survival, of resistance? I am aware that my community is slowly beginning to provide the kind of nourishment that a writer/an artist needs no matter what her or his creative talents may be. I draw on the gifts, the dreams, the creative talents that remain in circulation, those that did not dissolve in the wake of the middle passage, colonialism or neo-colonialism. At the same time, I draw heavily on a host of seasoned and committed writers such as George Lamming, Martin Carter, Merle Collins of the Caribbean, Ngugi Wa Thiongo, Ousmane Sembene of Africa, Alice Walker, Toni Morrison of the US. I believe their gifts are also mine, mine to share and keep in circulation.

Notes

1. Stuart M. Hall, 'Lamming, Selvon and Some Trends in the West Indian Novel,' *BIM* 6:23, June, 1955. Ed. by W. Therold Barnes and Frank A. Collymore. Millwood, New York: Kraus Reprint Co., 1977, pp. 172–178.
2. In Bruce King, ed. *West Indian Literature*. Hamden, Connecticut: Archon Books, The Shoe String Press, Inc., 1979, p. 96.
3. Caribbean Conference of Intellectual Workers, *Independence and Cultural Sovereignty*. Grenada, November 20–22, 1982. Impreso en El Palacio de Las Convenciones de Cuba, La Habana 1984, p. 3.
4. College of the Bahamas, *Bahamian Anthology*. London: Macmillan Caribbean, 1983, p. 2.
5. Frantz Fanon, *The Wretched of the Earth*. New York: Grove Press, 1968, p. 239.
6. Ralph Ellison, *Shadow and Act*. New York: Vintage Books, 1964, p. xvii.

'Pass the Word and Break the Silence' – The Significance of African-American and 'Third World' Literature for Black Germans

Sheila Mysorekar

Germany, autumn 1991. Sitting in front of the television, I'm witnessing the first post-war pogrom. In the small town of Hoyerswerda in Eastern Germany, a racist mob is attacking a foreign workers' hostel. The night is illuminated by the fire of the burning house. Through a splintered glass pane, we catch a glimpse of a Black face, one of the Africans who live there. Outside, a howling mob is gathering, more people are coming, 'ordinary' people from the area, spectators of an attempted mass murder. And not only spectators: they clap hands, they laugh, they agree, they encourage. The police don't stop the attackers. Buses come in, to evacuate the foreign workers. They hurry outside – Vietnamese, Angolans, Mozambiquans – followed by a hail of stones and screams. The mayor of Hoyerswerda states: 'This town is now free of foreigners.'

I switch off the TV. Only then do I notice that I'm trembling, my heart is racing. I'm overwhelmed by the pictures I've just seen, by fear and rage – and the feeling of an imminent threat by my 'fellow citizens.' I'm also German.

Black German.

Since this first pogrom against foreigners, the violence has increased. In 1992, the average number of foreigners killed was more than one per month; and worse is expected. We know who the potential victims are: non-white foreigners, especially refugees, including Turkish people, Sinti and Roma, to some extent also Jews, homeless people and Black Germans.

As Black Germans, we are painfully aware that in times of danger we have no community to turn to. There is no area in town where we can feel safe because our people control the streets, because they own the shops and run the business there – except, maybe, for the Turkish areas. We have no infrastructure, no radio stations, no schools, no churches, no Black cultural centres. Nor do we have money or weapons. There does not even exist an older generation who could teach us how to survive in a white society. The prominent feature of Black German life is its complete isolation.

Most of us are of 'mixed race' origin. Many of us grew up without the Black parent (that is, generally without the father), and therefore without contact with an Asian or African or Caribbean culture. As Black people, we have had to create ourselves; there was nobody to teach us, no place to go to. Considered as 'foreigners' by definition of our skin color, we do not easily come to terms with the fact that we have a right to call ourselves 'German.' In spite of never having been outside Germany, in spite of carrying a German passport, in spite of having German as our mother-tongue, many of us grow up calling ourselves 'Nigerian' or 'Pakistani,' or whatever nationality our father may have. The term 'Black German' was coined only recently. In a country which legally defines its nationality by the obscure and racist term 'German blood,' *Black* Germans are simply a paradox for most people, something impossible, a concept that can't really exist.

Consequently, we grow up with the sensation that we are the only Black German person that exists or, even, the only Black person in the world. On the other hand, we know very well there are Black majority countries, countries where people of all races live, where skin color does not matter, and even where racism does not exist – or so we hear. Many of us grow up with lonely dreams about New York, Brazil or, most of all, Cuba – dreaming of a society where we would blend in, where nobody would consider us as something rare. In real life, though, we feed on the snatches of non-white cultures we have access to, whatever they may be. A typical example is a young man who today is very active in the Black German movement: a Black German of Afro-Argentinian origin, who grew up with white adoptive parents, as a child he had close contact with a Korean family and through them, for the first time in his life, realized the possibility of living in a non-white culture. To this day, he feels very close and loyal to Korean culture.

The most popular traits of other cultures, those that are exported or are of some value to white societies, reach us first and give us the chance to connect. For instance, African-American music and Asian cuisine offer us the possibility of leaving the surrounding, all-white culture for a moment, and taking a little, solitary walk towards our roots. Through Muddy Waters or Lester Bowie or Public Enemy, Afro-America is talking to *us*; with spicy Indian masala or Vietnamese lemon grass, Asia is feeding *us*.

Much of the spiritual nourishment, though, comes through books. Pushed by the hunger to know more about the 'others,' guided by instinct based on vague information found in the bibliography of some history book – an instinct that also turns to certain names mentioned in left-wing flyers picked up at some demonstrations – we turn to the Word. Some of us start to read about Africa, until by chance we come across books by Cheik Anta Diop, which completely change our outlook on history. There exists a German translation of Walter Rodney's *How Europe Underdeveloped Africa*. Although there was no teacher at high school who could guide us further, although there was no fellow student to share the joy of the discovery with us, our world had changed – Africa was no longer a continent without history.

Others of us may have started with listening to Bob Marley, become involved with reggae and started to read everything available about Jamaica, beginning with travel guides, carrying on with New Age books that included a chapter on Rastafari, until, one day, we hit on the name of Marcus Garvey … there are many ways to become aware of Black politics, even without having anybody to guide us.

Black Germans who grew up in the German Democratic Republic at least knew about Angela Davis; and the officially pronounced solidarity with the down-trodden minorities of the capitalist world for us turned into something else: the realization that we, too, belong to a minority, and, more important, that we, too, may *fight*.

I remember one day, aged 17, I was browsing in the public library through books on Black American politics – books that attracted me, not knowing exactly why, not being able to draw the parallel between Black life in Germany and the United States. I picked up a book at random and started leafing through. When I turned over a page, there was a photo of a red-haired Black man, with 60s-style glasses, a non-smiling, serious face looking straight at me. The caption read 'Malcolm X.' 'X' as a surname? I took the book back home, compelled by an instinctive feeling that this was something important. And then lived with the frustration of not having anybody to share my discovery with.

More than anything else, books on African–American politics gave us a clue as to what was happening to us, by calling the problem by its proper name: racism. Black writers spelled out the subtleties of race relations, every cruel shade, the bitter details, and more than that: they told us how to fight. In Germany, where the word 'racism' is hardly used – usually only in connection with South Africa – this was a great step forward. In Germany, they talk about anti-semitism and xenophobia, but 'racism doesn't exist here,' they say. 'It's a clash of cultures. Different religions. Mistrust of foreigners. But racism? No.'

As Black Germans, we knew very well that we were not being discriminated against because of our ever-so-strange culture or religion. It was the color; that much we knew. We needed books to spell out the word 'racism.'

Of course, the experience of becoming conscious varied a lot, depending on family surroundings, on the intensity of the contact with the culture of the black parent, on education, and other factors. But in other ways our experiences were similar. For instance, many of us share an interest in Black and 'third world' literature; also people who, by temperament or education, are not used to reading.

Novels by Black authors were rare, but they existed. In high school, James Baldwin was mentioned; Salman Rushdie became famous. Those of us who went to London for a holiday came back with a bag full of books, all from the Heinemann African Writers series. But most of all, it was the Black women writers of the United States who talked to us in a way nobody had before. In the mid-1980s, the first books were translated: Alice Walker, Toni Morrison, Maya Angelou, Paule Marshall; more recently, Ntozake Shange, and the Asian-American writers Bharati Mukherjee and Amy Tan.

These authors gave us an insight into Black life and Black struggle in another country, gave us the chance to identify and, furthermore, envisage a future where a Black culture would surround us, where loneliness and isolation would be a thing of the past. These books connected us less with our roots in Africa or Asia but introduced us to the international community of the Black diaspora. Among other things, the African-American writers spoke about life in a hostile, racist society, about the art of survival; and the Asian-American writers reflected the experience of immigrants and the struggle for identity of the following generations. These were topics that touched our most secret, unshared feelings.

And these writers talked to us as Black women. Since most of the Black German women have white mothers, no knowledge about the relation between racism and sexism was transferred from mother to daughter. We didn't have words for the experience of sexist/racist oppression. The images that existed of Black women were images of prostitutes or mail-order brides. These books showed us there was more to life than this – something that we knew, looking at ourselves, but, without a positive context of other, especially older, Black women, we had hitherto missed the point that we were the rule, not a rare exception. Here it was: the novels pictured a rich experience, varied lives and self-assertion for Black women.

I remember very well, at the age of 22, reading for the first time a book by a Black woman writer: *Meridian* by Alice Walker. I had always been an eager reader, but this book hit me; I felt as if I had never read a book before. Though the story of the novel – the civil rights struggle in the American South – was miles away from my experience as an Indo-German in the Rhine area of (at that time) West Germany, there were many things I could understand and identify with. For example, the relations between Black and white women and men that featured in the book explained some of the things I had experienced or witnessed, without being able to understand what was happening. It needs a Black woman writer to capture the interweaving of sexism and racism, of struggle and survival on more than one level of life. It slowly dawned on me that, despite many books I had read before, I had always read books by white male (and a few white female) authors, in which my experience as a Black woman was not reflected and never could be.

As Black Germans, we are surrounded by silence; surrounded by a society that denies our existence and negates the fact of racism; surrounded by white peers who shut their mouths in incomprehension when we talk about humiliation and anger; surrounded by a wall of silence when we start to ask about our roots. This isolation was broken by the books that reached us, that connected us to the international Black community. Some of us did have other connections, via music, or travels, or meeting other Black people. But even if some of us didn't need to be introduced to Black life via literature, books remained an important connection to Black thinking and Black politics, that otherwise would not have reached us.

Now, that a Black German movement exists, in which Germans of African and Asian descent have started to work together on Black German politics, we no longer depend on word-of-mouth to hear news. Still, in a country without a cohesive Black community, information from Black communities outside remains very important; films, videos or books, anything that is easily available and not too expensive. We need to pass the Word. We owe very much to Black literature – African- or Asian-American, Caribbean, African and Asian novels, essays, drama, poetry, everything. And it was Black women writers who taught us to assert ourselves as **Black German women**.

Whenever Black European women meet – be it an Angolan German with a Tibetan-Swiss, or an Afrocuban-Russian with an Egyptian-Hungarian (and I tell you, all of these exist!) – we realize that many of us were initiated into the Black world by a book written by a Black American woman.

A special tribute must be paid to the novel *Quicksand* by the Afro-Danish author Nella Larsen, who talks about Black experience in Europe (in this case, Denmark) in the 1920s, that is, the generation of our grandparents. Since very, very few of us have Black European grandmothers who could tell us of their experience as Black women in Europe, Nella Larsen stands in to talk to us as one of the older generation of Black Europeans, generations that we know existed, but whose wisdom and experience has been lost, who died in German concentration camps, whose presence was wiped from the European history books. Thus, literature not only connects us to the present Black diaspora, but also preserves our past.

In countries with a large Black community, such as the United States, Great Britain or France, Black literature serves as a mirror to reflect and intensify and transcend experience. In countries without a cohesive Black community, such as Germany, Switzerland or Norway or, for that matter, any other northern European country, Black literature serves as a spiritual connection with other Black people, breaking the silence and isolation of the individual Black man or woman. Now that we have started to write ourselves, we do not only feed on the books that reach us, but we send out messages as well. Now it's our turn to help spreading the Word.

Over de Gekte van een vrouw
About a Woman's Madness

Astrid Roemer

'But the greatest Love remains misunderstood and no one has ever dared to say that it's there, where heaven started, the most desolate place ...'
(Albert Helman, Zuid-Zuid-West)

Nieuw Amsterdam, 26 May

Blue Alcaid

> YOU DRIFTED INTO MY DREAMS AT NIGHT
> DEVOID OF ALL CONDITIONS
> REGRETFULLY NOT UNCLAD
> MY FACE PERISHES WITH MY HANDS
> MY BREASTS AND MY THIGHS
> I RESERVE FOR YOU UNSCATHED
> MYSELF I DON'T LIVE MYSELF
> NOENKA LIVES IN ME

> YOUR GABRIELLE

> for
> Lam van Gisbergen
> Zamani, Safira and my boys
> and those who gave me the Word ...

Lelydorp, 29 August

Merak Mists

We have started the great year. Time has stepped aside from her straight line and has become a shrinking ellipse. Gabrielle and I orbit in opposite directions longing to meet in the zenith. Nature, meanwhile, rejuvenates itself in the harvest of oranges, colorful blossoms, moulting birds, bright yellow chicks, and seasons like rain in May and sunflowers in August. Even the sun lets the tradewind chase him unconditionally westward and I find the meteor shower alarming.

Since she slept with me, my Gabrielle, naked as the beat of the heart, and pure as the rushing of the blood, I felt I had conquered my primeval fear of the snake. There is more than enmity between his semen and me. Wherever I will meet him, I will crush him with my heel, even at the risk of losing a leg. But the rank weed makes me impatient, for it hides not a single snake.

I miss you, Gabrielle.

My love for you opens up like a flower. Amidst the overgrown weeds your seeds bloom and cannot wilt, for in a garden of shadetrees and swamogas I render the hermaphrodytical service exuberantly, yet devoutly, unmentionably tenderly and sensually.

There, orchids bloom in clusters, plumes and ears, with bizarre lips, wanting to kiss our earth. The white one with pink is called 'opening in the phallic vulva'. She reeks of mountains and frosty cold. She originates from the Rocky Mountains. Her petals are folded like hands in prayer. I have a blue one with a red lip. Six royal-blue sepals and a capricious runner. Seven petals. She shines like a star in the nebulous valley. I call her Big Dipper.

My clients come from far away, Gabrielle. They say that the whole valley smells of flowers. That gives me pleasure and I continue tearing while butterflies, bees and invisible creatures and the wind carry the pollen on to the sticky stamens until the whole country cries out for orchids: our days bear orchids Gabrielle!

Your Noenka

P.S. The hedge is dripping with sunlight in abundant forsythia to greet you.

Postscript

In 1875 the death penalty was carried out for the last time. The unfortunate one was a Chinese man. By the cast of the die he had been the one with two others designated to kill the foreman of the plantation 'Resolution', who had treated his racebrothers inhumanely.

During the execution the rope which was to cut off the airpassages broke twice. Fear spread. The death penalty was changed to 20 years' forced labor in handcuffs. The convict had to serve only part of the sentence and was paroled for good behavior.

Nieuw Amsterdam 19...

Gabrielle tends the vegetable garden. She loses her heavenly hands to the rough rope out of which she creates unusual basketry. She subjects herself to the punishment.

Via the OM I have appealed for parole. My ninth one. For years I am waiting for an answer now.

Tomorrow is the Queen's Day. Maybe they will release her too.

I wait at the gate.

Lelydorp 19...

The last train has left. The foldfields are exhausted. Vans from the city stop always with the same faces that breathe heavily in the wind. I too smell the orchids, which tremble, longing for the cold.

Weeks pass by and new ones arrive. Everywhere the same people. The same sun.

A month ago we buried Edith. Now children and workmen buy cooled orange from me.

> My eyes are tearing as I peel them.
> *Noenka e cre* (Noenka cries), they tease.
> Today they are right; I cry, Astrid.
> I am supposed to be with my Gabrielle on her fiftieth birthday.

My marriage lasted precisely nine days and caused a stir in our small state on the coast, which left me drifting throughout my life.

It started in the family circle when I awakened my parents, knocking that ninth night.

The rain pelted down commandingly and as the roof of our dwelling is not very steep, the sound of my knuckles on the wood never reached far inside; it was absorbed in the beat of the water pouring down. The house was silent, as if dead.

My hands hurt, more so than my head and my stomach, and I was drenched. And frightened, not only by the threat from the cemetery near the house, which looked like the stageset in a dream, but also by the dreariness of the sleeping city, which let the rain invade it, by the house of my father and mother, which refused to let me in on my escape to eclatpowder and brasspolish, the smell of tobacco and old newspapers, so as to rid me of the smell of blood about me. I no longer knocked, but pounded and screamed.

But the wind and the water giggled my cries back to my ears.

Pain! Pain!

Naked behind me was The Other Side.

Moments later I stood in the sparsely-lit kitchen, irritated, but relieved, wondering how long it had been since I had climbed through the window in disrepair, but memories were swept away by the urge to crawl quickly, as close as possible, near my mother. I felt a warm rush, and I groped my way, hungry, toward their room. Sacredly I put my hand on the marble doorknob and I turned it; pushed.

Years later I understood: it was behind that door that I crossed my threshold of pain.

They said I was a beautiful child. *Moi misi*, they called me and they took me in their arms, the women against their wide-pleated skirts, pressing my head to their bellies. Some smelled of fresh fish, but the smell of rot also penetrated my head. I'd moan and pull away.

'Noenka, Noenka,' they tried, shyly; but I stayed under the bed until my mother came to take me on her lap; fresh, warm and secure. There were aunts I rather liked if only because they did not spread their thighs to greet me but sat, their legs crossed next to me on the couch.

They spoke a soft kind of Dutch and wore plain-colored dresses with velvet bodices and narrow belts. Their legs shimmered silky through their nylon stockings and their dark shoes squeaked. These ladies were not received in the kitchen and were served tea in Delftblue cups and were offered thin, golden brown cookies.

While they talked about their honorable daughters, their intelligent sons, the lazy maid and the teacircle for charity, I inhaled the perfume, released with their every move. I heard about a bazaar, a fundraiser for the desk of the minister, that lovely, lovely man, with his darling blond wife, and to see if Mrs Novar, as usual, would provide all those delicious, delicious snacks and all that heavenly, heavenly cake like last time.

My mother blushed and I leaned proudly against her and she said 'Yes-of-course-I'd-be-delighted-to,' and if the ladies wanted to take a piece of pastry home with them … With that it immediately was handed to them wrapped in doilies out of a silver tin. But as soon as we had finished waving them goodbye she uttered a deep *tjoeri*;[1] she wildly pounded the cushions outside and, with my assistance, ate all the cookies that had been sacrificed to etiquette.

'Are you angry?' I asked, the fresh crumbs on my tongue.

'Not angry,' she smiled as she held me tight.

If the sun was so high, that you could stand on your own shadow, and Ma took in the bathtowels, Peetje came wobbling in. I ran to the gate, hurt myself on a rusty clamp, thrilled to take her hands stretched out to me.

She smelled of overripe sapotilles, bacoven, and the twig of sour-orange, which she chewed, would make me sneeze. She stood there for a moment, her widespread hand on my head, she'd stuff my mouth full of strange sweets which she carried in colorful corked jars in a wooden box on her head.

Hopping along against her white skirts, I reached with my shoulders up to the heavy pocket of her petticoat, where her coins were, so many for me, a fortune that no one else would possess.

On the backporch of our house she put down her box with a groan and conversed with my mother in a sing-song language which I barely understood. They drank gingerbeer with icecubes and ate small fried fish. Often they laughed boisterously: Ma highpitched and round and Peetje flat and broad.

And I, shifting from one lap to the other, I hoped that Peetje would never go away. She always did, muttering, the box on her head, the *koto*[2] stiff and full

---

1. *tjoeri*: an utterance of disdain.
2. *koto*: richly pleated dress, remnant of colonial days.

around her tawny body. I watched her leave, waved until the sunlight hurt my eyes and a swirl of schoolchildren scared me inside.

Apples, nothing but apples; soft, pink with white buttocks, which did more than quench the thirst when dipped in salt; deep red ones which reminded me of the angry, pouting mouths of the old, malcontented aunts, but which tasted sweeter; and the ones without much color, so delicious that convoys of black ants covered the endless road from their nest to push their way up the high branches, to crowd together in their large fold.

The apples ripened all at once. By the hundreds they lay at dawn on the dark backyard and they kept falling, all day long.

It was mid-May ...

The usual grey-blue sky was marred daily by the unshapely rainclouds which sailed in from the east. Then, something would make the greenery tremble, the wind would get moist and in no time there would be nothing but water. And apples. Amidst the shimmering leaves they hung in strong clusters, trembling as long as they did not fall and splatter apart like firecrackers.

I was staying at Peetje's, farmed out by my mother to help with the apple deluge. The whole day long I did nothing but gather apples, wash them under an enormous water faucet to clean them of mud and ants, and put them on a castle-like pile. Quite an impressive job when you are six and fond of everything sweet and colorful.

Emely, Peetje's only child, stirred all kinds of pots in the kitchen with wooden spoons.

After a few days a whole array of filled jars had taken shape which even the best stocked Chinese merchant could not rival. I helped bring the jars to Uncle Dolfi who, under a zinc roof, dealt in everything ordinary people need in small quantities. Two shelves were added and his selection was expanded with apple-butter, apple-compote, picked apple, apple-this and apple-that.

But most of all I delighted in announcing the small buyers with their rusty nickles for Peetje and toys, candy, and colored glass shards for me.

Yet I never gave away apples behind her back; I helped make Peetje's pocket heavier. Tired of gathering I fell asleep in her arms before dusk.

One night I awoke because the rain abruptly stopped and caused an asthmatic silence. I felt that I was lying on the floor and not in my bed. Confused, I got up. There was a light burning somewhere. I groped my way down the stairs in the half-dark, the living room, the kitchen, Peetje's bedroom. Wrinkling my pj's with my fingers I went to the bathroom with the cold cement to wee-wee, when a door blew open and Emely came storming in.

Everything went fast: lights out, me in her cool arms and the shudder, the hostile smell which attached itself inside me like an ugly scar.

'Ssh, quiet, quietly.' I was tucked in. It was the first time I wet my bed.

Stinkbirds around the house. On the roof, the rim of the well, teetering on the fence. Their broad, black wings packed tightly against their bodies, heads tucked in, eagerly searching eyes. I was sitting on the step of the backdoor, pitching the umpteenth halfeaten apple into the garbagebin. Even though the sun could be felt in the early morning the air remained heavy and humid. My cold feet made me long for home. It was wet everywhere and chilly. One vulture came closer and pecked at an apple without great interest.

'Shoo,' shouted Peetje coming back from the market and looking amazed at the strange visitors. 'What are they doing?'

'I don't know,' I answered, staring at the birds, whose number was increasing. Peetje rushed inside and followed with fascination the black invasion from behind the window over the stove. I found the birds funny and scary at the same time, I'd never seen them before. Slowly it dawned on me that they were looking for something. But what?

Peetje was searching too, sniffed and sniffed, wrinkled her forehead in deep doubt and sighed.

It seemed that hours went by. Suddenly the birds stirred nervously. Savagely they crashed into a bush of *tajer* near the john. They locked their claws on to something. A bundle tumbled out. Old rags, sheets. Peetje lost her self-control, ran into the yard and whacked a stick at the beasts to scatter them, away, away from the bundle which lay before her like a laid-out secret. She bent over, stirred it with the stick. From a small distance I watched with the vultures. A hysterical scream, flapping wings, a familiar odor, incoherent recollections, two long, long arms gather up the bloodstained sheets and flee into the house.

'Get Emely from Uncle Dolfi, quick, quick,' a mouth gasps and windows slam shut. The vultures stare at me with greed from the *tajerbush*. The bundle smells. I want my mother.

It could be the rain, the smell of blood, or something unclear which went with this night and kept fear and anxiety out of my reach. I saw Peetje as she was laid out in the coffin, a face of dried clay, full of cracks.

[The author acknowledges assistance from Dr Mary Harris with the translation of this article.]

From *Bajo la piel de los tambores/* *Under the Skin of the Drums*

Luz Argentina Chiriboga

Translated by Carol A. Beane

[Rebeca González, the novel's protagonist, leaves her small village in Esmeraldas, on the Pacific coast of Ecuador, for Quito in order to study in a convent boarding-school, a microcosm of society's class and racial prejudices, as well its hypocrisies. The novel opens in Quito, with Rebeca telling about the double life led by the boarding-school students: behind the walls during the day, their behavior dictated by books and strict moral conventions; over the walls at night, exploring and reveling in sensuality and worldliness. Early in the novel, her mother's words describe her as, 'not too good, not too bad; not too beautiful, not too common-looking; not overly intelligent, not excessively stupid; not too white, not too black.' The second part of the novel continues with Rebeca's life at school, now mediated by the presence of the revolutionary black nun, Sor Inés del Rosario. In the third part, as a prelude to her eventual and definitive return to Esmeraldas, she invites several of her schoolmates for a visit. This is the first time Rebeca's friends will see the places and people, and share the experiences that are, for her, home, origins, roots.]

It took me a good while to understand that my insistence on bringing my friends to Oriki was not the fruit of my having thought seriously about it, but of the memories. I was all too familiar with that constant breeze that carried the redolent shellfish smells of the beaches over the whole town, but I had forgotten the houses made from bamboo and palms that had the writing from many years engraved on them. The motor-boat whistle made me imagine a town that was not my own, a town buried in neglect. We walked towards the dock which was already filled with people.

The steamboat, *Pharaoh, El Faraón*, came chugging up and moored broadside; its name was faded and chipped; its hull wormeaten; its sails patched like the circus clown who passed through the place every once in a while. The planks of the wharf rattled and groaned. This wharf, for whose construction everyone in town had contributed experience and materials; indeed, this was the source of its discordant facade, which was utterly lacking any harmony of line. We saw several old men who seemed anchored to the dock, or the dock anchored to them.

That wooden arm was the heart of Orikí, a passageway of love; it was the means by which one walked towards other dreams, and the dead passed over it on their last voyage. *El Faraón* groaned like a wounded animal and woke those who were sleeping their siesta out in the open beneath the sun. The boat was a Noah's Ark where donkeys' braying mingled with the barking of several dogs; we also saw a cow with her calf, pigs, a horse, turkeys, ducks, roosters and parrots. Even though my companions were watching the unloading in amazement, I continued to think it had been a mistake in bringing them to get to know my hometown. Reviving memory, I searched for Julio Martinez among the crowd. I stretched out my neck and reached out with my eyes trying to discover him there among the passengers and the bundles of clothing, the boxes splitting at the seams, the baskets of fruits – as if taking inventory of the poverty of my town – but he was nowhere to be seen among the new arrivals.

In the dormitory, I had experienced the illusion of return. I remembered the blue sea with its seagulls, swallows' wings and pelicans high in flight; the palm-trees, their fronds dishevelled from the winds; the beaches lulled to sleep by the sound of the waves; and the snails I used to gather there. But now, as I fingered the deception of my nostalgia, I saw the town with other eyes. The last ones to get off the boat were men who were carrying a sick woman in a hammock. It's one of Las Mojadas, the Wet Ones, said a voice fading away into the noise of the crowd. Mother explained to Sor Inés that, like that woman, there were other victims of the effects of diving under the waters to obtain the shells from the mangroves. My companions, surprised at what they had just heard, scarcely noticed that a man was walking, balancing along the plank, a man in a brown suit and hat, carrying a small black bag. 'Pearl shell. *Concha de perlas*,' said Yazmin with a big smile. Jokingly they recognized the salesman from the Plaza 24th of May in Quito. Now that the mosquitoes roamed in clouds on account of the rains, and malaria was decimating the population, he had arrived. I recognized the man from the bus who had lost the money, since he was dressed exactly the same as on that earlier occasion.

By canoe the distance from Orikí to Sikán was only 20 minutes, but on horseback it was a much longer journey because my parents' compadres came out to greet us, and we would stay a while, tasting a specially prepared dish of venison, or tamales or sausages, since they were always killing hogs. They would start the horses moving at once and the mill would turn round and we would drink the juice from the freshly crushed sugar canes. [...]

My friends got into the canoe but they were afraid of the river in which small, naked boys dipped and dived, cutting intricate figures in the water and the sunlight; they hurled themselves from the top of the ravine into the water and landed in it with a great noise, like stones or tree-trunks. On one shore several heavy-breasted women with sun-darkened skin were washing clothes in troughs. When they saw us they covered their chests with the wet clothes and took off their hats, waving them to us in greeting. Along the opposite shore two rafts, carrying off the vitality of the once green forests, opened a pathway through the currents. The men waved their arms, saluting. 'Don Sergio,' they called out. Fascinated with the landscape that with every passing moment increasingly seemed to be one immense mural, my friends missed seeing the burnished, brown-skinned young boys who had thrown their fish-hooks into the river and held them in place with their toes.

Sor Inés intrigued me when she spoke about organizing the women who dived for shells into a union. The term 'Wet Ones' has stuck in her ears. I supposed that the shellfish we had waiting at home to serve her would not be as tasty as they would have been before, and that she would only remember the woman in the hammock.

We started the ascent to the house along a cobbled stone road. Napoleón and Sultan barked and welcomed us with their wagging tails. The banana trees had been propped up; the orange trees, the *zapotes*, the bananas, the avocados, the guava trees, the limes and lemons all mingled their fragrances. From the path to the road the stands of pine trees saturated the air with their scent. Adela Okú was standing in the shade; my friends were struck by her impressive height. *Si Adelita se fuera con otro, la seguiría por tierra y por mar*, they sang out all together. because everybody knew 'Adelita', song of the Mexican Revolution. She answered their greeting with that simple forthrightness that country people possess. When she had been a girl, Nicasio, agile and finely built, with his almost savage strength, used to go and visit Adela and they would run off deep into the fields where the colts were grazing to hide among the stands of guava trees. Adela came to live at our house when the police killed her father during a strike at the saw-mill.

Neither Mama nor I suspected that no sooner had my friends arrived they would be off into the kitchen to help our cook and maid as she prepared the *ceviche*, raw fish marinating in lime juice, onions, and chillies. When Sor Inés covered the table with the white linen tablecloth embroidered in cross stitching, I began to set out the glasses with rims of gold bought at the finest shop in town, the House of Tagua; I also arranged the set of porcelain dishes my parents had rented from Señora Restrepo. Father wound up the victrola so that we could listen to Carlota Jaramillo in a musical, *Sendas Diferentes (Different Paths)*. My friends began to sing. Mother went back and forth between the kitchen and the dining-room with quick steps. Afterwards she would escape to the room with glass windows and a view of the river from where she usually watched the sunsets contemplatively. A bed and a little table barely fit in her room; she always set books out on the table, since at home we were used to everyone having their own library.

On the wall hung a picture of her mother, and a small picture of herself before she was married peeked out from a corner in the frame; there was a third one, even smaller, as if those three photographs made up a *Matrojoschka*[1]. As the years passed, the concept of happiness had changed. There had been my grandmother who had travelled to Paris out of curiosity, wanting to see all the things that deserved to be seen: the gardens, the museums, the fine stores; she even went to the opera. Judging that her desires had been properly satsified, she returned home to her country and married a municipal tax collector, who, one afternoon when he was riding his horse along a deserted road, was shot point-blank and robbed of everything he had on him. From that time on mama wore silk skirts with lace flounces and ruffles, and blouses styled after those of Marie-Antoinette [...], everything my grandmother had set aside in the trunk which had remained unopened since her return from France. When mama turned 19 she took down the velvet curtains in order to sew up the dress she wore to her graduation as a teacher. For a year she trudged up and down to the Ministry of Education, trying to obtain a position, and when she got her post at Orikí she liked the name so much that she remembered the town without ever having been there.

It was there that papa met her and became consumed with the dream that she would become his wife. Watching Nidia Araujo walk by from beneath a leafy spreading ficus tree and feeling his heart change its tempo, he understood that he was in love with her.

Mama always used to say that her marriage to papa had come about on account of a misspelled word, since Sergio González had come up to her and shown her a piece of paper on which the word 'love' was written with a 'u' and without an 'e' and he had asked her if it was correctly written. Since the discussions about this word were lengthy, papa invited her out to dinner, and in between the different wines, Love is written l-o-v-e, without giving her time to protest, he kissed her, No, Nidia, l-u-v.

My father talked about Sikán and, amending the anthology of his memories, he told her about the Germans who were exporting tagua, the vegetable ivory, and rubber, and who were bringing in great quantities of fine, cheap goods; he never knew whether or not they were contraband from the House of Tagua. From that afternoon on papa thought that any time was a good time to tell stories about the old days. On the third day my friends besieged him with questions, and scarcely had he finished answering them than he scowled in order to explain to us the terrible designation that was decidedly racist, The Black List, names of those German, Italian, and Japanese citizens considered enemies by the United States; a list, by the way, developed by North Americans or North American residents in our country. One could not do any business at all with people from any of those countries for fear of being included on the list. The Black List, he said, in a hoarse voice, was called that because people attribute all bad things to that color black.

1. *Matrojoschka*: wooden Russian dolls which nestle one inside another.

Once papa had completed the first grades that were taught by a German professor who taught him everything he knew, from Algebra to Cosmography, my grandfather, in between the last hours of night and before the first hours of dawn, put him up on a horse and headed the horse for the nearest town where there was a school that went up to the higher grades. When he saw that he had left his father's house behind, his eyes filled with tears. Years later, papa laughingly remembered that as the animal was about to leave the fences of the homestead behind, he refused to go one step further since he had been trained not to stray off. My grandfather had made a mistake in setting my father on the back of a tricky horse. Pangs of sadness and longing for her absent son awakened my grandmother that night; she walked quietly over to his hammock. It was something to have seen. She cried out, frightened to death seeing the son she was imagining off at school lying there asleep.

One afternoon after listening to so many stories, Imelda, Yazmin and I went to see the cattle in the pasture near the house – the pasture belonged to the neighbor, but they didn't suspect a thing. Afterwards we rode horseback along the beach. As we were trotting along I let my thoughts drift back to Mariana Murat struggling to emerge from that tunnel she had entered without realizing it. Surely she was crying alone, sad to be waking up with such pronounced bags under her eyes because her sailor boyfriend was more distant every day. The movement of the saddle and the gallop made me vehemently desire something that right then I couldn't quite understand, but was a delicious sensation, as if I was on the threshold of some pleasure. When we reached the far end of the beach, a group of women was moving pans with sand in them from side to side and around in search of gold nuggets that would shine in the sunlight. The landscape, the river and the breeze carried me back to adolescence when I used to run around playing tag with Milton. It was Yazmin's idea to dismount and draw hearts in the sand while we listened to the conversations of the women panning for gold. They talked very loudly, almost shouting as if they were singing at a marimba dance. I put on my sunglasses and pulled my hat way down on my forehead so that they wouldn't recognize me. My friends approached the women in order better to examine the gold nuggets. They picked up the gold, brought it close to their eyes, and even sniffed it. It would all end up at the store, bartered for something to eat.

A black woman stared at me. Her father had been going to marry a niece of mine in Guayaquil, but then she found out that my niece was an Uyanga. Damn it!, I thought, just what I didn't want my friends to find out about, I'm done for. She stepped back, she said, trying to connect and document the memory with other information. But while the woman was speaking, my grandmother floated slowly before my eyes; I saw her teaching me how to get my kites high into the air, telling me songs learned in Africa to put me to sleep. I felt myself assuming a new identity, I had taken my place: I'm her granddaughter, I told the woman; and the words sounded like a challenge.

After that, everything was easy, that part of me that before, mistakenly, I had wanted to hide, no longer pained me. I felt myself a part of my grandmother, a part of everything that had ever happened to her; I was listening to her drums sounding beneath my skin. From then on I began to talk about her a great deal, and every time that I did so, I drew more strength from my memories of her.

Journal Entries Against Reaction: Damned if We Do and Damned if We Don't

Marlene Nourbese Philip

1. How does the writing of black women mesh with Canadian feminist culture?
2. Is it to be analysed as a part of feminist culture or as Other?
3. Is black women's writing to be included in this anthology because it is now the correct position to do so?
4. How many of the articles on architecture, theater, literature, the visual arts, video, and film will explore how these art forms impinge on black women, or women of color, or Native women, or even working-class women?
5. How many of these articles will explore the absence of these women and their realities from the practice of these art forms?

These were the questions I raised in a letter in response to being asked to write an article on black women's writing for an anthology entitled *Work in Progress: Building Feminist Culture* (ed. Rhea Tregebor, Toronto, Womens Press, 1987).

Here I answer these questions myself:
1. It doesn't. Canadian feminist culture is predominantly white – Anglo or Francophone. The writings of, and by, black women are, for the most part, perceived as immigrant, exotic, or ethnographic, all of which translate into exclusion or marginalization.
2. As Other – for the reasons given in (1) above.
3. Yes.
4. I don't know.
5. I don't know.

My letter continued:

> ... my observation of feminism as articulated in the media and the arts reveals a very specific type of feminism, which is continually articulated in an all-embracing fashion with the appropriate adjective – black, working-class – appended when necessary. What remains unacknowledged is that a very culturally specific sense of female identity is being manipulated – and one that is acutely ahistorical in its failure to acknowledge race and class as anything more than economic and social categories.

In an honest response to my concerns, I was told that 'as white women organizing an anthology of this sort, we're in a damned if we do and damned if we don't position.' This aphorism also sums up the dilemma black women continually face, though for very different reasons: they are seldom in the position of having to question their own power. Their damnation, on the contrary, arises too often from having too little choice. If the organizers were feeling damned at times – albeit for very different reasons – it was not a bad thing, I thought: it might help them to understand the no-win situations that often circumscribe the lives of black women.

My other response to this explanation was the thought that if some of the issues I canvassed in my opening paragraph and my letter had been analysed prior to the call for submissions, then these feelings of frustration and helplessness – this sense of trying to do the right thing, but not getting credit for it, which is undoubtedly the origin of the damned-if-we-do-and-damned-if-we-don't dilemma – could have been avoided. I have since come to believe otherwise. The aphorism *does* accurately sum up the position of those who have traditionally wielded power and are now trying to do something about it.

'Damned if we do and damned if we don't.' Can't we just hear the well-intentioned male uttering these words as he struggles with his sexism and offends everyone? And he *is* damned – whether he does or doesn't. By history, by his gender, by his class at times – by circumstances, in fact, which he himself may have had nothing to do with. And merely by virtue of belonging to a particular group, or class, or gender, at a particular point in history, he shares in a certain collective reponsibility, or guilt – a word I am very leery of using. If, however, we understand the historical underpinnings of his position, we must also acknowledge his frustration at not being accepted and at being challenged when he is being his most feminist. Damned he is.

I personally have done nothing to increase the misery and suffering of those who live in developing countries, but by virtue of living in the West, and partaking, however unwillingly, in some of the perks that come from living here, I too am implicated and share in the reponsibility the West must take for the plight of many of these countries. My morning cup of cappuccino is closely linked to the skewing of these cash-crop economics to the consumption habits of the West.

The organizers of the anthology may have felt, justifiably, that they were acting correctly in trying to include black women – and they were; but because of their historical position as white women at this particular point in time, and because of what this has meant and continues to mean in terms of power and exploitation, they *are* damned – if they do and if they don't. They have in fact joined the club of those whose choices have often, if not always, been the lesser of two evils. They are probably being damned for the sins of their forefathers and their foremothers and undoubtedly some of their own. However unfortunate it may be, we do live in times when a number of old scores are being paid off, and a white skin is often considered evidence enough that somewhere there are scores to settle. To cast it in less biblical and Old Testament terms, these are times when people's expectations concerning their human and civil rights run high – often outstripping the ability of society to fulfill them – and old oppressions run deep and rankle. The white feminist has, in certain situations, also been the beneficiary, at the expense of black women and women of color, of the spoils of patriarchy. She has been oppressed and exploited because of her gender but she has also benefited because of her skin, and continues to do so up to the present time. Consider, for example, that most affirmative action programs instituted by the various levels of government have now become synonymous with affirmative action for women – read white women, not peoples of other colours, nor the physically challenged.

No amount of good intentions, however well placed, will efface these historical and political realities; to pretend otherwise is to attempt to erase history. It was this evacuation of the historical and the political that informs the 'feminism' we read about – this attempt to present the articulation of feminism in Canada as something other than a predominantly white middle-class movement – that I challenged in my letter to the organizers.

Once again, however, I had found myself in a reactive position: I was putting out energy and joining issue over what is essentially a non-issue for me – white feminism. Before I could even get to the issue of the writings by black women (vis-a-vis black women's writing), I had to engage in a question of self-definition. For instance, if the organizers of the anthology had established such a category as black women's writing, didn't this imply that the other writings ought to be identified as white women's writing? Black women's writing can only exist as a category if white women's writing exists as a similar category. And who is defining whom? It was these questions which drove me back to an article I had written some months ago, but which addressed the core issue here for me – the issue of reaction and being reactive. In 'Why the United States,' Julia Kristeva writes, '[As] everyone knows every negation is a definition. An opposing position is therefore determined by what is being opposed. And in this way we arrive at two antithetical systems which internalize and reflect one another's qualities.[1]

Is not the category black women's writing an opposing position to white women's writing, and therefore determined by it? And don't these two categories

1. Julia Kristeva, *The Kristeva Reader*, ed. Toril Moi (Oxford: Basil Blackwell, 1986), p. 274.

then internalize and reflect each other's qualities, the one being what the other is not and vice versa?

Neither explanation nor instruction is my purpose, and continual self-definition 'in opposition to' is an exhausting business. To deny while at the same time affirming is often an impossible task, and so as a writer who considers herself doubly blessed in being female and black, my chief concern has been to create a place where I can write from a position of statement first and not reaction, because reaction implies that I am being determined by what I oppose.

No writer ever truly makes a first statement; we are all engaged in some form of dialogue with history, with literature, with the past, the present – even the future – expanding, clarifying, or modifying what someone else has already said, or trying to say it in some new way. 'First statement' implies not so much the original or new statement as a perspective from which I seek to write; a perspective that tries to embrace the full range of human experience in my work: struggle as well as love, politics and pleasure, sensuality, passion, sexuality, hatred, the grime and gold of the human spirit. As I write these words, I recall Toni Morrison's *Song of Solomon,* a work that seems to me to encompass this profundity of human experience.

It is difficult, if not impossible, for black female writers in the West today to ignore issues of racism or sexism in their works, particularly in realistic works, without making them seem untrue to life. The problem is not that we black and female writers should be seeking to avoid these issues, but how to manage them within our work so that, when we are done, the work is not consigned to the ghettos reserved for us (even in literature) where we become mouthpieces for the guilty white liberal conscience. As black women writers we are particularly challenged today to subvert those restrictions that subtly and not so subtly suggest we should write only about certain topics, in certain ways; we will have to find new ways of including our wholeness in our work while maintaining our integrity as black women. In my own work I have witnessed a poem move from the raw, brutal emotion arising out of the absence of a mother-tongue, to a poem that now contains and sustains that grief and moves beyond it even to celebration.

Surrealist forms, the magic realism of Latin American writers (which those of us from the Caribbean can lay claim to), post-modernist eruptions into the text of other discourses, all offer the possibility of embracing the unembraceable – our struggles *and* our passions. Whatever method is chosen to elaborate our realities, the imperative is a discovery and reconstruction of ourselves piece by piece in our own images. This perhaps is the best way the black female writer has at her disposal to expose the lie that has constructed her as Other, *without engaging in reaction.*

'Journal Entries Against Reaction,' which follows, speaks to this issue – a central issue in my life as a writer circumscribed by the two political realities of being female and black. It is not a piece *about* black women's writing since that would

be a reaction to white women's writing. What it attempts to do in this context
is to convert negation into affirmation. It prescribes no answers, but merely charts
the terrain and raises issues. It is one writer's statement – a writer who often
feels equally damned if she does and if she doesn't; a writer who is continually
assaulted by the tenets of sexism and white supremacy, and who, for that reason,
struggles to resist the temptation to reaction in her writing.

Journal Entries Against Reaction

Day One

We bleed therefore we are. In opposition to the *cogito ergo sum* of Cartesian
philosophy, which would have us believe something as simple and reflexive as
thinking proves our existence. Surely only a man – a white male at that – could
have made such a suggestion. Images which confront me daily in the media suggest
that for 'the Others' – blacks, people of color, the native peoples, women, gays
– my aphorism is a more accurate one: we bleed therefore we are. We have,
after all, been thinking ever since we *were*; much of the time it appears that we
still *are* not. I take liberties with Descartes' maxim, but for me it is not only rooted
in his philosophical ideas on the certainty of doubt, but also in a patriarchal matrix.
I think therefore I am. Only a man.

Day Two

'[T]he first impulse of the Black man [sic] is to say no to those who attempt to
build a definition of him. It is understandable that the first action of the Black
man is a reaction.'[2] Much the same may be said of women: their first action is
a reaction to those who 'build definitions' of them. It is difficult not to react –
as female, as black – when much around conspires against these very realities.
And why shouldn't one react?

Day Three

There is nothing wrong in reacting. We must. But there are dangers for the writer
who has roots in these twin realities: blackness and femaleness. The danger is
that one's writing can easily become persistently – I am tempted to say perni-
ciously – reactive. Can writing which is always reactive ever succeed beyond
the immediate and particular? Can it ever be more than a rallying cry to action?
Should it be more? or less? or different? Rallying cries are absolutely imperative.

2. Frantz Fanon, *Black Skin, White Masks* (New York: Grove Press, 1967), p. 36.

But if we consistently write from a reactive position, are we not still responding to someone else's agenda?

Day Four

Racism, sexism and all the other 'isms' call forth and inspire reaction. To write from a place of wholeness and integrity – is such an ideal utopian in today's world, writing as a black female?

Day Five

The white male thinks and therefore is. He seldom, if ever, says or needs to say, I am; I am white; I am male; I am human. Everything around him conspires to transform mere attributes into qualities of apparent permanence and universality synonymous with privilege. We might say these arguments are hackneyed and old hat – we are, after all, in the age of post-feminism. But these issues crash in against the writing which is rooted in the word – 'the "paternal Word" sustained by a fight to the death between the two races (men/women).'[3] Not to mention the father-tongues imposed on us, the colonized peoples of color. How to use the 'paternal Word' to issue forth first statements – of wholeness?

Day Six

The black, female writer faces a dilemma. Integral to the qualities of white maleness is a denial – at times more explicit than at others – of all that she is and represents. She must respond and react. The conundrum: how to transform what is essentially a response and a reaction into its own first statement.

Day Seven

To transform writing from reaction to statement. To oppose Woman to Man, according to Kristeva, is to impose a 'fixed sexual identity which is counterproductive to understanding and action.'[4] Woman is not a reaction to Man; she is not a response. She is her own first statement. Black is not a reaction or response to White; it is its own first statement. I am only black and female, if you are white and male. I think therefore I am – black and female.

3. Kristeva, *Kristeva Reader.*
4. Ibid.

Day Eight

How to convert the mere attributes of blackness and femaleness into first principles as gratuitous as whiteness and maleness? Or are feminism and black consciousness but moments, spasms in the history of *mankind*?

Day Nine

I am. Not in defiance and response to your pretending otherwise, but simply because I am. *Not* because I bleed – unless you bleed with me. But because I think. I demand the utter luxury and privilege of claiming existence merely by virtue of my thoughts – they have not been sufficient to date – not even my blood. Is it possible to think and so be? Probably not in our time. But as I write, I am constantly establishing my self, my being, my reality, as center, not Other. To echo Kristeva's question about women: what will they write that is new? What will I write that is new?

Day Ten

A Caucasianist (as in Africanist): a specialist (not by choice) in Caucasian affairs. I once introduced myself at a poetry reading in this way: a Caucasianist. A stab at the constant imposition of the white western expert on the rest of the world's peoples. We who have lived in the belly of the whale – shark is maybe more accurate a symbol – for so long, surely we best know its internal workings and their outward manifestations; surely *we* – 'the Others' – are the true experts. One seemingly absurd attempt at positioning myself at center, not periphery. There are more serious attempts: developing a language more attuned to expressing my reality; creating written forms of the demotic languages of the Caribbean – in which I am most at home as in Heidegger's sense of language being the house of being; 'playing with' language to arrive at that place where life and death meet within the language. Language itself – symbol of death and life for me. To arrive at the center. To write from the center.

Day Eleven

There is no law against dreaming. So writes Winnie Mandela. Dreaming – the imagination – the one faculty of the human that can resist colonization. To construct imaginative and poetic worlds as if we were at the center. To design imaginative and poetic scapes with us at the center. We speak from the center and are whole.

Day Twelve

How to transform reaction into statement. Transformation or metamorphosis: 'the action or process of changing in form or substance, esp. by magic or witchcraft' (OED). All art is about transformation and metamorphosis, which requires sacrifice: one form or shape, one reality given up or sacrificed for another. All art is about sacrifice of one sort or another: the artist lets go, literally gives up on the faith that something else will appear. Magic? Witchcraft? It often does. To transform reaction into statement, what must be sacrificed?

Day Thirteen

Call and response. An African art form. Together the call and the response make up the whole expression or the expression of the whole. Denial and response. They can never coexist: they can never coexist because denial implies death of the Other, and there is no response to death. Denial and response – mutually exclusive.

Day Fourteen

We are, however, more than the sum of all our parts. To believe that our reality is circumscribed by the words 'black' or 'female' is to connive and collude in our own prisons. But. But. But.

Day Fifteen

Writing cannot be in defense but in acceptance – of life, of death. It must transcend – but how to find the center from which one can look out, all around, transcending gender, race, class, yet still belonging to all those things – because we are, after all, human *and* flawed.

The Bilingual to Quintulingual Poet in Africa

'Molara Ogundipe-Leslie

Very often, foreigners express surprise that one writes in English at all. Americans, in particular, seem to think that language use is related to color. One wonders if there is any thought about their black compatriots who speak English as a mother-tongue. Perhaps it is because many do not think of their colored population, most of the time. It appears, however, that people like the Scandinavians tend to understand better our language dilemma in Africa in the same way that Asians seem to do because both groups have had to resolve the situation of living in the modern world with mother-tongues which are not world languages. Asians and most Scandinavians understand the condition of working with foreign, imposed or adopted languages.

Perhaps such understanding comes from belonging to cultures where it is known that language is a cultural artefact and not a genetic, biological or racial (whatever that means) possession. You do not speak a language because you are of one color or the other, you speak a language because you are socialized to speak it. Africans seem to know this more than any other peoples, perhaps because of the age of the continent and because of the centuries of interacting with peoples of varying races and nations, ethnic groups and identities, well before the Arabs or the Europeans entered Africa. Today, most Africans are at least bilingual if not polylingual to the fifth degree; and so my title.

Why do some of us write in English which is not our mother-tongue? And what is the experience of writing in English, particularly for a poet? We gained a facility with English and achieved a proficiency well beyond that in our mother-tongues, due to the colonial experience. The proficiency varies from person to person. Some are able still to speak their mother-tongue better while they remain fluent in written English; others have their fluency in both the writing and the speaking of mother-tongue permanently interfered with by the colonial experience. Still others end up not being able to speak the mother-tongue at all.

I was fortunate to have had a forward-looking mother who felt that children should speak their mother-tongue at home because they would inevitably gain a proficiency in the colonial language from the schools. It was the heyday in their time, the new day of imitating Victorian English families by speaking English at home all the time (mercifully only in the middle classes) and calling your parents 'Mummy and Daddy.' We kept in our home the older Victorian form of 'Papa and Mama.' You will still find the 'mummy/daddy' pattern in most former Anglo-colonial countries today. My parents' generation could be said to have taken over from the British in more ways than one. My parents were born in 1896 and 1906 respectively; educators both who continued the traditions of school and church, directly gained from white teachers. My parents set up and ran many mission schools across Nigeria as far east as Cross River and Ogoja States between the 1920s and the 1950s. My mother was one of the earliest women professors in teachers' colleges in Nigeria, and she was for a long time the highest qualified female teacher in Nigeria, the first woman to pass the highest exams for teachers in the 1930s. The positive impact of our parents' lives and cosmopolitan nature was that we, the children, grew up with the same inclusionary and broad-minded attitudes towards other cultures and a disinclination to think 'tribally.'

While we were young, though, my mother ran the junior section of our mission school where my father was the bishop and superintendent of the schools. Perhaps my mother did this to stay near us while the family was young and to cooperate as always with her Romeo, my father. Through all this we spoke Yoruba, my language, at home and we spoke a particularly refined form of it; that is, without curse words. It took my going outside our home and meeting girls from other social classes, particularly girls with mothers who spoke the mother-tongue, only for me to realize what cursely things my language could do and how altogether bawdy the language could be.

Fortunately, also, the education policy in Nigeria, at that time, was to teach every subject in the mother-tongue in the first five years of school. For this reason, the first books I read as a child were in Yoruba, while I studied Yoruba all through grade school and high school to graduate with high distinction in it. Still there were girls who came from the working classes or whose mothers were mother-tongue speakers only; and girls who belonged to Yoruba sub-ethnic groups noted for colorful and imagistic Yoruba, who spoke a more beautiful and idiomatic Yoruba than I could have dreamt of speaking at that time. These girls, more linguistically blessed in Yoruba and more adroit in their use of her, did our trans-lation exercises in class with aplomb, rhythm and gusto, striking the rest of us with envy, admiration and joyful laughter. We used to tease those little Yoruba experts in our classes then, calling them 'little witches' or 'little old women' because you expected such Yoruba expertise only among the elderly and the old.

I can say that I survived the attack on our minds and identity, which the colonial education was, due to the nationalism and natural intelligence or foresight of my parents. Nonetheless, English comes to me more easily in certain situations while Yoruba does in others. A great deal depends on the emotional situation, what I am trying to say and to whom. We have not suffiently studied the bilingual experience, particularly in its emotional functioning. Situations such as living abroad for a long time or marrying a mother-tongue English speaker (in which case English is spoken for twenty-four hours a day in the home) can bring the bilingual speaker almost to the point of first-language expertise. The language user may find that he or she speaks, even thinks, in English all the time. The same situation may go for the person married across ethnic groups in a situation where the couple does not or cannot speak a common African language together. A return to a home context or an existence in a mother-tongue setting can, however, make the spouse of a foreigner remain fluent and adept in both languages, in English and the mother-tongue.

In the colonial scheme, getting the best education often meant getting the best alienation, the best aggression on your mind and the best attempt at cultural erasures in your world and psyche. The will to survive and be happy in dignity is perhaps the surest protection we adduced, often unknowingly, against this sometimes insidious, sometimes brutal onslaught. Many of us were both 'bad' (read: rebellious) kids. Racially demeaning texts had no meaning at first or were just funny; something to read and laugh about, tumbling in fun and innocence in the dust or grass; something to forget about thereafter. When racially demeaning texts first began to *mean* in our maturation process, then began to *hurt*, and then finally commence to *generate* intellectual reactions worthy of research by us. The colonial intention was to produce the nearest imitation of the master culture. Apologists for the colonizers would say that there was no negative intent in the colonial workers, only their-all-too human aspiration to produce what they considered excellent. Research has, however, shown how there was a concerted colonial effort and language policy to create and appropriate faithful and loyal local elites, by seemingly admitting them, through the educational process, into the master class at the metropolitan center. The use of English and English literary studies were to be some of the mechanisms for this cultural and spiritual onslaught while India, Nigeria and Uganda were some of the colonial laboratories for these human experiments. The theoreticians of this intellectual banditry go back to the seventeenth and eighteenth centuries in colonial history; to imperialists like Grant, Hastings, Trevelyan and Lugard among others.

Now we find that African families are themselves carrying on the heritage of denuding their children of mother-tongue expertise in their bid to enter the international workforce, I suppose, or to share the benefits of belonging easily to a cosmopolitan culture. What does this early apprenticeship do to the African child, however? I hear that recently there were almost ethnic riots in Nigeria at the suggestion of the introduction of a mother-tongue education policy in the early years of school. This was seen as anti-nationalist in the sense of affirming ethnic identities; yet what happens to the psyche of the child in the process, the child who speaks English from age zero? What does that produce in the individual?

It produces a mental and emotional situation where the person does not think wholly in his or her mother-tongue, if at all. A situation of informational mixture; a capability only for a situational and positional use of language. We need not speak here of the cultural losses or absences. Let us instead return to my early questions.

Why do some of us write in English? I suppose part of this question has been answered by my long sociological clarification. English comes more naturally in speaking of certain subjects, in certain modes and to certain audiences. A great deal depends on whom you are trying to address about what and their openness to whatever it is you wish to communicate.

My second question is more interesting for us here. What is the experience of writing in English, particularly for a poet? English has a relational usage, among others, for the bilingual speaker. Cultural signs and usages resonate from the mother-tongue culture depending on the addressed, her situation and the effect you are trying to have on the hearer or hearers. English can also be used to distance if you do not like a person or if you wish to reject a person emotionally by interposing a foreign language between you and that party, as could happen with a suitor or a loved one, for instance.

I have always wondered in what language we think our deepest emotions and in what language we naturally express them? Some emotional situations you express in English; in others, you burst out in your head and, later, through your mouth in your language. In what language do we dream, for instance? And in what language do we make love? An African colleague of mine once laughingly said to me that a person who made love in English was truly colonized! In what language, therefore, do you have an orgasm, if we dare to be truly Rabelaisian or down to earth here?! Do you cry out in your mother-tongue or in English, dear bilingual to quintulingual writer? That seems to me like a deep test.

In what language do you genuinely cry out to the universe in poetry? In what language do you spill forth the music in your soul to harmonize, integrate or counterpoint it in order finally to dissolve it into the music of which the universe is made, to echo Okigbo, a Nigerian poet?

But, poetic expression is not always an atavistic, pristine and cosmological affair. It also relates simply to the question of audience. Whom do you want to reach and what is the best way of reaching them? Are certain audiences even remotely interested in what you have to say? Is your subject their issue at all?

I have written things in Yoruba, my mother-tongue, attempting things in poetry and fiction. I found my voice completely different from when I write in English. I become a different person or persona while the sentiments expressed are different, flowing from another part of me because through the language, I am harking back to another philosophical store of knowledge, to a different view of life and the meaning of that view of life, in a process which could only percolate that meaning in my use of English. This view of life sometimes has to be forced through your English as you strive with all your linguistic might to avoid sounding merely quaint or exotic because you are speaking from within a living and lived culture, despite all the social science fantasies about vanishing, not evolving cultures. As you write in your mother-tongue, you understand more deeply than theory that how you speak is determined by who you are speaking to and what you are thinking of as you are speaking. Even if you think you are speaking to some vague posterity as many of us writers like to claim, that posterity must have some kind of ears, if no face; and definitely a cognitive store to which you must relate.

More deeply than theory too, you realize that language carries its own cultural baggage which you may not necessarily care for, share or believe in any longer, even in simple everyday phrases, conventional turns of language and, more importantly, sentiments, which are considered idiomatic, beautiful or expert but which are fraught with concepts you no longer accept intellectually. The scramble for an authentic voice which is you as a writer then becomes doubly strenuous and more time-consuming in a situation in which you are hurrying to get heard before mortality intervenes; in a real-life drama in which you are running alongside Death against your own temporality. I suppose, finally, it is a question of commitment to a particular kind of mode.

If you feel you do not have the existential time nor the interest or commitment to work for the success and acceptance of a new way of using the Yoruba language in a new mode which may not be immediately but only eventually accepted; if you cannot wait to create a new language and build up a new audience, what do you do? You become a bilingual to quintulingual poet, writing in borrowed tongues, singing to ready-made and familiar audiences. I have used the term quintulingual, therefore, to indicate that Africans often have to be many-tongued, speaking not only European languages but also several local African languages, in order to interact and communicate, even in their own home setting.

If I were to write a love poem in Yoruba now, I would find myself using accepted and conventional phrases and images which may be far removed from my experience but are considered classic and beautiful. My mind would immediately turn to another world.

Listen:

> Oko mi, eleyinju ege
> adufe mi, aduduyemi
> pagbo yi mi ka o
> gbe mi ro
> gbe mi leke, gbe mi ro.

It translates as: 'My husband/ of the balanced eyeballs/ you, whom they struggle over to love/ you, of the befittingly black skin/make a human fence around me/hold me enduring upright/hold me triumphal/ hold me enduring, upright, and stayed' – or something to that effect. It is difficult to translate the emotional and aesthetic nuances of the eyeball image; the fencing to protect, a fence made of people standing around you to defend you, and the sense of *ro*, upright and stayed, still and enduring, all impacted in the same word. The husband idea comes in because there is hardly a concept of love outside an approved social union; expressed publicly at least and approved, while the concept of husbanding seems to be the most intimate way in which a woman may convey intimacy which also includes the deep sense of physical husbanding. The word for lover *olufe* is a post-colonial neologism. But who says we can only write in old pre-colonial words. Nonetheless, the colonially-constructed words tend to sound scribal and emotionally false to me. An in-audience is obviously required for this kind of poetry and a particular kind of audience which may not always be different from the English-reading audience because there are experiential overlaps in multi-lingual communities.

Perhaps it is the commitment to waiting for one's results and perhaps never getting them; the commitment to forging a new language, literary tradition and audiences, which are some of what distinguish the genius from the merely good or great writer – and certainly from the everyday 'writer.'

Part II

Women Weaving Words:
Raised Poetic Voices

SISTER NETIFA

I am a Poem

I am a poem
written in anger
I can comfort
or cause u pain
you've nought to lose
all to gain
so read me
fill your soul
I'm a poem
silent like a stream
running to the open
sea to be free
touching coast to coast
in any tongue
sometimes written. sometimes
a song of liberation
or frustration at
a corrupt system
I'm a poem
take me. read me
fill your soul
I'm a poem
in my words
I can hush a baby
or start a war
I am a poem telling
the world of the truth
which nothing
is new
I'm a poem
sometimes happy
sometimes blue
I'm a poem

I was written for
you. take me
read me!
fill your soul
I'm a poem
written in anger
silent with scorn
I am the writing
on the wall
what is covered
will be exposed
for the eye to see
take me! read me
fill your soul
I am the word on the wind
blowing along

I am a poem
sometimes sullen
sometimes bold
I can be smutty
erotic
stinging hard
like the fruit of the earth
I am the poem for all
nations
who want to be free
take these words to you
from me
take me! read me!
fill your soul
take me read me
fill your soul

daughters of the soil

we are daughters of the soil.
look at us, feel our anger.
        feel our pain.
            feel our sorrow.
eyes weeping blood, blood
flowing into rivers.
staining the earth.
our nose breathes in the injustice
that hangs over the world
like a cloud
ears hearing abuse, so freely rendered.
oh feel our anger
        feel our pain
            feel our sorrow.
YET!
What started as a whisper from our tongues
has become a shout
from every conscious mouth
still!
you rape us
still!
you abuse us
again again again ...
shoot us! shoot us! death cannot kill the spirit
our spirit, which will rise,
rise like a mist to smother the downpressor.
then fall like dew,
to nourish the land
that gave we birth.
we are daughters of the soil.
look at us.
See Africa.
feel our anger
        pain
            sorrow.
i must be free.

sister

the large colorful head wraps you wear
in soft pastel colours
bright
loud
long skirts
swishing around your knees
silver and gold bracelets
tinkling on your wrists
making soft tunes as you move
singing sad songs
humming the tunes
laughing with the baby
cross with an older child
you're like the wind outside
swaying gently to the music
sometimes your eyes closed
dreaming of far off lands
places you never even heard of
will never see
dancing rhythmically to faster beats
remembering
when you were younger
when dreams
were not dreams
but visions
stand firm sister
we are your family
and here in places you never heard of
will never see
are fighting by your side
for all of our freedom

SHANTA ACHARYA

Words as Places

Images of retreating words
mirage our unexplored thoughts,
travellers in an alien country,
unprotected self-portraits.

The images come straight through the masquerade,
from the bottom of this immense pool of seeming.
This the defect of our too great nearness,
attributing to one experiences of the other.

I can only have my own awareness of you,
a ritual out of myself I must provide for.

You pinned all your metaphors on me,
ferocious alphabets sprawled upon my limbs.

Anywhere I grow, I have to find a place elsewhere.
The landscape alters irrevocably with my coming.
I cannot have direct knowledge of it before my coming.

For the Dispossessed

Each passion in my sinews' landscape
strives to encounter itself articulate.
Consciousness is captivity, held in silence.

So have you recreated my womanhood
in the tradition of whoring goddesses
treading this *cultured* sunshine
in a processional of marionettes.

Nor am I exactly my self-conferred queen.
I cannot even define this becoming.
These syllables are familiar to me.
Here is my space, but I cannot lie in it.

Then I must speak for the dispossessed,
for the exploration is no longer the same.

A Giddy Mannequin

A giddy mannequin discreetly naked
I pose for you in a glass cage,
out of your reach, perfect and undefiled.

I learnt the use of facades
when you began destroying my porcelain dolls
so long treasured behind the purdah of my self.

Dead images and my mirrors in pieces
I strive to escape continually
the incarnation of my several selves
strewn casually over our encounters in time.

They glisten into life mocking me at multiple angles
as I puppet-dance to your discordant tunes.
I pretend not to take notice of such things.

Even this discerning unconcern
I stole from your eyes unaware,
perfected to an art of survival

As you, in perpetual ambush,
prefer to remove your glasses
before you come forward to splinter mine.

I have nothing to be sad about
as our images crackle and drag.
My body remains silent and complete,
a giddy mannequin discreetly naked.

MIRIAM ALVES

En-Tarde-Ser[1]

A tarde sorriu elegância
matinal fragância invade espaços
A tarde sorriu elegância
a tampa da emoção explode
                    nos atos
Reconfortantes movimentos
encostados a tempos
                    cedem
A matinal fragância
                    fecunda a tarde
O sol instala fervor
                    suor seca roupas
incessantes ataques lubrificam
A fragância matinal
                    sonoriza-se
Anoitece eternece
          torna-se...
                    femeal

Dente por Dente

Foi tráfico
vidas desnudas nossas
                    postas
a mesa canibálica insaciável
lupas garfos culturais devorando-nos
          palavra
                    por
          palavra
          sílaba
                    por
          sílaba
ãfa glutão consumindo-nos realidade
era cilada

---

1. A word play with *entardecer* which means afternoon, sunset, becoming dark: *en* = in; *tarde* = afternoon, evening; *ser* = to be.

Becoming Night

The afternoon smiled elegance
matinal fragrance invades space
The afternoon smiled elegance
emotion's cork explodes
              in action
Soothing movements
propped up on times
            stop
The matinal fragrance
           fecundates the afternoon
The sun installs fervor
          sweat dries clothes
incessant attacks annoint
The matinal fragrance
        reverberates
Night falls softens
       becomes…
            female
(Translated by Celeste D. Mann)

Tooth by Tooth

It was business
our naked lives
    placed
at the insatiable cannibalistic table
cultural magnifying glasses forks devouring us
    word
        by
   word
      syllable
      by
      syllable
gluttonous anxiety consuming us reality
was a trap

(Translated by Celeste D. Mann)

Tempos Difíceis

As cores mudam
sorriso debochado
          flutua na cara da saudade

Retenção e medo
          imperam
          enrolam-se no manto vaidade
sorriem

As cores mudam
Todos disfarçam esbranquiçados

Difficult Times

Colors change
jeering smile
    vacillates in the face of 'saudade'[1]

Retention and fear
    reign
    wrapping themselves in the cloak of vanity

they smile

Colors change
All wear pale white masks

(Translated by Celeste D. Mann)

1. saudade: longing, desire, homesickness and nostalgia.

Pedaços de Mulher

Sou eu
que no leito abraço
mardisco seu corpo
com lascivo ardor

Sou eu
cansada inquieta
lanço-me à cama
mordo nos lábios
o gosto da ausência,
sou eu essa mulher

A noite
no eito das ruas procuro,
vejo-me agachada nas esquinas
chicoteada por uma ausência.
Desfaleço
faço-me em pedaços

Mulher
sou eu esta mulher
rolando feito confete
na palma de sua mão

Mulher – retalhos
a carne das costas secando
no fundo do quintal
presa no estendal do seu esquecimento

Mulher – revolta
Agito-me contra os prendedores
que sequram-me firme neste varal

Eu mulher
arranco a viseira da dor
enganosa.

Pieces of Woman

It's me
who embraces in bed
slightly chews your body
in luxurious heat

It's me
tired restless
who plunges into bed
bites in the lips
the taste of absence
I am this woman

At night
in the blue of the streets I search
I see me crouched around corners
whipped by an absence.
I dismay
made into pieces

Woman
I am this woman
rolling just like confetti
in the palm of your hand

Woman – rags
the flesh on the back drying out
in the back of the backyard
tightly stretched in your forgetfulness

Woman – rebelled
I struggle against
whatever holds me tight to this clothesline

I, Woman
Throw out the blinkers of the pain
misleader

(Translated by Zenaide Djadyle)

Quando

Quando nada mais restar
ficam meus sonhos
dependurados vazios
presos nos prendedores de roupa

Quando nada mais restar
ficam minhas esperanças
de prontidão na curva
        da rua
tingindo o azul do horizonte
com meus gritos de fogo

Quando nada mais restar
ficam minhas lembranças
de mãos dadas
cirandando
com o que eu poderia ter sido

When

When nothing else's left
my dreams will be
hanging empty
held by hangers like clothes

When nothing else's left
my hopes will be
readily on watch by the street
        curve
dyeing the horizon in blue
with my fiery cries

When nothing else's left
my remembrances will be
holding hands
circling 'round
with whatever it is
that I could have been

(Translated by Zenaide Djadyle)

Carregadores

Carregamos no ombros
feito fardos
a luta, a dor dum passado

Carregamos nos ombros
feito dardo
a vergonha que não é nossa

Carregamos nos ombros
feito carga
o ferro da marca do feitor

Carregamos na mão
feito lança
as esperanças do que vira

Carriers

We carry on our shoulders
like burdens
the struggle, the pain of a past

We carry on our shoulders
like targets
the shame that's not ours

We carry on our shoulders
like cargo
the marking iron of the overseer

We carry in our hands
like a spear
the hopes of what is to come

(Translated by Zenaide Djadyle)

Revolta de Desejos

Nossos desejos
sufocam os braços
    que nos prendem
    nos convencionais
      aquecimentos
        chamados Amor

Nossos desejos
inconformam-se todos
    abrem as pernas
    fecham antigas
    trincheiras
estimulando novos passos
    no ritmo do desconhecido

Nossos desejos
dão-se as mãos
    unem os umbigos
    num novo bailado
estalando os medos
    antigos
chicoteiam-nos aos gritos
    de LIVRE
expurgando as Grandes Mãos
    que nos querem
    domar.

Rebellion of Desires

Our desires
choke the arms
    which arrest us
    in the so-called
      warm-ups
        named Love

Our desires
themselves all unconform
    open their legs
    shut old
    trenches
estimulating new steps
    on the beat of the unknown

Our desires
hold hands
    link navels
    in a new swing
clapping old
    fears
whipping them at shouts of
    'FREE!'
expurging the Big Hands
    which will to
    tame us.

(Translated by Zenaide Djadyle)

AIDA CARTAGENA PORTALATIN

¿Cómo llorar la muerte de una rosa?

'De todos los hombres que están vivos, quién sabe algo?' — ECLESIASTES

¿Cómo llorar la muerte de una rosa,
si los amaneceres han desdoblado el Mundo,
y en la hierba que tiembla cerca de los rosales
se han quedado las albas vueltas gotas de agua?

Sólo desde la tierra
tienen brillo de ámbar las estrellas.
A la tierra amarga vuela
la lluvia del color de los rosales.

Sentir cómo los musgos se asen a las piedras;
Hay un rencor en la brisa viajera.

Hombres no han llorado
porque caen los hombres.
¿Cómo llorar la muerte de una rosa?

How Can One Mourn the Death of a Rose?

'Of all men living, who knows anything?' — ECCLESIASTES

How can one mourn the death of a rose,
if sunrise has unfolded the earth
and in the grass trembling near the rose trees
dawn has turned daylight into droplets of water?

Only as seen from the earth
does the starlight shine golden.
And to the bitter earth
the rose-colored rains return.

To feel as the moss clinging to the stones;
a reproach is heard in the traveling wind.

Man has not mourned
because men have fallen.
How can one mourn the death of a rose?

(Translated by Daisy Cocco de Filippis)

Una mujer esta sola

Una mujer está sola. Sola con su estatura.
Con los ojos abiertos. Con los brazos abiertos.
Con el corazón abierto como un silencio ancho.
Espera en la desesperada y desesperadamente noche
sin perder la esperanza.
Piensa que está en el bajel almirante
con la luz más triste de la creación.
Ya izó velas y se dejó llevar por el viento del Norte
en fuga acelerada ante los ojos del amor.

Una mujer está sola. Sujetando con sueños sus sueños,
Los sueños que le restan y todo el cielo de Antillas.
Seria y callada frente al mundo que es una piedra humana,
móvil, a la deriva, perdido en el sentido
de la palabra propia, de su palabra inútil.

Una mujer está sola. Piensa que ahora todo es nada
Y nadie dice nada de la fiesta o el luto
de la sangre que salta, de la sangre que corre,
de la sangre que gesta o muere de la muerte.
Nadie se adelanta ofreciéndole un traje
para vestir su voz que desnuda solloza deletreándose.

Un mujer está sola. Siente, y su verdad se ahoga
en pensamientos que traducen lo hermoso de la rosa,
de la estrella, del amor, del hombre y de Dios.

A Woman is Alone

A woman is alone. Alone with herself.
With open eyes and open arms.
With a heart opened by a wide silence.
She awaits in the desperate and despairing night
without losing hope.
She believes herself to be in the leading vessel
lit by creation's saddest light.
She has sailed away, fleeing from love,
the North wind guiding her flight.

A woman is alone. Binding her dreams with dreams,
the remaining dreams and the open Antillean skies.
Thoughtful and quiet, she faces a stony, aimless world,
lost in the meaning of its own word,
its own useless word.

A woman is alone. She believes everything to be nothing.
And no one speaks to her of the joy and sorrow to be found
in the blood that leaps, that flows,
in the blood which nourishes or dies of death.
No one comes forward to offer her clothing to dress
her naked, self-defining, weeping voice.

A woman is alone. She feels and her truth drowns
in thoughts which speak of the beauty of a rose,
of a star, of love, of man and of God.

(Translated by Daisy Cocco de Filippis)

Otoño Negro

elegía

'Redoblado tambor redoblando...'

Sé que era otoño sin alondras ni hojas.
Yo que lloro al árbor, al pez y a la paloma
me resisto a los blancos del Sur
a esos blancos con su odio apuntando a los negros.
No les pregunto nunca, porque responderían
que en Alabama pueden florecer las dos razas.
Mas, después del Verano de Medgar W. Evers
hicieron un Otoño de cuatro niñas negras.

Ese cortejo de tantos ataúdes.
Ese cortejo nublando la alegría
redoblado tambor redoblando,
¿hasta cuándo? aquellos cuatro cuerpos.
Su luz de carne negra iluminando el Orbe.
No es hora de un grito jubiloso.
Afligida la tierra, hasta la tierra llora...
¡Hasta la muerte llora las cuatro niñas negras!
¿cómo habitar sus huecos? Malvadamente muertas
porque la muerte es propia, otro no debe usarla.
Sus tiernos esqueletos levantarán su raza.
Con sus cabellos crespos se tejerán banderas.
Cuatro fueron las niñas en una iglesia muertas.
Antorchas inmortales sembradas en el Sur.
¿Cómo se escribe en Alabama L I B E R T A D ? – pregunto.
Yo que lloro al árbol, al pez y a la paloma.

Black Autumn

elegy

'Echoing drums, echoing on …'

I know it was already autumn,
without leaves and a lark's song
I, who cry for the trees, for fish and doves,
reject the white men of the South,
those whites with their hatred aimed at black men.
I'd never question their motives
because they would answer
that in Alabama both races can blossom.
After the summer of Medgar W. Evers,
came the fall of four black girls.

The funeral procession of so many caskets.
That procession clouding happiness
the beaten drums, echoing on
Until when? Those four black bodies.
The light of their dark skin brightening the earth.
The time for joy has gone.
Afflicted, even the earth cries…
Even Death weeps for these four black girls.
Who can fill the empty place they leave? Brutally murdered.
Death owns death and no one else should dare to use it.
Their tender bones will lift up their race.
Their curly hair will knit flags.
Four were the girls murdered in the church,
four immortal torches sown in the South.
How can one spell F R E E D O M in Alabama? – I ask.
I who cry for the trees, fish and doves.

(Translated by Daisy Cocco de Filippis)

Memorias Negras

tono I

Vertical camino derribado
reducido a esencia original
fatalidad: el hombre
su problema inherente
simplemente la raza

el verbo de los ágrafos
betún de la piel negra
la cama en el pajal

el reclamo del vientre
la insistencia del sexo
responso lloro pena la nube

llueve

tono 2

oh
negación del amor
quién habló de soledad y esperanza
llorar llorarllorar
no habéis la muerte preparado
llora la muertellora el cielollora el negro

ooooooh amor
amor asesinado

Black Memories

tune 1

Vertical road trampled
reduced to its original being
misfortune: Said simply,
race is the problem
man inherits

The word of the wordless
shoeblacking of a black skin
the bed in the haystack

The claims of the womb
the insistence of sex
I cry for the death the cloud pines

    it rains

tune 2

Oh
denial of love
who told of loneliness and hope
to weep to weepto weep
You have not made ready for death
death weeps heaven weeps the black man weeps

ooooooh love
murdered love

tono 3

era tanta la lluvia en sharpeville
la nube cerró el ojo
para no verse mojar los cadáveres

era tanta la muerte en sharpeville
la lluvia se tapó el oído
para no oirse caer sobre cadáveres

tono 4

son las noticias y memorias negras
destroza el cuerpo la metralleta   repartiendo plomos
oooooooh

asesinando a la magnolia negra
compás a contratiempo los disparos

cobardemente explotando a áfrica
ooooooohooooooooh
tres días la muerte horizontal tendida
responso lloro pena la nube

    llueve

tono 5

sharpeville
en esa tierra se llega al hambre
en esa tierra el hambre saluda el día
los plomos queman
la sangre aúlla
revelará el secreto de la memoria negra
el polvo de los huesos calcinados
  ay,ay,ay,ay
asesinaron otra vez a áfrica
otra vez en sharpeville
ooooooohooooooooh
OoooooooooooooooooooooooH
nadie grita: castigo

tune 3

There was so much rain in sharpeville
the cloud closed its eyes
not to watch itself wetting the corpses

There was so much death in sharpeville
the rain closed its ear
not to hear itself fall on the corpses

tune 4

There are the news and black memories
the machine-gun destroys the body sharing lead
ooooooh

murdering the black magnolia
the syncopated rhythm of bullets

cowardly exploiting africa
ooooooohoooooooh
For three days death has lied horizontally
I cry for the death the cloud pines

   it rains

tune 5

sharpeville
one arrives at hunger in that land
hunger salutes daylight in that land
the bullets burn
blood howls
to reveal the secret of black memory
the dust of calcined bones
   ahahahah
they murdered africa again
once again in sharpeville
ooooooohoooooooh
OoooooooooH
no one shouts: curses

(Translated by Daisy Cocco de Filippis)

NANCY MOREJÓN

Grenada Woman

I am a Grenada woman.
I planted nutmeg
under the constant shelter
of the wild poinciana
and I cast my nets once more
in the summer blue.
Herbs, stones and shells
cradled the heart of my villages
and the sky was witness
to how all my children
hungered in the harbor.
I am a Grenada woman.
I saw the hearths, suddenly,
now alive amidst the dead,
amidst the range and the lightning flash.
I have discovered that essential tomorrow
while I dig a grave for the marine
who dared dig mine after his unpunished assault
against a young St George's girl.
I am a Grenada woman
and here you lie, stretched out
awaiting the snakes damnation.

So the Legends Say

The hoofbeat of the antelope, as it approaches in its elegance,
alerts the hunter
who waits crouching and nervous.

So the legends say

But

what of your footsteps?
And your silent appearance?
These take me by surprise,
they attack me for ever,
crouching like the hunter,
nervous like a leaf,
without clear words, without tongue,
like a new slave in the nineteenth century.

Lianas, Fish and Algae

I walk on the river
sunlight gently glows.
Rocked by a net of strange flowers,
lianas, fish and algae, I go sailing.
A force pushes me and I am unaware.
Naked, a copper sailor gazes at me.
Rocked by a net of strange flowers,
he goes sailing amongst fish, lianas and algae.
We are alongside each other, looking to the shore.
There are some women talking, there are other women
singing.
You and I, sailor, let ourselves be taken along,
I walk on the river. You walk on the river.
Those eyes point us out,
their pupils cast the deepest flame.
A force pushes me and I am unaware.
A force in the water drags us along.
There we go sinking
There we go drowning
There we go beautifully
into the sweet river water.

Spinning Woman

Who doesn't read, at some time,
about spinning women?
In fairy tales
beautiful spinning women appear
reaching sure clouds
with their unending threads,
pushing silk into space
where we hear music
rising from their white cones.
The lively eyes of this spinning woman
hold the magic of bread.
Their humanity, steeped in the thread-work,
would bring us eternally
the gusting winds of Lyon,
the perfumes of Persia.

I want us all
to read once more
those tales
of spinning women.
Bear us off, spinning woman, once more
to green castles,
to draw-bridges,
to the illusions that you create today,
amidst mechanized looms
that make you more powerful,
more tender, more earthy.
Bear us off
with your hands,
towards those childhood dreams.
Bear us off, spinning woman, and give us your joy.

LISSETTE NORMAN

natural thoughts

as I lay in my bed trying to fall asleep
my fingers found themselves in my hair
i parted it searching remembering
my ancestors as they brushed the roots
i felt the chemically straightened hair
and avidly searched for the roots again
after having passed the deadline
for a perm
i felt the 'new growth'
what was truly mine
and had oppressed for many years of my life

(i wore an afro in my younger days
before I was introduced to straightening
chemicals hot combs and curling irons
believing the european 'white hair is good
hair and african-american hair is bad
hair' ideology that was instilled in me)

i continued parting my hair and felt this
'new growth'
i wondered about it
i tried to measure it with my finger:
about an inch
an inch that was probably worried when
its oppressor was coming
it was late this time
i felt it
my eyes closed
i wondered about it
i thought about every little curl
imagining a story
with every bend and curve of the curls
stories deeprooted in africa
followed by more and more
stories of latin america

and then I ran my fingers to the very edges
of my hair
you know – those areas where the perm
never quite straightens no matter how long
you leave the perm in
results: good hair with burned roots and a sore scalp

i combed through my hair with my fingers
and again traced the bends of the curls
my eyes closed
i imagined them to be some sort of design
something artistic
I traced them back and forth
and suddenly felt movement
waves
waves came to mind
the feeling was refreshing
my fingers stood with the waves
it was flowing
flowing
flowing suddenly into melody
a melody desperate to be heard
a melody from a blues song
        bessie smith
ma rainey
        billie holiday
so sweet

i felt around all night
wondering what it would be like if
my whole head was embodied with this
new growth
'my' hair
i couldn't stop thinking about it
i thought about it all night
i thought about it so much that it
is now months later
and the 'new growth' has grown to be
many inches long

although it takes a little
more work
in trying to manage it
i have come to accept its existence
and am learning to love 'my' hair
more and more
i have gotten so much from this experience
and cannot explain it any further than this

i've been confronted by sistahs
(who perm their hair)
who cannot understand my
going natural
they can't seem to understand this change
that I have chosen for myself and
constantly tease me
about my 'nappy' hair
but I laugh along with them and say
'aint my naps beautiful?'

i no longer feel a need to defend
the very existence of my hair and
no longer bother to explain
why I chose to go natural
but if you really must know
i'll tell you
that i do so as a
cultural spiritual and philosophical
                    expression!

EINTOU PEARL SPRINGER

On Becoming a Woman

for my first-born, Denise

Watching you grow
to womanhood
seeing you
venturing into life,
questing,
hoping,
brings back
memories
of the pain
the love,
that bore you,
makes the pain
swell again;
reminds me
of that first pain
signalling
birth.

Your birth;
A pain
so sharp
so intense
in fear
in terror
I cried out
stood on my head
held tight
to my own mother
bathed in tears,
wanting to take
my pain as hers
knowing she could not

And if my love could cushion you,
then never
would you know
the pain
of being
WOMAN;
Never
would you know
the pain
of hurt
rejection
betrayal
as I.

And if my love
could protect you
from all
who would come near you
and then hurt you
from all
then life for you
would be
the happiness
that flooded me
when first
I held you

My baby,
you were
so beautiful.
You are
so beautiful.
Flesh of my flesh
mirror
of my dreams;
like my mother
could not
shield me
alas!
My love
and hers
cannot hold back
the march
of years
inexorable.

And so
I feel the pain
again;
that pain
heralding
your eagerness
to be born.

Again
I felt that quickening
inside me
that said
you moved
you lived.

First child
child
of my first love
no longer
cocooned
in my womb;
I cannot
protect you
from the pain
of being
WOMAN

BUT
I can
with a mother's curse
that is
like no other
DAMN
all who
would hurt you.
I can
with a mother's curse
that is like no other
DAMN
all who
would take your dreams
your hopes
and sully them
betray them

I can
with a mother's love
that is like no other
give you
the sum
of my pain
the sum of my joy
in being
WOMAN
and wish you...
LOVE.

Caribbean Man

Prolonged infant,
suckled
in matriarchal relays,
twixt breasts
of stifling fondness.
Growth to manhood
stunted
in perennial milk.
The cock let go
spews the sperm
scattered
over wide expanse
of irresponsibility
makes
a new generation
of breasts
atrophy;
and tears fall
as milk flows
for infants needing
paternity;
for manchild
suckled
in matriarchal relays
twixt breasts
of stifling fondness.

Come Close

Come close.
The night
is time
for closeness

It's not
to force
your smile
that I am here
with you

The times are grim.
If, I am true
there'll not be much
to tickle you;
but, stretch your hand,
when it meets mine
we both may smile.

It's not
to beg
for love
that I am here
with you.
But, spend a while,
maybe with time,
we'll see
love's there to find

It's not
to chastise you
that I am here
with you.
I can but hold
the mirror
to me
as well as you,
and, if we see
some things
for change
we both
may grow

Come close,
push down
the walls
touch me.

It's not
to fill
a space
I say
to you
come close.
Share with me
but leave me
room
to grow.

Out of the Shadows

Out of the shadows,
leaping
into the light
of self-knowledge.
Out of the shadows,
into sharp focus.
Out of the shadows,
out of the shape
and images
pre-ordained
super-imposed,
moving now into
clear vision,
a mission even
for self
fulfillment.

Out of the shadows
into focus,
clear visibility;
image no longer
shrouded in shadow
of he
behind whom
it is said
I should walk.

Out of the shadows,
out of oblivion
demanding
clear compensation,
clear recognition,
of roles
of functions.

Out of the shadows
spitting
in the eye
of those who want me
still
as burden bearer
of the race;
spitting
in the eye
of those who say
only helper supporter;
screaming chanting
I come.

Out of the shadows
into sharp focus,
standing alone,
nowhere
to lean,
to rest.

Once – long ago.
I leaned
on the man
who walked
beside me.
His knees wobbled
and I
balanced us both.
Balanced, he quickly
moved
from my side,
leaving me
screaming.

Out of the shadows
now
I come
screaming chanting
no longer despair,
but personhood,
bare humanity,
saying it is time
I share
this burden.

At even time,
head bowed
feed shuffling
back aching
I have walked,
for centuries
from fields
of labor
to beds
of labor
Still – everywhere
the sun goes down
upon my shame;
my double curse
black – and
woman –
scraping the barrel
of humanity
wallowing
in my shame
my chains
wound tightly
over my mind,
receiving
savage kicks
propelled by agony
by anguish
from a bruised
bleeding castration
a running sore
for centuries.

I come now
out of the shadows,
of inarticulate
beast
of burden;
weary
of taking strain
on my back
in my belly;
knowing now
to take the kicks
is not
to heal
the wounds
of centuries.

Out of the shadows
I stand,
focused,
strong and knarled
like rock
buffeted by centuries
of harsh wind and rough weather.

Out of the shadows
standing alone;
nowhere to lean.
No longer though
are the screams
those of despair,
of fear.
Defiant now
in sunlight
I walk
chanting personhood.

I balance myself
against the buffets
of harsh winds
and send out
a word
to sistren
groping still
to find a way
in the darkness
of
self negation;
seeking
seeking
a way
out;
seeking
seeking
simply
PERSONHOOD.

GLORIA WADE GAYLES

Letters to Our Ancestors

To Sojourner Truth

you wear your name well
sisterwoman of truth

riding your chariot
hard and fast
through mud puddles
leaving brown tracks
on the faces of men
ashamed to show their arms

hard and fast
with your skirt raised
by your own hands
and your Bible raised
and your anger raised

hard and fast
through the births
and the thefts
and your mother's pain
which none but Jesus knew,
and understood

you wear your name well
sisterwoman of truth
whose dressed-down words
rode hard and fast
through the centuries
arriving in time
and on time
to dressusup
for change.

To Phillis Wheatley

a million regrets we owe you
singer of songs
dancer with words denying
truth in every couplet
pain rhymed

they decorated you for royalty
we hanged you for treason

they stole your life
we threw away your art
which was the only life
you owned

a million regrets we owe you
sister poet
genius woman
mother of the free ones
writing freely

NOW

To Harriet Tubman

Time means nothing to those
whose suffering continues time
and time again to be ignored
by Time which takes no time
to end the seconds, minutes
hours and centuries of
our pain

It is time, I say,
to close the books
which lock you in a time
called yesterday
so removed from now that
only somebody else's words
can tell me who you were
and what you did
then

today
this moment
this second
(not a century ago)
but today
this moment
this second
I see your anger silencing a chorus of fears
your skirt brushing the earth clear of tracks
your courage calming the waters
your teeth
     biceps
       legs
         arms
            pulling the train to freedom

To Ida Wells Barnett

from your womb
the children
you held with love
and released
for others to hold
while you held
the race

from your mind
the words pressed
into action
and history

from your rage
the knife
that cut the rope
and the gun
your woman hands
would have cannoned
even at moving targets

To Mary McLeod Bethune

your dark skin and body
too large for dainties
meant by their definition
beauty was not yours

but it was not beauty you sought
or needed in their conference rooms

wearing the aroma of pies
passion
and the people's dreams,
you walked in
thunderously
sat down
proudly
took off your white gloves
ceremoniously
and moved your dark hands fast
like scythes cutting through
thickets of lies

your lips
pursed with Africa
preached the plans
and sang the alma mater
yet to be

when you finished
talking and singing
          (you never danced for them)

you
left sane
with your bodacious hat
cocked arrogant
     and
       victorious

it was their world
their game
even their words

but your school

To Zora Neale Hurston

I want to resurrect you
the way you were
when you shook up
the patrons
and the writers
and the world
with your feisty genius
which didn't give a damn
about anything
except your truth

I want to remove
the pounds and the lies
and set you up somewhere
anywhere you want to be
with money
happiness
baaad hats
and a hundred Phoebes
holding your hand

To Fannie Lou Hamer

in Mississippi where
bosswhite men walked the earth
like gun-shaped shadows you
couldn't hide from
even in the dark

everybody knew
a black woman didn't have a chance
to be free

in Mississippi where
the exact don't-miss-a-comma
recitation of the preamble, the
Constitution, the by-laws, and
Adam Smith's principles of dee-
mock-cracy were the hiddenbuttons
you had to push before the lever
would move,

everybody knew
an unschooled black woman
couldn't go to Dee-See
and shatter the
chandeliers with her husky
you-gotta-listen voice for freedom

in Mississippi where
power wore white faces
and unzippered pants
or blonde hair teased
high like the hoods
they wore

everybody knew
a woman like you
had to sit down
stand back
give up...

you refused
to
listen

DONNA M. WEIR

A Sister Needs Love
and Other Weapons ...

1   Rage has tied my tongue
spun a web of silence
round my pen
I walk this cold night
naked, unarmed, searching
for my lost words
trying to resurrect the active-anger
spilling from my pen
for Tawana Brawley
Michael Griffith
but for you, my Brother
I can find no words
locked up in the image of your cage
long skinny hands handcuffed
behind your back
your seventeen-year-old righteous defiance
demanding to know *since when*

was it a crime to play REGGAE
music from a boom box at the bus-stop?
I sit in the court house screaming
silent curses at the cold white
rightness, SOWETO
seeping into Queens, New York
My brother, another innocent victim.

2   He used to tell me I was
merely prejudiced
When I warned BEWARE
of white cops
white laws, white lies
last night I called to assure him
that I would cut my class to be there
he said, he knew!

He said everytime now
he sees a white face in the neighborhood
terror rises in his throat
threatening to choke
I remind him of the time
I was five and he was one
and it was election season in Jamaica
there were the usual riots in the streets.
someone threw a smoke bomb
and I panicked!

I didn't know what to do with that
beautiful, brown-skinned
roly-poly, real live dolly baby
Mama had left in my care
So I lay him on the ground
and covered him with my body
I revived moments later to find him
screaming like a siren in my ear.

But that was when he was one
small enough to hide behind my body
at seventeen he's six feet tall
and black and male and threatening
and the hungry white wolves
are howling for his blood
and sistah love is not big enough
Sistah love is not deep enough
Sistah love is not enough
enough to protect him!

For Kerry

Outside Chile

Outside chile, yes!
Born outa wedlock
one stormy October morning, you know
cause her Mammy say
she was too beautiful and proud
to force-marry the chile no-good,
run-around, not so pretty daddy
although him did come from a good family!

Well, this chile come find
her daddy well married-off to some
stay-at-home, wash the clothes
maager woman[1]
not so nice
was she step-mammy.

Outside chile, she was
the outsider child
used to visit
at Birthdays and Christmas time
to watch for the crumbs falling off the plate of the inside,
bellyful children dem.

---

1. *maager:* means meager, too-skinny, not a desirable characteristic in Jamaican society.
Jamaicans consider fatness a sign of beauty and good living

People used to ask,
is this Watler outside pickney
Bway, but she almost pretty
look a little like her mammy
and a whole lot like her daddy
side a people dem,
But de family don't accept her, nuh?

Big-bright eyes,
pretty, white smile
long, skinny legs
short curly mop a reddish brown hair
(Mammy used to catch her and rub black shoe-polish in her head,
nasty up de whole a de pickney white school-blouse)
smarter than a whip lash
gentler than a Mama's tit
sensitive like a raw-nerve
exposed to cold and rain.

Big nation-wide exam
only ticket to high school for
non-class-privileged Jamaicans
little brown-dusk pickney passed
with flying colors
name in all the papers, you know?

The whole generation on daddy-side
come running now, yes!
chile, what you need
books, clothes, shoes, money eh?
pickney don't want nothing but
that they all clear out of
her grandmother piece a house
right this minute
so she can hug up
to her mamma Daisy a little bit
look up in her flowers pretty face
ask her,
Did I make you proud!

For my mother Daisy

Leaving

'Who shall kindle the fire now
and pick the coffee at harvest time
feed the chickens
water the cows and goats
and boil green herbs
to bathe away
the baby's fever?'
'not I' – she said
'surely, not I'
standing half-in/half-out
the door
The years falling naked
from her face!

*For Lluvia and Curene and all the women
who had the strength to walk away*

Jigsaw Noose

1   I know a man whose words
form a jigsaw puzzle
in his brain
jump from his mouth
in a superfluous jumble
to lie listless
on the startled air
his Mama boasts him brilliant
cause she never understands
a word he says.

2   I know a man
whose chiseled words
shoot from his mouth
red hot with razor
sharp edges
to lodge in the brain
to lodge in the brain like
a splinter of truth!

3   I know a man
    who sculpted words
    mold them soft and round
    like a lullaby
    to settle gently
    round women's necks
    like a widow's shawl
    or a hangman's noose.

MAYA CHOWDHRY

Atta

Her white hands
burrow through *atta*,[1] she calls brown flour,
and he adds *pani*[2] laughing and she says water, he *namak*[3]
and adds the salt

Her gold thread sari border shines like
her newly wedded laughter,
he taught her recipes and words and threw Indian customs across
oceans and floors, she learnt to bow her head
and raise it only for *Angrezi*[4] parties.

Some of her children slipped from her, clotted blood sliding
between her legs and
girl children flowed like monsoon rain until a boychild she
thought she'd delivered happiness but
nothing changed.

Her *kheema*[5] learns to fly,
she scrubs
the stubborn *haldi*[6] from the walls, it smiles
yellow like
the August sun on her wedding day.

1. *atta*: wholewheat flour
2. *pani*: water
3. *namak*: salt
4. *Angrezi*: English, Western
5. *kheema*: curry made from minced meat
6. *haldi*: tumeric powder

Mother Tongue

My mother's tongue
is pink and mine
is English
rose
red.

In my mother's tongue
I learn to read
write
say words for home
house
makhan.

Garden

Knots of heather twisted, glints of
purple separate flecks of green,
beside an old rose
steady frame that harbors guilt all year,
cut back
in early spring
and bursts red and soft and scent
to make a thousand princesses sleep
and peas the flowers sweet and
bright like the 7 A.M. sun in April wet.

She plants
each seed safe in the dark wet earth,
whispers growing words
while in her belly
her seeds float without earth
and water
to make them grow.

Property Section

I look
for home in advice books on destiny,
the language my mother
speaks/accents I hear around me.

I look for
home on the shelves of my mother's
cupboards, amongst garam masala and tomato ketchup, in
her top drawer beneath lipstick and nail varnish, in
the back wardrobe behind sequined saris and embroidered shawls.

I look for home
in the horoscopes on the back pages of magazines,
the classified columns of Scene Out,
the property section of the Guardian.

Skin

My skin is brown,
I die,
my flesh is
arrested.
I am more angry than all of these fires,
than a dusk curfew,
an armed patrol,
than the subtle racism from a white
journalist's lips,
than skeleton buildings and melted desires,
than the blows which crack my skull,
than speeding bullets,
than the words
no justice/dead on arrival/arson/payback time.
I am angrier than the dense black smoke
I suck into my lungs,
than relentless helicopter blades whipping the air,
than pools of blood and glass,
than the taste of hatred in the wind.
I am angrier
than the zip-up bag you dump my body in,
the chalk line you draw around me,
the fatalities list where my name appears.
We die,
we are arrested.
Our fragile bodies
have no home.

SONIA SANCHEZ

haiku

For domestic workers
in the african diaspora

i works hard but treated
bad   man. i'se telling you de
truth   i full of it.

Song No. 3

For 2nd and 3rd grade sisters

cain't nobody tell me any different
i'm ugly and you know it too
you just smiling to make me feel better
but i see how you stare when nobody's watching you.

i know i'm short black and skinny
and my nose stopped growing fo it wuz 'posed to
i know my hairs short, legs and face ashy
and my clothes have holes that run right through to you.

so i sit all day long just by myself
so i jump the sidewalk cracks knowin i cain't fall
cuz who would want to catch someone who looks like me
who ain't even cute or even just a little tall.

cain't nobody tell me any different
i'm ugly anybody with sense can see
but. one day i hope somebody will stop me and say
looka here. a pretty little black girl lookin' just like me.

under a soprano sky

1   once i lived on pillars in a green house
    boarded by lilacs that rocked voices into weeds.
    i bled an owl's blood
    shredding the grass until i
    rocked in a choir of worms.
    obscene with hands, i wooed the world
    with thumbs

                while yo-yos hummmed.
    was it an unborn lacquer i peeled?
    the woods, tall as waves, sang in mixed
    tongues that loosened the scalp
    and my bones wrapped in white dust
    returned to echo in my thighs.

    i heard a pulse wandering somewhere
    on vague embankments.
    O are my hands breathing? I cannot smell the nerves.
    i saw the sun
    ripened greeen stones for fields.
    O have my eyes run down? i cannot taste my birth.

2   now as i move, mouth quivering with silks
    my skin runs soft with eyes.
    descending into my legs, i follow obscure birds
    purchasing orthopedic wings.
    the air is late this summer.

    i peel the spine and flood
    the earth with adolescence.
    O who will pump these breasts? I cannot waltz my tongue.

    under a soprano sky, a woman sings,
    lovely as chandeliers.

ABENA P.A. BUSIA

Counter-Coup

Harshly aware of the brightness of electric light
against the dark January sky,
in the ominous silence of the harmattan night
we kept vigil
for the final shots.
From guns to guns again:
again.

Fissures in Old Friendships

i admiration

In your sure-footed stride
across troubles and joys
do your steps ever falter?
when you think to whisper secrets
to we who were there,
do you stop to turn and see
if we have not fallen by the wayside
or turned back?

On this your certain journey
Do you ever doubt
you have a beauty to match the strength
of those of us who carve
a strength to match your beauty?

ii   Walking Distances

A shadow falls this twilight
as we watch gulls fly on their way
passes between us in our talk along this path
and leaves you wondering what happened.

iii   Demands

It's not that I don't want you with me,
I just wish you wouldn't *assume* I do.
Perhaps I want to sleep.
Perhaps I want to walk alone
without you
angry
or whimpering
behind me.

iv   Roommates

Sometimes, I waited,
anxious to hear
your footsteps on the stairs;
and I heard laughter
and there was sunshine in your eyes.
Other times, I watched you
turn the kitchen dark and cramped
closed-mouthed in your agony of silence.
And I have stamped your name in anger
on the stones of Port Meadow,
and you have brought me
pink roses, out of season.

Exiles

Funerals are important
away from home we cannot lay
our dead to rest
for we alone have given them
        no fitting burial.

Self-conscious of our absence
brooding over distances in western lands
we must rehearse
the planned performance of our rites
        till we return.

And meanwhile throughout the years,
our unburied dead eat with us,
follow behind through bedroom doors.

For Anyone of You Who Knows I am Your Sister

I know the story of a man, who happened to be Catholic,
behaved like a Good Samaritan and saved a brother from drowning.
At least, he tried.
And the drowning was literal, not metaphorical.
But by the ocean's edge he realized,
there being only so much beating a body can bear,
he needed to offer another salvation
and he asked for rites for the dying.

This prayer became controversy.
What if the dying man were Muslim?
What if, even if another Christian, he wasn't a Catholic at all?
What if he had some other Faith? What if ... what if ...?
And amidst all this speculation and burning anger
no one seemed to reach out and celebrate
this one simple fact.
He had acted out of love.

Death is our final necessity.
But alive we resist it with every living breath,
until in the face of defeat, and grievings out of season,
we reach out with passion with what we know
and give ourselves in rituals.
Not necessarily what is needed, but with what we have inside us,
when that is all there is left to give.

There is always anger at the loosings,
and a generation of our brothers is dying
on the concrete battlefields of city streets,
the suddenness of their deaths unmarked
by any rituals of departure.
Dead they are called a 'lost generation',
Yet not in concession to that naming, but as a battlecry.
Not in acceptance of that horror,
but in a calling out the greater crime
that permits their murder
and coldly counts the dead.

There are so many discrepancies of gesture.
We none of us know each other's language
or learn identical rituals.
Yet can we living embrace transgressive actions
which flout all conventions, even our own,
that have their source in love?
For in the end, we are all beaten by the wayside,
bleeding broken on city streets,
or drowning.

And in the end, in the end,
I'll reach for the hand of anyone
who even cares I'm dying.

For Audre Lorde

CHEZIA B. THOMPSON-CAGER

Singing in the Choir

Somedays our mutual colors
portend more than the duty
that calls us to work
and we come prepared
to have church
to walk the halls chanting
Allelujah
amidst the tribulation
of fiscal instability
epidemic divorce
newly wed frenzy
and the absence of
the Pastor

Brown Ladies in Black Dresses
Singing In The Choir
making music out of unimaginative
grinding anguish, poverty and
distraught laughter
Florence Nightingales
with hands to hold and heal
and the will to be present
as an anchor
in body and spirit
in a time and a Place
standing between a hard fought past
and an uncertain future
moving silently
their working hands sing
'We are soldiers
In the Army
'We have to Fight
Although we have to Cry
We gotta hold up the
Blood-stained Banner
We gotta hold it up
until We Die.'

For Hattie and Margaret

broke bitch blues: a choreopoem (because of L.C.)

'Why would I wanna fuck that broke bitch?'

going down baby
down the old wharf land
i'm going down baby
down the old wharf land
i remember pennsylvania avenue
been there and back again

say i usta love you
but can't no more
say i usta love you
but i can't no more
you new woman
campaigning
and i gotta go

call me a broke bitch baby
cause i got my self and my child
call me a broke bitch baby
cause i got myself and my child
born and raised in the graveyard
you better watch where you walk
for a while

remember when you called me baby
it sounded so sweet
remember when you called me baby
yeah, it sounded so sweet
you gon eat those words baby
like you eat real meat

you're a mean
motor-scooter
and you know that it's true
i say you're a mean
motor-scooter
and you know that its true
but you're gonna miss
this angel
before your life is through

egungun speak
and nobody deny
when egungun speak
ain't nobody gonna deny
what goes around
comes around
darling
and i'm gonna be fine

call me a broke bitch baby
cause i got myself and my child
call me a broke bitch baby
cause i got myself and my child
born and raised in the graveyard
you better watch where you walk
for a while

It Looks Like a Woman
But It Walks Like a Man

the pink
tailored men's shirt
that she had taken off of him
fit her perfectly
and sliding into
the Pierre Cardin
double-breasted wool suit
made her feel
at home
when she was not

What is it?
It looks like a woman
But it walks like a man

innocuous
in black gray stripes
resplendent in
tailored elegance
she smoothed
her bushy eyebrows
lined her lips
with brown color
and laughed
at how much
she looked like her father

broad shoulders
straight lined
into the hateful look
that passes as
male arrogance
she revolved once more
making the sign of Shango
and passed bodies
in the malestrom of time
in preparation for war

'Gentlemen', she said
entering the meeting
and yes they thought
she was all so corporate cute
till she opened her mouth
and a man stomped
around the room
leaving discernable tracks
in the eyes of all present

    tactful
        aggressive
            intelligent
                and correct
she took no prisoners, today
but reconciled the attack
with a control and a
goodwill that was astonishing

but it wasn't obvious
with that weird name
what she was anyway
      'She looks like a woman
      But only a Man walks
      Like that and is allowed
      to live'

watching her
I took note
of the dilemma
and prayed

MAYRA SANTOS FEBRES

Las yerbas y los ríos son para mí
para esta negra que nació en Carolina
que ha vivido en urbanizaciones
en satélites hermenéuticos
una avenida hacia la boca propia
hacia el líquido poema que se sueña
cada noche en mi cabeza.
con las yerbas
un urgarme superficies canceladas
un temblor de pestaña entumecida
más allá de la memoria en el olfato
de la saliva memoriosa
buscando dimensión de ojos –
dimensión de viento.
la historia siempre huida
1950
no recuerdo nada más
y para esta hembra urbanizada
universitada
blanqueada y reblanqueada sin éxito
las yerbas y los ríos son
autopista cosmogónica
hacia el pecho común.
la sal iodizada en la cabeza
no es progreso
abuela, madres, no es progreso.

Roots and rivers mean to me
to this black woman born in urban Carolina
to this one right here
who has lived in suburbs
in hermeneutic satellites
the road towards my own mouth
towards the liquid poem that dreams itself
nightly on my tongue
Roots help me find canceled surfaces
tremors of tumid lashes
the smell of memory
the remembered spit
With roots I search for eye's new dimensions –
wind directions
fugitive histories
(1950, I don't remember anymore)
and for this urban bushwoman
college female
made to whiten and rewhiten
but without success
roots and rivers are
the primordial freeway
to the common heart.
the taste of iodine in tamed mouths
grandma, mother, is not progress
believe me
it isn't progress.

El instituto de cultura dice

que las puertorriqueñas somos
taínas, españolas y africanas.
tal vez
y también tal vez somos obreras
que orinamos de espalda al viento
sin memoria más allá
del traje que compramos
hace una semana
del retoque que debemos darle
al alisado, al tinte
al esmalte de uñas más perfecto.
el censo demográfico de última hora dice
que las puertorriqueñas somos
nueve mujeres para cada hombre.
tal vez
y talvez también somos
una confusión de sudores en el aire
un tratar de mirarnos la vulva
sin asco, sin pena
sin risa, sin furia, sin lástima
cómo se mira desde el balcón
a un transeúnte
que acaba de tomarse un café
y se sonríe;
una guerrilla contra la soledad
contra los hombres punzantes
como aguaceros
que siempre se van con otras
más altas, más finas, más rubias
el miedo a querer demasiado
a otras mujeres
a preñarnos de lagartijitos ciegos,
a engordar.
la comisión de asuntos de la mujer dice
que las puertorriqueñas constituimos
más de un 37 porciento
de la fuerza laboral del país.
tal vez
y también tal vez
somos las que mantenemos

The Institute of Culture says

that Puerto Rican women are
Taino, Spanish and African
perhaps
but perhaps we are also those
who squat with our backs to the wind
without memory of anything but
the dress put on lay-away a week ago
or the touch of relaxer we should apply to our
hair, maybe some highlights
or to find the perfectly matching nail enamel ...
The latest demographic census says
that Puerto Rican women are
nine for every man
perhaps
but perhaps we are also
a sweaty confusion in mid air
attempting to look between our legs
without shame, or scorn,
without fury, or sorrow
just as one watches a passerby
finish his coffee and smile,
a guerrilla warfare against loneliness
against pungent men
who always leave us for
taller, thinner, blonder girls
against a fear to love other women a bit too much
to get pregnant, to get fat.
The Commission on Women's Issues says
that Puerto Rican women are
more than 37 per cent of the country's labor force
perhaps
but also, perhaps we are those who support

tres hijos y un esposo
con salarios de miseria
las que vendemos cosméticos
y toperwear
a la hora del almuerzo
para poder pagar la luz y el teléfono
las que aguantamos
los dedos tiñosos del jefe y nos reímos
nos reímos desesperadamente
para no mandarlo todo al infierno
para no correr y correr
hasta el centro de la furia
lejos de las estadísticas
que jamás podrán cuantificar
el aguacero que no para
que deja todo sin rostro y sin aristas
que corroe el clavo de colgar
el último quinqué de calma.

three children and a husband
with miserable wages,
or we who sell cosmetics and tupperware
on our lunch breaks
to pay the phone and electricity
those who bear the bosses' stained hands
and laugh
laugh desperately
we who laugh to keep from sending all to hell
to keep from running
towards fury's eye
away from statistics
that can never quantify
that inner rainstorm that never ends
that leaves everything faceless without edges
that corrodes the nail by which we hang
our last hope, once we get home.

(All translations by the author.)

DOROTHEA SMARTT

Connecting Medium

i.   Sea of lights heading into JFK at night
     scaled-up mega-mix
     of everything I knew to be
     'industrial' 'urban'
     I started my period on the descent
     full moon following me
     reflecting in a winding river below
     guiding me
     thru' sets off t.v. cop shows
     and a Black bourgeoisie
     the Black town of Harlem
     up Lenox to 132nd

ii. Sparks-flying
meeting …
feeling reverberating vibrations
static electricity in the air
life-to-life resuscitation
in the presence of ancestral spirits
beckoning
voices and rhythms
BlackAmerican cousins
meet
BlackEnglish sistah
connecting beyond cultural colonization

iii. Early
this morning
I remembered the glass fish
typical of so many West-Indian households
in shades of blue green and brown
when I was how old I don't recall
I took the fish
put pennies in its mouth
did this whole little ritual in 'african'
did this on my own in the front-room
maybe I was home
sick from school
maybe I was home-sick.

Just That Minute…

she went to kiss me
full in my mouth
and hugged me so …
caught me by surprise
could stream and curve
with her
soft
sweet
strong tide
washing me

HUSH!

... and perhaps,
If I were not your daughter
we could talk together
woman-to-woman
sistah-to-sistah
and we could learn what hides behind
we could learn the secrets
of one another's hearts
together we could shatter the silence
of centuries
but, you are my Mother.

JEWELLE L. GOMEZ

Sir Raleigh

I see them as I turn the corner of 105
on my friendly Raleigh three-speed.
It's not French or Japanese
but sturdy, light and fast
Gift from an ex-boyfriend.

I see first four
then two more standing,
shifting on the stoop
restless with their beers
and clean tee-shirts.
They've dressed up
to be unemployed.

I wipe sweat from my face
and fix my eye on Broadway
steady Raleigh
bumping over bottle caps
trapped forever in greasy street tar
like them.

They whistle and call as if I
am a child, a pet, a game.
I clench my jaw and pray
between my teeth in the deepening dusk:
please don't let them be angry
because I won't smile, don't answer
to the many names they have for me
a woman, happy, alone and flying.

Their words are spit in the air
raining on me as I pedal.
One steps into the street
waving a red scarf and an empty grin
sucking air between his teeth
demanding I be pleased.
I stand and pump faster
letting the wind whip my thighs.
They grunt and groan as I pass
with my eye on Broadway
leaving them in my city dust.

Now laughing
on my steady, sturdy Raleigh,
the only thing a man ever gave me
that was always good
between my legs.

Reunion

I met my mother on an untraveled road
She carried the burden of my abandonment
like those bloody rags
we are all so eager
to flush away
I knew it was she
by the way
she looked just like me.

Her fingers were strong, circled in gold,
she held my face looking
for the small one
she'd said goodbye to long ago.

Steel light fell harshly on days we could not relive,
years that strained to come together
but my need for nurturing is much too
sporadic.

The young girl she had been was there once again alone
watching her choices dwindle
like a burning taper,
that Greyhound bus disappearing down an open
road away from me.

She holds my arm
I feel a cradle rock
and hear a bluesnote lullaby.
The way is unfamiliar
but her hands are warm,
I know it is she
by the way she looks
just like me.

IRÈNE ASSIBA D'ALMEIDA

This is an English language based text so there are translations.
Some writers see translations as the imposition of a hierarchy in
which English remains dominant and it was decided not to
translate the French poems. Colonially-imposed language
separations, and the boundaries they have installed, are fundamental challenges for anyone wanting to pursue black women's
writing cross-culturally.

Afrique

Je me suis laissé dire
Que l'Afrique était belle
Comme les grandes femmes du Sahel
A la peau de bronze
Et aux cheveux de jais

Je me suis laissé dire
Que l'Afrique était forte
De ses hommes d'antan
Fiers et valeureux guerriers
De ses amazones belliqueuses
De ses charmes et de ses talismans

Je me suis laissé dire
Que l'Afrique était grande
Comme le furent les Béhanzin,
Samori, Chaka, Dan Fodio
Et tant d'autres encore

Je me suis laissé dire
Que l'Afrique était riche
ivoire or diamants,
Terres généreuses, fruits en abondance

Je me suis laissé dire
Que l'Afrique était fraternelle
Que pour elle l'invité était roi
Et le seuil de l'autre sacré

Je me suis laissé dire
Que l'Afrique était sage
Qu'elle avait depuis la première lune
Accumulé la sagesse des Grands
Et qu'elle l'avait semée dans ses chants
Ses porverbes, ses contes féeriques et fascinants
Et que cette sagesse avait germé
Et grandi, et rejailli
Sur ses nombreux enfants

Je me suis laissé dire
Que l'Afrique était droite
Que le fil des ans
Avait donné à ses Anciens
Le sens de la justice, de la probité
Profond, enraciné pour jamais

Je me suis laissé dire
Que l'Afrique était pure
Comme le regard limpide
De l'enfant nouveau-né

Je me suis laissé dire
Que l'Afrique était vivante
Vivante et gaie
Remplie des cris de joie
Résonnante des mains agiles qui battent avec fréenésie
Des pieds souples qui martèlent la glaise
Vibrant des reins possédés par le rythme
Des dos qui ondulent
Des poitrines qui s'enflent
Des voix qui s'enflamment

Et j'ai voulu moi-même dire
Toutes ces choses de l'Afrique d'aujourd'hui
Mais je n'ai vu partout que
Faiblesse et misère
Charlatanisme et jalousie
Vol, viol et vilenie
Et j'ai pleuré sur ce continent
Des larmes de douleur.

Cendres refroidies

Comme une vague
sans cesse roulée
par l'immense océan
Elle est toujours
Rejetée
sur le rivage.
Rejetée
non point brisée
Elle se relève péniblement
Et court vers des terres plus hospitalières
A la recherche d'une grande flamme
Elle no trouve jamais que cendres refroidies

Le toucher du regard

D'un regard tendre
plus expert qu'une main
je caresse
le velours frémissant
de ta peau.

FAWZZIYA ABU KHALID

Six Short Poems

Suicide by Blaze

When you left me
I did not need an elegy
Because you sowed in my heart
A swarm of butterflies.
Now I follow their track as a Knowing Bedouin
Tracing his strayed mare.

Secret Diaries for Children

These words from the diaries of Gamilah Buhered and Lelia Khaled
In the days of my country's children:
  – Now it is the role of woman to abolish the role of
        her breast ...
  The tiny lips starve ...
  The earth is breast, lactating blood,
    Oil,
  Into pledged bottles.

Prayers of the Moment

Moment,
Human skin is smaller than the space of my kiss,
I am gnawing my lips.

Running in Your Eyes

That night
There was an equator between you and me
Your eyes crossed it
My sighs crossed it
But it did not end

When Your Silence Says I Love You

I entered you without paper, without pen
In you listening is more painful than speech.

May My Comrades Know

I went into you on a winter day
I went out to my friends
Proud of the shawl of suns that you spun
From cocoons of fire in your chest.

VELMA POLLARD

Belize Suite

I   **Sea Wall**

Only a gentle swish
where waves would touch the land
no wind no turbulence
along this wall arranged by man
dividing land from sea

No cruise-ships light this harbor end to end
only that cluster
where the army lights
ride there at anchor...
cool darkness and deluding calm

houses sit silent near the water's edge
their calm precarious like our peace
hoisted on stilts
like mokojumbies in the carnival
listening to the oceans's gentle murmur
hearing its angry wail
what seems like decades now
when death rode loud and furious
on the hissing waves

From storm and earthquake
Lord
deliver us
and us
and us

II   Xunantunich

The gods will ask
tell them I left my offering there
three handspans to the left
of that dread corner where the two slabs meet
under a stone
set in a threadbag
that I kept between my breasts
so that my hands could help me
timid goat
climb half way up
no more

it isn't strength that matters
courage to climb
is what the old hearts lose
my children's children never now will know
what sights the high-priests saw
undizzied by the dizzying heights

Power is always from on high
lookouts where pirates guard the harbor
rivers that tumble down from angry hills
cloud tops for cherubim
and Maya priests' Xunantunich

For Roy W

III   Road from Xunantunich

Dusk settles in
first near the edge
where towns like pale mirages sit
and slowly shrouds us
shocked to silence by the stillness here ...

Where are the night sounds
that begin at dusk?
not here or just not yet?

King trees with long and hairless trunks
reach green and fertile locks
towards the sky

no mountains here
no rocks
no green between those thick locks
and the close cropped kinks
that can't protect the land
cracked now with long unsightly breaks
(the geolog unstraps his EYE and clicks)

Who would be king
but with no subjects
who would grow strong and perfect
but alone?

This silence sobers us
and sends us feverish
seeking home

YANICK FRANÇOIS

Rapine

The seizing and carrying away of things by force; pillage: plunder.

Spring 1986

Whenever a man thinks he's
making love to me –
I end up in the end of it all
feeling as if I'd been raped
I hold the world's record
the single most raped woman ever

My mind's been raped
My heart's been raped
My body's been raped
My time's been raped

What is rape anyhow
A seizing by force
A stealing
Whatever it is, it is against my will
something I did not want, nor plan
He thought the date afforded him
privilege, so he raped my mouth
ravishing it as he tugged at my tongue
pinching it with his teeth and hurting me
Yelling and punching frantically
I told him to leave
He intended to get the value of his date
it was a rude awakening
to suddenly learn how much
one date can cost when a woman
doesn't pay her own way

I felt as if I was being beaten by my father
his teeth were welt-making instruments and
his tongue was the leather strap
striking against my skin
Disbelief was my bondage
the element of surprise
arrested my strength and
rendered me invalid
inform the cops of what?
I can barely believe it myself
how can I convince a jury?

I'm bleeding in the shower
the water cleans painfully
but the tears shed nothing of the mind.
    I'm just a medium
    in his making love
    to himself.

Something's Missing

I could not move my tongue in rhythms I have never heard
to speak a tongue I have never known.
I could not speak a language I was kept from learning
so, forgive me, my Mother, something's missing.

I could not tell tales and stories of people and places
I do not remember ...
but I could not remember tales and stories
of a people and a place long forgotten, long lost.

I cannot think of thoughts which my life's experiences
have not brought
It's not as simple as corrective surgery
to learn to love what one had been conditioned to hate
It is not simple to identify beauty
when being sought through ugly eyes.

When my feet's soul has known no other
than the pounded concrete pavements
I dug beneath the shell clear through to the wet soil
to add reason to my injured sole
and now the grass of my roots are as a bed of grapes
beneath my journeyed feet
I hear the rhythms of my speech now
rhythms I have learned to recognize

I have found the missing things
the knowledge which was not passed on
because of self-hate, the legacy of slavery
the struggle against which distracted many
from appreciating themselves and therefore
neglecting to teach us to love ourselves
Through my nostrils blow Alaskan air
and the carcasses of
Lion-feed,
but no longer am I a victim of missing things.

Amputee

I came out of El-Barrio
a place not easy to let go
with a grip so strong – you understand
but I had a dream
and I had a fear

A ghetto is a place bearing scars
the living remembrances of past to future pains
the filth is not dirty
but unclean none-the-less
and cleansing is a painful deed

El-Barrio is a spirit
with life – flowing light through me
having heart will travel
to the ends of dreams pursued

I fear the darkness
of a dream removed

and now I must place in perspective
what light has been removed

when I came out of El-Barrio

STORME WEBBER

artist's exam (take home)

question #1: will you agree to be a conductor of electricity?

to act as a catalyst/a lightning rod
i will put my hand upon you/be *fearless*
the crucible is one of the most important parts
you will burst forth invincible vibrating energy
all you need i've given you/faith heart courage
patience strength & ACHÉ
the power to make things happen
grows strong/through flame ever hotter
ocean ever fathoms deeper
grows strong fierce sweet and sure

pledge:
for all the sounds wandering
for all the souls lost
for all the spirits never set free
this light will come through me.

i stepped through razor sheets

i stepped through razor sheets of
translucent/opaque blood
& endless sporadic madness/to bring you this message
STOP LOOKIN AT ME LIKE YOU DON'T KNOW ME
you fear yr own intensity/yr own rage
& the spirits of yr ancestors
whisperin whisperin commanding
what sets our feet/to our own particular path
i'll wait for you in the next world
but we have to travel together
some more/through this one
so let's take some time & thought
and talk with each other
stop dipping yr pen yr brush
yr fingers into my blood
making a dance of my voyage

& leaving me/huddled against the wall
my tears fomenting an internal implosion
my lips thirsting for a taste of the cool water/you hoard
i am strong/my soul bruised but calloused/but am not an island
a metaphor/a case study/or grist for yr creative mill
i am a woman/ancient spirit/straddling cultures
climbing slowly & painfully up a ladder made of my ancestor's
splintered bones
each rung a sliver of their submerged lives embeds
in my living flesh
drives me on
STOP LOOKING AT ME LIKE YOU NEVER SAW ME
they beat us until our languages fell shattering
from our tongues
but you/you who call yrself 'griot' 'artist' 'poet'
you know the sounds
don't fear what you know instinctively
spirit don't lie/when you listen
i don't lie/when the voices come through me
i try to give truth a sound
in this steel wanderground.

heritage

i am the daughter of my mother my father
both my grandmother's child
i am the scream echoing down the tunnel
generations of anguish built
i am the warrior
handed the broken sword
bidden to remake its edge
in mounting flames of destruction & despair
burning from the inside out
i am the howl the shriek
whirling into larger & larger concentric circles
through the long tunnel of history's recording
these bloodlines joined at the point
i was produced
to ride & be ridden by the spirits
of ancestors/wronged
seeking redemption
seeking retribution

demanding a retelling of the tale
their voices/strangled stilled
never born whole
my story is written in blood/it seeps
from my tongue & out of the tips
of my fingers
& i will sing/until the blood stops
welling up in my throat/sing strong
till it ceases & pure startling color light
& sound flowers.

AFUA COOPER

Memories Have Tongue

My granny say she have a bad memory
when I ask her to tell
me some of her life
say she can't remember much but
she did remember the 1910 storm and how
dem house blow down
an dey had to go live with her granny
down bottom house.

Say she have a bad memory, but she remember
that when her husband died, both of them were thirty,
she had three little children, one in her womb,
one in her arms, one at her frocktail.
She remember when
they bury him how the earth buss up under her foot
and her heart bruk inside
that when the baby born she had no milk
her breasts refused to yield.

She remember how she wanted
her daughter to grow up and be
a post-mistress but the daughter died at an early age
she point to the croton-covered grave at the bottom
of the yard. Say her memory bad, but she remember
1938
Frome
the riot
Busta
Manley
but what she memba most of all is that a
pregnant woman,
one of the protesters, was shot and killed by soldiers.

Say she old now her   brains gathering water
but she remember
that she liked dancing as a young woman
and yellow was her favourite color.
she remember too
that it was her husband's father who asked
for her hand. The parents sat in the hall and discussed
the matter. Her father concluded that her man
was an honourable person and so gave his consent.

Her memory bad but she remember
on her wedding day how some of her relatives
nearly eat off all the food.
It was alright though, she said,
I was too nervous to eat anyway.

To Jamaican Women

To those women who rise
at five in the morning to prepare
food for their children and send them off to school
while their men lie
in bed

To those women who have no food to give
their children, cannot afford to send them to school
and whose men have disappeared

To those women who, in order to raise their children,
sweat inside oppressive factories
lie on cold sidewalks
hack an existence from rocky hillsides
take abuse from men who are their only source
of survival
this poem is for you

To those whores at Half-Way-Tree
with their mobile hotel rooms

To the young office girls who think
they hold the key of life in their hands

To those schoolgirls with their bright faces
whose dreams are sometimes betrayed by men
twice their age
to the unnamed
who by their unceasing work and action
cause life to flow unbroken

To those daughters of Nanny
who are beginning to realise the power
they hold in their hands
This poem is for you

Aunts

Aunts sometimes are life-savers
they make sure they tell you things like the facts of life
bloody things like your period
and what to do when it comes
and what that means for your whole life
and some aunts will even tell you what to drink
to lessen the flow
I mean they tell you, that if you go with a boy
you can get pregnant
Aunts sometimes are life-savers
I mean they tell you
carry yourself like a woman with integrity
go to school and learn so that when you become
a woman

you don't have to depend on nobody
and not to sell yourself for 30 pieces of silver
not to put up with no-good men
one aunt had told me
that she married such a man
she fell in love with his looks but he was in fact a beast
he abused her for many years
until one day she packed her bags
threw stones and eggs behind her (a sign meaning she will not return)
and forever left the beast.
He came many times begging her to return
but for him her heart had turned to stone.
Another aunt told me how she spent 20 years in
England and was ready to return home. She had
had enough of the cold of the climate and the people.
But her husband was not ready to return.
So she simply packed her bags and came home and
built a house in the sun.
Aunts sometimes are life-savers
they provide themselves as role models for you
and tell you every day that your life need not be as
hard as theirs have been.

Womanhood

We who were thrust out of dark caverns
into a maddening light
We who know no truth
    no honor
we who go through this madness called life
into the estate of adulthood
crossing no dividing line
experiencing no period of transition
having no celebration of our puberty
        our blood
No rites of passage
no lovesong
only a shameful quietude
an impatient sadness
Now here we hang – suspended
between madness, agony and absolute truth
becoming women
suddenly thrust into a sphere we do not understand
becoming women

Sunset

Your face begs what I cannot give
you want my laughter, I give you tears
you want my joy, I give you sorrow
I have abandoned you, you say

We are standing at the doorway
and I do not want to leave
yet I do leave and hide my face.
You must not see me weep.
When our eyes meet they plead
for an embrace we dare not
share
Our silence is a pain we dare not
speak

Perhaps, there is still time for us
but there are dawns we must wake to alone
and not be afraid.
I leave you now
I always leave
yet I never leave you

MARLENE NOURBESE PHILIP

Meditations on the Declension of Beauty by the Girl with the Flying Cheek-bones

If not   If not   If
Not
If not in yours
              In whose
In whose language
Am I
If not in yours
              In whose
In whose language
Am I   I am
              If not in yours

In whose
           Am I
(if not in yours)
                I am yours
In whose language
                     Am I not
Am I not   I am yours
If not in yours
If not in yours
                In whose
In whose language
                     Am I ...

Girl with the flying cheek-bones:
She is
I am
Woman with the behind that drives men mad
And if not in yours
Where is the woman with a nose broad
As her strength
If not in yours
In whose language
Is the man with the full-moon lips
Carrying the midnight of color
Split by the stars – a smile
If not in yours

           In whose

In whose language
                Am I
                Am I not
                Am I   I am yours
                Am I not   I am yours
                Am I   I am
If not in yours
           In whose
In whose language
                Am I
If not in yours
                Beautiful

PATRICIA TURNBULL

The Curse of the Domestic

they deport Marie Helene
yer child, they fired her
they send her home to stay
well, when the fact did hit
my girl was hot with rage
so hot she choke 'pon slow insult
that scream what pierce her head
and cut her tongue
refuse to let her speak
in her defense:
you people do not want to work
you do not have respect
you cannot run this place

What a showdown this was
that bossman lately come
already licensed, tried and true
and Mae-Mae pending permit still
faking it for so long
on this domestic front
Marie Helene Joseph
short-order cleaner
confidante and bo-bo kisser
cook and fly chaser
was charged since overtime
when she take back her tongue
that hot hot day, she say
I will not lick no arse, no way
yes child, she gone
she gone back home to stay

Business Letters

Dear Father:
        How are you? Hope your divorce is fine.
        I really used to miss you long ago.

                All Grown Up.

Dear Government:
> I right here all this time
> When will I get these papers
> and a little raise
> and water in this pipe
> and one of those scheme houses
> and teachers who like school
> and children with ambition
> and work that don't kill
> and people who can see me?
> None of all you getting
> my vote again.
> I am

Fed up

Dear macoumere,
> What I do you?
> I still is
> your child nennen

Your ex-friend

Dear Mr Man,
> Your children need you
> Me too. Maybe
> Ai chye
> I is

Woman

Dear Mam,
> You pospone your dreams
> till you forget them. Sorry.
> We are fine. Don't worry.

Your child always,

Truly

Unbalanced Equation

Alas. We're not at all harmonious.

My darling daughter sleeps and wakes
in every t-shirt that I own
plus her father's
three times and more her slender size
minus the frills and pastel prints
of nighties on which I waste my money.
She stashes them away in drawers
that spill over with odd things
divided by her brother's snooping

the whole thing is
                    carrying me over
taking me away
        remainder   nothing

I am totaled by this girl
this woman-child of mine
who'd rather be my equal
and fight me like her foe

For Harmony

Rugged Vessels

I've picked up many vessels
since that cracked one
was chucked away
the same for which I paid
too high a price.
There are the ornamental ones
gifts from the children
in fancy, gilded, oriental styles
with swirls and wings and petals
selected to appease.
There are the little ones
relieved from cluttered
gift-shop shelves
quaint souvenirs squeezed in

from places I can only
hope to see again.
And lately, I have learned
to make my own

> pat-a-clay
> pat-a-clay
> maker's hands
> make me a new woman
> as fast as you can

molded in my image
more than my children
want to be
the rugged beauty of each piece
holds my primordial sense
to make and multiply
to fill, to store, to know
to keep, to carry, to show
and yes, if it should be to this
to let weak vessels go.

ATSANGO CHESONI

Sitting Manners, for Proper African Girls

'One leg in Mombasa,
the other in Nairobi,'
that's what they say about you.
They say you take up
too much room.
They say, your habit of 'catching air,'
takes too much space
be like molded matrons,
they say, who sit with their legs stretched
out before them, projected in one
plane and still, with straight back.
Fill only the dimensions
we want for you.

A Coming of Age Poem,
a Story Untold

I

I remember Sophia,
sapling amongst the sprouts,
too tall –
Sophia.

I remember Sophia,
searing a pitch,
tar melting at her toes.
Sophia, launching a ball,
soaring, a goal.

II The damming of the tide

'Sophia,'
the school master said
'good girls do not talk
back,' I remember
the detention of Sophia,

the damming of the tide,
the Monday she was late.
Ten strokes of the cane
ordered by Sir.
I remember the uprising
of the skin of your palms,
Sophia.

The welts you swept
in the Master's yard,
Sophia.
Furrowed –
Sophia – patterned
like the arcs
of earth you made with your broom.

I remember your uprightness
Sophia. The bracing
of your back
as you fetched
water
for the Master's meal.

III The breaking of the waves

I saw you Sophia
as you weeded.
Doing time for forgetting,
Your swollen ankles
Sophia,
the swift become a snail.
Sophia,
the headmaster now says
'you wanted to become – Sophia,

a butterfly before a cocoon!'
Sophia,
I saw the uprising
of the skin,
the ridges
formed on your palms.

Sophia, I heard
the lashing of the water
as you labored and bore
the slosh
of cleaning Sir's house.

ESMERALDA RIBEIRO

América

América do Sul, Rhythm and blues,
Chicago, África do Sul, Capitalismo
pobreza, lixo, vício, ismos

AMÉRICA
na terceira margem
sou azul
e me sinto só

mas eu sei quem sou:
samba, rap, capoeira, blue
e tenho soul

America

South America, Rhythm and blues
Chicago, South Africa, Capitalism
poverty, garbage, vice, isms

AMERICA
on the third line
I'm blue
and I feel alone

but I know who I am:
samba, rap, capoeira,[1] blue
and I've got soul

(Translated by Celeste D. Mann)

---

1. Capoeira: an Afro-Brazilian martial art, practised during slavery as defense;
performed today in folkloric shows and in competition.

A Rainha Ayò

AYÒ
Rainha da Cidade de Xangô
na quarta espalhou cinzas
na cinzenta avenida
e o público a cultuou em *nagô*

AYÒ
Entre plumas e pulhas desfilou
a filha de Xangô[2]
irada ficou quando um tolo
a chamou de mulata

AYÒ
Mulher da riqueza e beleza
lendas espalhou com seu agogô

AYÒ
na cinzenta quarta evocou
raios e rios
das águas um mar de fantasia e cor
e assim a Iaô transformou
a alegria em bela pomba que voou

Queen Ayo

AYO
Was queen of the city of Shango[2]
She scattered ashes on Wednesday
on the ash colored avenue
and the people praised her in nago[3]

AYO
Amongst feathers and thugs she
paraded
this daughter of Shango
and she became enraged when a fool
called her 'mulata'

AYO
A woman of beauty and riches
legends were spread by agogo[4]

AYO
It was on ashy Wednesday that she
evoked
rays and rivers
a sea of color and fantasy came from
the waters
and so it was that Iaô transformed
happiness into a beautiful dove that
could fly.

(Translated by Celeste D. Mann)

2. Shango: deity (orixa) of Afro-Brazilian religion of Yoruba origin, associated with
fire and thunder.
3. nago: Yoruba.
4. agogo: percussive instrument of African origin.

SÔNIA FATIMA DA CONCEIÇÃO

Hermafrodita

mulher negra És.
Sua prole prolifera
promíscua
    Ratos
habitam becos
lambem sarjetas
    Peçonhas
Ameaça ao bem estar
    social
Determinação
    extermínio
    maioridade aos
    16 anos

Hermaphrodite

You are a black woman.
Your prolific offspring
promiscuous
    Rats
they live in the alleys
they lick gutters
    Poison
A threat to the social
    well being
Determination
    extermination
    majority at
    16 years old

(Translated by Celeste D. Mann)

Antropófago

Mastigaste-me
voraz nas esquinas
da noite
Saciado
lançaste-me ao
vento na
janela do dia

Cannibal

You chewed me up
voracious on the corners
by night
Satiated
you threw me to the
wind
out the window by day

(Translated by Celeste D. Mann)

Navio Negreiro

Por força e comando
do ORIXÁ Maior[1]
mudou-se o rumo dos ventos
desenharam-se nuvens no céu
E o mar foi colocado
em nossa direção

Slave Ship

By the force and command
of the Major ORISHA
the course of the winds changed
and clouds were drawn in the sky
and the sea was placed
in our direction

(Translated by Celeste D. Mann)

Devolver a Alma Branca

Há que se
vomitar
o inquisidor
e fazer brotar
o homem

Give Back the White Soul

Have to
vomit
the inquisitor
and make the
man
come forth

(Translated by Celeste D. Mann)

Ausência

Limitaste teu
mundo
já não me
vês

Absence

You limited
your world
you no longer see
me

(Translated by Celeste D. Mann)

1. ORIXÁ Maior: Afro-Brazilian deities of Yoruba origin.

CONCEIÇÃO EVARISTO

Eu-Mulher	**I-Woman**
Uma gota de leite	A drop of milk
me escorre entre os seios.	runs between my breasts
Uma mancha de sangue	a blood stain decorates my inner thighs
me enfeita entre as pernas.	Half a chewed word
Meia palavra mordida	escapes my mouth
me foge da boca.	vague desires insinuate hopes
Vagos desejos insinuam esperanças.	
Eu-mulher em rios vermelhos	I-woman in red rivers
inauguro a vida.	inaugurate life
Em baixa voz	In a soft voice
violento os tímpanos do mundo.	I violate the world's eardrums
Antevejo.	I foresee.
Antecipo.	I anticipate.
Antes-vivo.	I live before.
Antes – agora – o que há de vir.	Before – now – what must come.
Eu fêmea-matriz.	I the original-female
Eu força-motriz.	I the moving force
Eu-mulher	I-woman
abrigo da semente	shelter of the seed
moto-contínuo	prime mover
do mundo.	of the world.

(Translated by Celeste D. Mann)

Vozes-Mulheres

A voz de minha bisavó ecoou
crianca
nos porões do navio
Ecoou lamentos
de uma infância perdida.

A voz de minha avó
ecoou obediência
aos brancos-donos de tudo.

A voz de minha mãe
ecoou baixinho revolta
no fundo das cozinhas alheias
debaixo das trouxas
roupagens sujas dos brancos
pelo caminho empoeirado
rumo à favela.

A minha voz ainda
ecoa versos perplexos
com rimas de sangue
    e
    fome

A voz de minha filha
recolhe todas as nossas vozes
recolhe em si
as vozes mudas caladas
engasgadas nas gargantas.

A voz de minha filha
recolhe em si
a fala e o ato.
O ontem – o hoje – o agora.
Na voz de minha filha
se fará ouvir a ressonância
o eco da vida-liberdade.

Women's-Voices

My great-grandmother's voice echoed
child
in the ship's hold
Echoed laments
of a lost youth.

My grandmother's voice
echoed obedience
to the white omnipotent 'massas'

My mother's voice
echoed soft revolt
in the back of strange kitchens
underneath the bundles
dirty white men's clothes
by the dusty road
that leads to the favela.

Yet my voice
echoes perplexed verses
with rhymes of blood
    and
    hunger

My daughter's voice
preserves all our voices
preserves itself
the mute quiet voices
caught in our throats

My daughter's voice
preserves itself
In speech and in acts.
Yesterday – today – now
In my daughter's voice
one can hear the resonance
the echo of life-freedom.

(Translated by Celeste D. Mann)

ROSELI DA CRUZ NASCIMENTO

Engulo	**I Swallow**

Engulo o engôdo
fático, fálico
o verso indigente
soldando sonhos
engedrando letargia

I swallow the bait
factual, phallic
the impoverished verse
welding dreams
engendering lethargy

Redizê-lo em sensatas
Emoções
metáforas do gênio
transfunde sílabas
eugenia para a reincarnavalização.

To say it again touching
Emotions
ingenious metaphors
spreads syllables
myrtle for reincarnivalization.

(Translated by Celeste D. Mann)

Deglutição	**Ingestion**

ávida
consumação
de letras
nos papéis embruxados
INÉDITA e patética
deglutição
sem convérsão
convulsão

avid
consummation
of letters
on the rolled-up papers
UNPUBLISHED and pathetic
ingestion
without conversion
convulsion

(Translated by Celeste D. Mann)

LIA VIEIRA

Auto-biografia	**Auto-biography**
Nasci grande	I was born adult
nasci escrevendo	I was born writing
Já Negra bela	Already a beautiful black woman
Já Mulher.	Already woman
Passei por mãos que me burilaram a forma	I passed through hands which adorned my form
E me conservaram a essência.	And conserved my essence
Trilhei caminhos	I tread paths
Virei mundos	I turned worlds
Busquei céus	I searched for heavens
Construí vidas	I built lives.
Cantei cantos	I sung songs
Chorei desencantos	I cried disillusions
Edifiquei sonhos	I constructed dreams
Fiz revoltas	I led revolts
Pratiquei vida.	I really lived.
Ousei, questionei, debati	I dared, I questioned, I debated
Encontrei na escrita	I found in writing
A forma, força, feliz	Form, power, happiness
E nela sobrevivi.	And within it I survived.

(Translated by Celeste D. Mann)

Mãe Negra

Mãe Negra
Tu tens que ser bamba,
tu és Baobá.
Não nascestes para a servidão.
Te diluíram na história
e conceber fostes
nem sempre por opção
nem sempre em 'família'
mas na dura realidade,
oprimida, resistente – Mãe.
Nunca serás chamada rainha
muito menos representarás
perfil para comerciais.
Em tua trajetória e projeto legítimo;
o triunfo de nossa alforria
que se perpetua em tua maternidade.

Black Mother

Black Mother
You must be chief
you are the Baobab
You weren't born for servitude
History diluted you
and you were conceived
not always by choice
not always one of the 'family'
but in the harsh reality,
oppressed, resistant – Mother.
You will never be called 'queen'
even less likely to
be plastered on billboards
In your path
the triumph of our liberation
is a legitimate project
perpetuated by your maternity.

(Translated by Celeste D. Mann)

Fiz-me Poeta

Fiz-me poeta
por exigência da vida, das emoções, dos ideais, da raça.
Fiz-me poeta
sabendo que nem só 'se finge a dor que deveras sente'[1]
e crendo que através da poesia posso exprimir
a arte do cotidiano, vivida em cada poema marginal.

Fêmea/Mulher

Às vezes meu coração fala
minhas mãos, estas-estão sempre
traduzindo meu pensar
Meus olhos têm imãs
mas poucos, só poucos conseguem percebê-los
Minhas pernas se expressam pelo movimento
querendo da mesma forma que os pés
impedir que os detenham em seu percurso,
passando veladamente a cabeça
O ato da ação
refletidos
em palavras,
gestos,
na própria vibração
Todo meu Eu corporificado...
centralizando no umbigo
a Fêmea/Mulher em constante vigília

1. Perhaps a reference to 'Autopsicografia' by Fernando Pessoa. See Fernando Pessoa, *Sixty Portuguese Poems* (Cardiff: University of Wales Press, 1971) pp. 24–27 for the original poem and translation.

I Became a Poet

I became a poet
because life, emotions, ideas and my people
demanded it
I became a poet
knowing that one can't just 'feign the pain that one really feels'
and believing that I could express myself in poetry
the day-by-day art
alive in each marginal poem.

(Translated by Celeste D. Mann)

Female/Woman

Sometimes my heart speaks
my hands, they are always
translating my thoughts
My eyes contain magnets
but few, only few are able
to perceive them
My legs express themselves
through movement
wanting, just as the feet,
to not be
detained on their course
covertly passing to the head
the act of action
reflected in words,
gestures,
in vibration itself
All my I incarnate
converging at the navel
the Female/Woman in constant vigil

(Translated by Celeste D. Mann)

SHEILA MYSOREKAR

Black Rage

I've known this
since I know Germany
since being a child
known always
the bitter taste
of being treated as an idiot, again
once again not having been taken seriously.
On my cheek still burns a mark
of all the fingers that wiped through my face:
'Is this color real?'
For years
only words as weapons, for defense.

Then a new feeling
at the beginning uneasiness
the wind got colder
and blew straight in your face.
At the beginning news of individual attacks
more graffiti on the walls.
After reading the newspaper
I crinkled the pages into a ball
but in my head
the headlines
were burnt in already.
The fear grew
as life changed:
be ready for defense
buy weapons
to banish this feeling from your throat
that's squeezed up tight from all the screams
which never leave.

A new everyday life
life in the new Great Germany
Somebody spit in my face
I wiped the muck away with my sleeve
and fear was joined
by cold hate.

Now instead of cold
the fire:
fire of bombs
gun fire
little flames that run along a petrol track
to the drums
to the explosion.

But I won't wait
until they come to get us
until our bones burn to ashes
not this time!
Before my face suffers burns
I'll lay fire myself.
Times have changed:
It's the Black rage
that catches fire

It's Nation Time

Chicago Angola Tamil Eelam
fine threads of gold and blood
but now
   now is the time
too long
   we have been waiting
we are everywhere
   just turn around
In the metro in Paris in Marseille in Lille
dark lips twisted rings
a sidelong glance
The same kind of understanding in the supermarket of
Leicester Liverpool Notting Hill
kinky hair with glittering gel
slow smile and hands slapping
there we are we are here
what's the time
rumba in Dresden
in the crucible of the Ruhr
spicy sauces are being mixed
Black voices in Berlin and Koln
   ... and clenched fists

what's the time
   what time
what's the time
   now
beat the drum
   dance
   dance the nation dance
It's NATION TIME!
We are many
and now
   now is the time
   now the time
has come

(Translated from German by the author)

ISHA McKENZIE-MAVINGA

Identity Parade

Speaking of Yellows, Reds, and Greens
and in betweens
of the revolutionary mixing of color
Greys
Browns
Sepias
half Black half White begonias
Half
which half on which side
which half claims the birthright
Mulatto on Africa
Mulatto on Europa
of the revolutionary mixing of color

The dark side
the light side
the Europe Africa divide
Coconut and caramel
pure Whity white and Black as night

Speaking of color matching
shading and tinting
sperm squirting color flirting
shapes that entwine
no elusions straight down the line

Purity purity White
Purity purity Black

Speaking of Yellows Reds and Greens
and in betweens
of the revolutionary mixing of color
Greys
Browns
Sepias
half Black half White begonias

Fair skinned picknee baby
Quadroon mystery
nice nice hair
bad beautiful
reproduction of sin

Speaking of the dread of night
the dread of light
the dread of procreating
Black and White
Africa and Europa
India and Europa
Worse still Africa and India

Speaking of color matching
shading and tinting
sperm squirting color flirting
shapes that entwine
no elusions straight down the line

Purity purity White
Purity purity Black

Dont look Black
Dont look White
Cant look White
Cant look Black
Cant look back
Dark in light skin
Light in dark skin
Whose kin?

The kin of day and night
The kin of night and day
The kin that's here to stay

Abandoned

Dark girls
borrowed from our parents
with borrowed clothes
belonging to everyone
and no one

Dark, borrowed
parentless
torn hair combed
with steel teeth
groomed by no one
and everyone

colored by a world
of crying babies
searching for our parents

Dark women
sisterless children
found in our birth giving
bedmaking, husbanding

Dark sisters
mothered by time
and season

Mixed Marriage Collusion

My father

would you have loved her
had you been
striving with the ultimate force
of your Anti-imperialism

If you had resurrected
the rights of inheritance
of slavery
and thrown open
the gates closed behind
emancipation

would you have exposed her
as a perpetrator

My Mother

Would you still love him
had you been
charged with your part
as an   accomplice to plunder

If you had
experienced the turmoil
of facing a stage beyond
the gates closed in front
of his liberation

would you have exposed
your true association

Harmony with slavery
Harmony with destruction
Would there be any reconciliation.

Time

The week begins as it ends
rushing into the carriages
ferrying us to the day

The ark is familiar
We enter two by two
Its purpose and route
never change

The soul
is fading from our eyes
we have lost sight of things

Human excreta
is blown
out of the sky

The statue
does not look like
Nelson Mandela

It frowns through
white pigeon shit.

The week ends as it begins

Identity

I search for my identity
in this deep, deep
sea

I look for answers
I find questions
is this me
is this me

The echo resounds
my jumbled waves
murky with mortality

I search for mother
Pale queen
herstory in me

I search for father
Ebony king
History in me

My hair is Afro curly
My skin is brown

I eat rice and peas
I eat white history

The wounds of hatred
churn within
this translucent gulf
drowning my story

I search for black father
white mother country

In this deep, deep
bottomless confusion

JOEL HAYNES

Mamie Never Cried

You who have scrubbed, *Far* too many
White Woman's Floors
You who have cleaned too many
White Man's shit
With your teeth clenched tight, and jaws set,
you took your pay, knowing it would not be
enough to feed your five children
So ... you cussed when you came home

Mamie
you are the reason for my survival
you are the reason why I lived so long.
you have given me the gift.
It is a gift that is used every morning and
night
by young girls, daughters and mothers

Before you went back,
cleaning Shit and Floors, you used the gift for your survival
I watched you from the corner of my bedroom
door,
hoping you would snatch me from my invisible
world,
rendering me visible
and
full of your mother's tongue
But you had your Black Women's work to do,
and ... So did I.

AND STILL YOU NEVER CRIED A TEAR
when Con-Ed came to smother us in darkness
making us aware of our invisibility
when the boiler broke down and
you had to put your tired hands into a
sooted bag of coals ...

knowing ... burning blisters would appear.

You understood that crying was a privilege,
        you could not afford. It cost too much.
        So ... you broke pieces of wood over your knee,
        stuffed newspapers and old clothing inside the
        already broken boiler and poured
Kerosene, giving warmth to your five
        hungry children

OUR SURVIVAL WAS AT STAKE ... AND SO YOU NEVER CRIED
No one helped carry you up fourteen flights of stairs,
        when you slipped, breaking your hip in two
places,
        on your way to work as a Nurses Aid
        but, really as a maid.

Mamie ...
        only the isolated darkness within my bedroom,
        knew of my silent screams

AND STILL ...
When you knew, all the protection,
all the silent conversations
    (only for adults)
didn't save your daughter from her ruined innocence,
    from a virginity broken too soon,
you flew into a hot ball of rage, knowing you could not
risk the chance of becoming 'soft' with emotion
you held onto the gift

Handed down from generation, onto generations
    and lashed out, at the violence, inflicted
by an all too common weapon of brutality.

Mamie ... you knew
all your careful manipulations, to form
with all your brown mother's hands
a blossoming daughter,
full of orange mixed with yellow laughter ...
    were in vain.

you watched your flower turns into wild dandelions,
>   lost among the thorns.
>   crushed, trampled, underneath the earth's womb,
>>   in silence.

Huddled in my dark corner, I waited for my
withdrawal symptoms to fade
>   Like an addict I wanted to die
Soiled panties,
>   Blood, seeping, slowly out of my childhood
>   my life depended on the lessons and gifts

So, I learned
>   Never to speak of the fire that ran hot through
my veins
>   Never speak of the quick, sharp, pain that runs
>   like electric shock,
>>   with remembrance
through my Child-like,
>   Woman, Now
>>   Womb
>>>   exploding into my brain.

I've learned

>   Never speak of the times when you actually, *Knew*
>   I was crazy, not wanting to believe in my reality,
>   wanting only to commit myself
>>   to be safe
>   hidden among the other dandelions

Mamie ... you never cried
>   for my lost spirit,
never cried ... for the forgotten child,
>   your yellow blossom ... Who held the stars in your eyes

So with my lowered eyelids, I lived my life silently
>   hoping no one would notice me in my world
>>   and ... I resumed the work given to all young black
girls
>>   who never made it over the rainbow

AND SO ... I NEVER CRIED
  For that lost child among the torn
I never cried for the soul ...
   searching for her forgotten home
forgotten through her nightmares
   through her years of blood and pain,

AND SO ...
    After setting the plates for you, Mamie, and you
'Mista'
   INVADER
    VIOLATOR
     ABUSER
      RAPIST,

MISTA ... since I was told to give respect to
 all my elders and parents, no matter their faults
Mamie ... you spared me not a glance
 knowing I would be at your side
 adopting new skills,
 of how to survive in a world,
 so full of dangerous
 weapons

JACQUELINE BRICE-FINCH

Rite

Soul Mate is what I felt
When we talked
Kinetic energy crackled as we
Sequed into each other's life
Instant joy hearing the bass of you
Combining intellect with interest
Multivalent and imploding
  The physicality of you awe fully
Comforting and intense

Passages II

Searching for a distillation of emotions new
A filter for experiences old
Sifting, shifting through ideas confusing
Impulsively voicing a contradiction, a truth
Paradoxical in the making
Awash with tension uncontrollable

Day/night time jabs of sleep
Punctuating the subconscious defenses
The thin scabs, scars of heartache, rupture

Surcease on the horizon a rainbow of friendship.

One Evening

A sweet caring smile peaks,
    Under the weathered cap
        As he sits expectantly happy.

The music undulates – a joyful mood mix.
    We meander allegro toward the lightness
        Of a strong, sustaining bond.

Perspectives

Words so carefully spoken,
        so softly voicing emotion new.
Restraint, caution, a slip into
        the forbidden zone of possibility/probability
Action on hold until the pattern
        of honesty is,
                until the fantasy of freedom becomes a reality.

ROSEMARI MEALY

Patterns

Here, my mind touches the stillness which speaks silently to me/
caressing my womanspirit
and touching my soul
with a delicate kiss, planted
there, by an invisible design of the forever
-unknown which during these
days seem to be tracking my destiny.
In this place I write poems about love
and feeling and spirit
and dreams and love things,
only to retrench in flight
every now and then to another part
of yesterday's terror – separated from tomorrow's
anticipation,
where people fight with the police on the street and in crowded
subways, men rape
WOMEN –
Here I come to the temporary reality of telling myself
that I don't have to
play darting eyes with strangers because they have tasted
the real meaning
of freedom – they know what it is like to walk the streets,
sing songs, run in
the wind, build real castles to the sky, transforming an
entire society into
gardens where Mariposas grow and their fragrance becomes
the perfume's
struggle.

A Natural Guide to Serenity

In the midst of eternal greens on one side of a
space/separated from the
mountain terrain
Palm trees stretch out their beauty like a lover's arm –
Ceibas clump in natural file, whose outstretched
branches are a haven to
mortals escaping the fire of lightning bolts. Even this
sacred tree gives the
horizon that feeling of time immortal.
The red dirt of this land
with its natural hue
becomes another reminder to
the sacred spirit where the Siboney
are encased in burial grounds long
lost to the eye.
How may I touch the butterfly of life
who perches so gently upon the
delicate branches in the lemon groves,
symbolic of tomorrow's children who
will ride these roads
totally free
from the threat of a cowardly mosquito
known all over the world as imperialism.
Tomorrow's sunshine breathes life
into the dancer's spirit. Her leaps cascade
across the shadows like the windmills who still draw
earth's waters
alongside the streams which flow into the veins of banana
plants, both
nurtured by an unseen source.
I saw birds fly over lakes which have been caressed in the
spaces created by
organized time – while the boheos of yesterday are there to
remind one of a
distant past, when sunshine only breathed life into the
dreams of the poor.

AMELIA BLOSSOM PEGRAM

Declaration

F
R
E
E
D
O
M
three
hundred
fifty
unfranchised
years
long coming
to sardined townships
where children treasure-hunt
in dungheaps
grandmothers patch peopled pants
slow coming
to crowded
sacrificed for
chalk and talk classrooms
never came to gone generations
in poverty
beaten down to menial jobs
cupped hands received
wages from sneering pockets
painfully coming
through splintered dreams
of humanity
warrior red sunsets
F R E E D O M
should be big.

Cityscape

Children of our streets
unfamilied
from society
broken
pieces drifting through the day
surviving
on hand-outs or take-outs
from have-it pockets
Children of our cities
mazing
with the can't-be-scared
hip-hop swagger
through the you're-on-your-own
we-don't-give-a-damn
rejection
laid out in somebody's civilized plan
Children forgotten
not resting
on high oak limbs
after care-free chases across green
fields
not lullabied
cradled in warm mothers arms
Children
discarded
on day-warmed sidewalks
huddling sleep
under tattered cover-ups

For Johannesburg

Quiero

I want to stretch my body
on your rolling undulations
Inhale your smells
fresh pine, heather
Feel your breath on my face
bare arms, legs
Let your substance drip
through my fingers
I long to be with you
in the Springtime
when Table Mountain sports
fresh green grass
and daisies white, yellow
The sea wafts
salty damp warmth
fanning me
as I burrow my body
comfortably into your
contours
Let your rich earth
fall through my fingers
squish between my toes
I yearn to be home.

OPAL PALMER ADISA

The Word

in the beginning
was the word
the word
the word
it comes up
from my bowels
the word
the word
laced in pasteurized
blending of all
i have ingested
the word
the word
it comes up
these words
slide from my throat
after i receive
a thump in my back
the word
in the beginning
was the word
from the navel
of my center
the word
trapped
on the roof of my mouth
between the crevices of my teeth
the word
the word
the word
lost
knocking at mouths
twisted from years of mis-stories
the word
shaping meaning
back into
the vowels/consonants
the word

before it was spoken
the word
that i try
to speak
the word that
cries
the word
that destroys
like hurricane gilbert
that leveled my home
the word

in the beginning
was the word
i try to find it
render it free
like this freedom
i've been seeking
the word
that lost its voice
in the cargo of a ship
perfumed in feces
and the confused
state of a people
tricked/lied to
deceived by greed
and shiny glass
the word
that now stutters/stammers
the word
the word
in the beginning
before
woman and man
laid together
before the race
was set in motion
the word was god

and ruled the land
the word was the dream
and made day follow night
the word was love
and was seen
in the blue-tipped wings
of the jay

the word
the word
in the beginning
before
we discovered
duplicity/to take words
like spit
to tease/trap/defile
my word was the order
and in the order
was the word
the word
the word

the word
that sings
i mean to shape
back its form
find the house in which
it once lived
give back the truth
listen to what
i know i must say

from the beginning
was the word
and the word was me
the word echoes
the notes of the
talking drum
echoes the love
of beating hearts

echoes the rhythm
of dancing feet
the beginning
all i had was
what i gave
i gave my word
and it was understood

the word
was respected
the word
was the light
the word
the word
now i stumble
my fingers
grope dirt
trying to replant
the soil in which
the word has taken refuge
the word
crying beside
my dead child
in the homelands
of south africa
the word
that is sown
in the moving lips
of these homeless street walkers
those beggars of selfhood
the word
that my not yet
four year old
uses to spur me/taunt me
demand of me

the word
that has lost its feet
and whose leathery soles
no longer leave foot prints

the word
that those kidnapped
children all over
the world voice
this is my name
where is my mommy
why are these people
keeping me from my mommy

the word
that those silent parents
with pregnant eyes
weave in their heads
questioning their negligence
reaching for hands that
do not respond
voices that do not
cry out in the night
seeking comfort

the word
that politicians use
to make mockery
of the plunder
the power mania

in the beginning
was the word
the word
the word
that i keep seeking
the word
still in my navel
the word
nurtured in my menses
the word
that lives always
at the edge of my
finger prints
the word
that i still must find
to speak
the word
the word
the word

My Work Speaks to
Those Other Women

i am
wo/man
i woo, i walk, i wail, i talk

my poetry
are legs and breasts
thighs and swinging behinds;
the poems cry of neglect,
laugh with the sun,
dance under the blazing flamboyant trees
raise dust with bare feet
and use the hem of dresses to wipe sweat,
wipe odor from brows and sweating
underarms

these poems are women
reeking of the blood
that drips monthly
that some women put in their food
to keep what's theirs theirs
singing of troubles locked in boxes
that females are always left to guard

these poems are about women
who have always worked
in soil, at river banks
in beds, in kitchens, on street corners
working without writing down their poems
working so that others can study and
write about them
working because they must

these poems are of the Shes
she is there
for the supporting,
for the unplugged microphones,
to produce;
she is there
and gives birth of new poems
some stored in the after-birth
some postponed/denied by the pill,
the bush tea,
the condom, the withdrawal, the abortion;
theses are women's poems
defined by their roundness,
their backs tall and hard,
their lips pulled tight
to quiet screams

these are female poems
wet with vaginal juice
and the loving eyes
that women keep for each other

in each shape of a leaf
in every song of the moon
with the rising waters
each is a poem
feminine define
these poems are herstory

Women Weaving Stories

their diasporic ripples
stretch
intertwine
with the ocean weeds

they travel
sculptured goddesses
rejecting anguish
their arms
shut out confusion
soft
caressing
the space
where rape knew
no limits

they are not
amazons

godmothers
we call them

each birth pain
pushes
releases
push
release

their tongues
might well
be amputated
for their stories
have no words

just the sounds
their bodies
make
as they work
wherever they work
doing whatever work
needs to be done.

GINA AMARO

Ave Maria

Spirits dance   Bathed within sanctums   Chambers
SoulsOur Souls Flying Tangling   Spiraling Outward
Powerful   possession of Rebellion

Our External Shells Sweating   Panting to Drums that
Scream Singing Songs   Bitter Sweet Sweat Sweetness.
Sensual Cantations of Struggle   Journeys   Stories Mine
Yours Her Story of Standing Unified Free

Free from Pain   Struggle   Break from grappling
Hooks   Hands white from above which Scratch with rusty
Nails   Tear Her bloody flesh which has been Shed for Us

Beautiful Petals formed richly red Profusion lick away the
shackles from Her Body   Freeing Her Spirit once again.
The red Essence leaks from Our Hands   Our tool of caress
that soothe longing Dead Roses baptized for Rebellious
Realm

Here pure Black swells transcending Here Hear Drum;
Never an ephemeral Heart Beat Singing Beating Free Freedom
Within our Heart Dancing with cause for the religion of the
Movement   Rounding the tree of burning Bush   We Womyn of
Culture shake eat drink Swallow its Fruit   Feeding our Soul

Richly Raped Roots grown Strong Drum with no skin I have
shed Upon You   The Skin falls I gain my boundaries   We
Rest in pain   Strength

Tic Toc Tic Lock   Confined to Pure Clarity
of Vibrant Shallow Seclusion Crave Fight Silence
Black Bare feet will Never tire For Screaming
Drums continue to play.

Notes on Contributors

Shanta Acharya lives and works in London. Her poems have been published in India, where she grew up, and she was one of 18 poets published in the anthology *Contemporary Indian Poetry* (Ohio University Press, 1990) and in the *Journal of South Asian Literature*. In the UK, her work has been published in *ArtRage, Feminist Art News, Delhi London Poetry Quarterly, Spokes Poetry Magazine*, and *Acumen* and *Wasafiri* (forthcoming). She has a D Phil in English from Oxford University (1983) and has been a visiting scholar at Harvard University.

Catherine Obianuju Acholonu was born in Orlu, Imo State, Nigeria, in 1951. She is on the faculty of Alvan Ikoku College of Education in Owerri. She has written poems, plays, scholarly articles and some children's literature in English and Igbo. She is the editor of *AFA. Journal of Creative Writing*. She has produced a poetic drama, *Trial of the Beautiful Ones* (1984), which incorporates dance, ritual and spectacle and is based on the Igbo *ogbanje* myth. Catherine Obianuju Acholonu has also researched and published *The Igbo Roots of Olaudah Equiano*, in which she uses oral history, linguistic and other research to trace the family of Equiano. She is working on a novel. The story, 'Mother was a Great Man,' developed from her grandmother's life.

Opal Palmer Adisa is a Jamaican-born poet, short-story writer, storyteller and playwright. She has lived in California since the end of 1978. She has a collaborative poetry collection, *traveling women*, with San Francisco-born poet Devorah Major (1989). Her other published works are *Bake-Face and Other Guava Stories* (1986); *Pina, the Many-Eyed Fruit* (1985); *Tamarind and Mango Woman* (1992). Her poetry has appeared in numerous journals and books including *Making Face, Making Soul*, ed. Gloria Anzaldua (1990); *Adam of Ife: Black Women in Praise of Black Men*, ed. Naomi Long Madgett (1992); *Erotique Noire: Black Erotica*, ed. Miriam da Costa-Willis et al. (1992); *Voice Print*, ed. Stewart Brown, Mervyn Morris and Gordon Rohlehr (1989); *Caribbean Poetry Now*, ed. Stewart Brown (1984); *Perspective on a Grafted Tree*, ed. Patricia Irwin Johnston (1983);*Caribbean Woman*, ed. Lucille Mathurin-Mair (1977); *Caribbean Women Writers*, ed. Selwyn Cudjoe (1990). Journals in which her work has appeared include *The Black Scholar, Nimrod, New England Review and Bread Loaf Quarterly, Day Tonight/Night Today, Sub Rosa, State of Peace: The Women Speak*.

Miriam Aparecida Alves

Born 6 November 1952 in São Paulo, Miriam Alves is employed as a social worker. She has written a variety of works including poetry, short stories, and drama.

Her works include two volumes of poetry, *Momentos de Busca* and *Estrelas no dedo*. She co-authored a play with Arnold Xavier and Cuti (Luis Silva). She has published much of her work in various issues of *Cadernos Negros* (São Paulo). Her work also appears in *Axe. Antologia Contemporanea de Poesia Negra Brasileira* (1982). A theoretical essay on the nature of Afro-Brazilian literature appears in *Reflexoes sobre a literatura afro-brasileira* (1985). She has also contributed to a number of other collections including *Criação Crioula, Nu Elefante Branco*; *Mulheres entre linhas II – concurso de poesia e conto*; *A razao da chama*; *O negro escrito* and *Schwarze poesie/poesia negra* as well as *Encontro de Poetas e Ficcionistas Negros Brasileiros* (1985). A member of the Quilhomboje writing collective, she was prompted to begin asking the question 'Where are my sisters?' and finding answers to that question in her work and in the works of others. To that end, she has edited an anthology of works by Afro-Brazilian women titled *Emfin Nos. Todas Negras Brasileras Contemporaneas*.

Gina Maria Amaro is a Puerto Rican poet and community activist born and raised in New York City. She is a graduate of SUNY-Binghamton University in English literature and rhetoric and a member of the Progressive Alumni Network, National Latina Caucus, Muevete and a founder of the Sistah Project, an international Womyn of Color organization for which she is developing a young women's anthology. She is coordinator of Aspira, of New York's AIDS/HIV Prevention Education program.

Carol A. Beane is an assistant professor of Spanish in the Department of Modern Foreign Languages at Howard University. She has published articles on Afro-Hispanic authors and subjects, translated poetry from the Spanish, and is writing a book on the representation of slavery and freedom in Latin American literature.

Marion Bethel comes from Nassau, the Bahamas, where she still lives and works. Her writing includes poetry, prose, drama and essays. She was awarded a James Michener Fellowship in July 1991 by the Caribbean Writers' Summer Institute of the University of Miami. Her work has appeared in *Junction*, an anthology of Bahamian prose and poetry; *Lignum Vitae*, a journal of the Bahamas Writers' Association; *From the Shallow Seas*, an anthology of Bahamian prose and poetry published by Casa de las Americas of Havana, Cuba, and other periodical publications.

Carole Boyce Davies has research and writing interests in African, Caribbean and African-American women's writing and black feminisms. She has studied and/or lived in Africa, the Caribbean, Afro-America and most recently Brazil. She has a commitment to making accessible and 'spreading the word' as it relates to black women's writing, thought and politics. Besides numerous articles, chapters and essays on black women's writing, she has edited two collections, *Ngambika. Studies of Women in African Literature* (1986) and *Out of the Kumbla. Caribbean Women and Literature* (1990). Her most recent book is *Migrations of the Subject. Black Women, Writing, Theory and Identity* (London, Routledge, 1994). She is working now on building her expression in creative writing.

Jacqueline Brice-Finch is Professor of English at James Madison University. She received her PhD in English from the University of Maryland, College Park. Prior to her present position, Dr Brice-Finch was an assistant professor of English at the St Croix campus of the University of the Virgin Islands. She has lectured on her area of specialization, Caribbean literature, and written articles which have appeared in *Black Books Bulletin, Caribbean Quarterly, Dictionary of Literary Biography, MAWA Review, The Caribbean Writer* and *The Literary Griot*.

Abena P.A. Busia was born in Accra, Ghana, and spent her childhood in Holland, Mexico and Oxford, England. She is an associate professor at Rutgers University. She has a substantial record in publishing critical analysis which appears in a variety of journals such as *Cultural Critique* and in collections such as *Ngambika. Studies of Women in African Literature* ed. Carole Boyce Davies and Adams Graves (1986); *Out of the Kumbla. Caribbean Women and Literature* ed. Carole Boyce Davies and Elaine Savory Fido (1990); and *Changing Our Own Words* ed. Cheryl Wall (1991). Her first collection of poems is *Testimonies of Exile* (1990). Her poetry has appeared in a variety of anthologies and collections such as *Daughters of Africa* (1992). She recently co-edited (with Stanlie James) *Theorizing Black Feminisms* (1993).

Luz Argentina Chiriboga of Esmeraldas and Quito, Ecuador, has been a participant in many conferences on black culture and black women held in Latin America, and is the author of two novels, *Bajo la piel de los tambores / Under the Skin of the Drums* (1992), English translation by Dr Mary Harris (forthcoming), and *Aguas turbulentas* (1994). Selections from the former appear in the anthology *Erotique Noire* (1992); her own collection of erotic poetry, *La contraportada del deseo / The Backpage of Desire* was published in 1992. Her prize-winning short stories and articles have appeared in numerous journals and magazines in Latin America. She is presently at work on another novel.

Maya Chowdhry, a black feminist artist of Asian/Scottish descent, is a writer, film-maker and photographer who works across, through and over these art forms, covering a wide range of experiences, issues and concerns. Her published poetry includes *Putting in the Pickle Where the Jam Should Be* (1989) and the *Climbing Mountains* tape. Her poetry and controversial radio play, *Monsoon*, were selected for the 1991 Young Playwrights Festival, broadcast on BBC Radio 5 in 1992. In 1991 she was awarded a SCC Script Development Fund Loan towards developing a drama, *Broken Promises*. She directed *Running Gay*, a documentary for Channel Four's 1991 'Out' series. Her photographs have been published in *Feminist Art News*, the *Guardian*, in magazines, books and on cards, and appeared in the Viewpoint Gallery Exhibition *None But Ourselves*. She has worked on residencies and workshops in community centres, schools and colleges. She has performed and facilitated writing workshops at festivals and other events from Vancouver to Edinburgh with Jean 'Binta' Breeze and Essex Hemphill.

Atsango Chesoni. 'I was born and raised in the republic of Kenya. Most of my writing is in the form of poetry and short stories, though I would like to explore other genres such as the novel and the essay. I write for the daughter I may never have.'

Afua Cooper is one of Toronto's most consistent and perspicacious young poets, known for her lively and sensitive readings. Afua is of African-Jamaican origin and her first book of poetry, *Breaking Chains*, was published in 1983. *The Red Caterpillar on College Street* was her first book of children's poetry and *Memories Have Tongue* (1992) is her third poetry collection. She is now in the process of completing *Greengage Days*, a collection of short stories, as well as a series of children's stories, entitled *Fatima's Nightgown*. Afua has had her poetic works published in several anthologies in Britain, the United States, Canada and the Caribbean. She also recorded her dub poetry on the album *Womantalk* (Heartbeat Records, 1984) and on the cassettes *Poetry is Not a Luxury* (Maya, 1985) and *Your Silence Will Not Protect You* (Maya, 1986). Her solo cassette, *Sunshine*, appeared in 1989. An avid student of African people's history, she is enrolled in the PhD program in history at the University of Toronto. Poems in this collection are from *Memories Have Tongue*.

Irène Assiba d'Almeida comes from the Republic of Benin in West Africa. She spent most of her childhood in Dakar, Senegal, where she was born. She studied in France where she obtained a Licence d'Anglais from the University of Amiens, in Nigeria where she received a Master of Philosophy degree from the University of Ibadan, and in the USA where she received a PhD from Emory University. An associate professor of French and Francophone African Literature at the University of Arizona, Tuscon, her book *Francophone African Women Writers: Destroying the Emptiness of Silence* is published by the University of Florida Press, 1994. She is also involved in creative writing, particularly poetry. She has written a few poems in English but writes primarily in French. At present she is working on a 'lighthearted' autobiography.

Sônia Fátima da Conceição was born in 1951 in Araraquara, daughter of Jovelina Pereira da Conceição and Francisco Caetano da Conceição. She has a degree in social sciences and is a member of the Conselho de Participação e Desenvolvimento da Comunidade Negra. Her works are included in the following anthologies: *Cadernos Negros* (1979, 1981, 1983, 1985, 1988–9); *Reflexões sobre a Literatura Afro-brasileira* (1985); and *Marcas, Sonhos e Raízes* (1991). Her work has recently been discussed by Carolyn Richardson Durham in 'Sônia Fátima da Conceição's Literature for Social Change' in *Afro-Hispanic Review* (1992).

Daisy Cocco de Filippis is Professor of Spanish in the Foreign Languages department at York College, City University of New York. She has published many articles and translated the works of Dominican women writers. Her most recent publications include *Sin otro profeta que su canto: antologia de poesia escrita por dominicans* (1988), *Combatidas, combaticas y combatientes: Narradoras dominicanas* (1992) and *Stories from Washington Heights* (1994).

Nawal el-Saadawi was born in the village of Kafr Tahia on 27 October 1931, the eldest daughter in a family which was later to be composed of nine brothers and sisters. She worked her way through the successive stages of primary and secondary education, then through medical college from which she graduated with distinction in 1954, despite difficult economic circumstances. After graduation she worked as a physician in the rural area to which her family belonged. Deeply moved by the misery and suffering of village people, especially women, she started expressing what she felt through writing short stories and, later, novels. She quickly established herself as a talented writer and a rebel against the bureaucratic practices of the health system. Her activities made life difficult and precarious, especially as her rebellion against the system and its values vibrated in all her writings, but it is through her work as a fiction writer and later through her studies of women in the Arab world that she became the most widely read writer in Arabic-speaking countries. She first emerged on the international scene with her now famous book *The Hidden Face of Eve in the Arab World* (English version, 1980). Since then this book and twelve others have been published in thirteen languages all over the world. In 1972 she was fired from her job as director of public health because of her outspoken book *Women and Sex* and the publication of a magazine called *Health* which addressed itself to the socio-economic, psychological and sexual aspects of health of a vast readership composed mainly of youth. For over ten years her books were banned from Egypt and a number of Arab countries. In 1981 she was imprisoned for three months because of her views. Undaunted by her short but tough prison experiences she came out with a new book written on scraps of smuggled toilet paper and entitled *Memoirs of the Women's Prison*. She also came out with the firm resolve that women should be organized and in 1982 founded the Arab Women's Solidarity Association. Still active in community organizing in her village and other communities, she is also a founding member of the Arab Organization for Human Rights (Tunis, 1983).

Conceição Evaristo (Maria da Conceição Evaristo de Brito) was born 29 November 1946 in Belo Horizonte, Minas Gerais. She has been writing ever since she was a child, and at eleven won a school literary prize for an essay. She moved to Rio de Janeiro in 1973 where she graduated in Luso-Brazilian literature and then did graduate work in Brazilian literature at the Federal University (UFRJ). Presently she is working on her Master's degree in comparative literature. She achieved Honorable Mention in the First Literary Contest (Primeiro Concurso Literário da Faculdade de Letras da UFRJ) of the Department of Letters at UFRJ in 1990 with her stories 'Di Lixão' and 'Maria.' Her published works are included in the *Cadernos Negros* (1990 and 1991).

Yanick François was born in the capital city of Haiti in 1956. In 1964 she and her siblings migrated to the USA. She entered college at the University of New York, Center at Binghamton in 1982 after which she divorced her husband of twelve years and proceeded to struggle through college as a single mother. Yanick François has been published in *Black Women's Writing: Crossing the Boundaries* (1989) and numerous other publications.

Gloria Wade Gayles is a native of Memphis, Tennessee. She earned a BA at LeMoyne College, MA at Boston University and her PhD at Emory University. She is the recipient of several grants and fellowships, among them the Woodrow Wilson and the Mellon. Her publications include *No Crystal Stair. Race and Sex in Black Women's Novels, 1946–1976* (1983); *Annointed to Fly* (1991); 'The Search for Balance in the Fiction of Alice Walker,' in *Southern Women Writers* (1990); and essays and poetry in *Sturdy Black Bridges, The Black Woman* and *Double Stitch*, among others. Her poetry has appeared in *Essence, First World, The Black Scholar* and *Catalyst*. She is an associate professor of English and women's studies at Spelman College.

Beryl Gilroy was born in Berbice, Guyana, and migrated to England in the 1950s. A teacher for over forty years, her experiences are documented in *Black Teacher* (1976). She has written poetry (*Echoes and Voices*), short stories, professional essays, reflections and novels such as *Frangipani House* (1986), *Boy Sandwich* (1989) which won the GLC Black Literature Prize, and *Stedman and Joanna* (1991). She was recently awarded the Guyana Medal. Beryl Gilroy has written over fourteen children's story books in the Nippers reading series, London.

Jewelle L. Gomez is the author of two collections of poetry, a novel, *The Gilda Stories*, and most recently a collection of essays, *Forty-Three Septembers*. She is a former director of the Literature Program at the New York State Council on the Arts, and currently lives in San Francisco.

Joel Haynes was born in Trinidad and Tobago in 1969. A graduate of Binghamton University, she is currently in graduate school for a Master's degree in African studies. 'I hope to continue the work that our ancestors have left for us as women of color struggling to survive within this colonial society. It has become imperative for us as black women to begin the process of closing the gaps that have kept us separated for so long. We must continue struggling for our liberation as women, black women. We must link up our fight for freedom for all oppressed people all over the world. That is the only way we can be truly free as a people, as black women.'

Fawzziya Abu Khalid was born in 1957 in Riyadh, Saudi Arabia. She has an MA in sociology from King Saudi University, Riyadh and has worked as a lecturer in the university's sociology department. She has published two books of poetry in Beirut (1974 and 1984). Some poems have appeared in *Women of the Fertile Crescent* ed. Kamal Boulatta and *The Literature of Modern Arabia* ed. Salma Khadra Al Jayyusi (1988). She has presented papers, such as 'The Participation of Women in Modern Arabic Literature,' at professional conferences. 'It's a warm and supportive feeling to know poetry from the heart of the desert is included in your collection. Your efforts in *Moving Beyond Boundaries* will be *(inshallah)* appreciated all over the world.'

Patricia McFadden is an African feminist, who has lived in Senegal and East Africa, who writes on gender issues; with special interest in Southern Africa. Currently she is working on the reclamation of 'herstory' in the African feminist experience, and on nationalism and the political marginalization of African women in post-independence societies on the continent. She now works for SAPES Trust, Zimbabwe as coordinator of the Gender Programme.

Isha McKenzie-Mavinga is a black British woman of Afro-Caribbean and Euro-Jewish descent, raised in care. A mother and grandmother, she works as a mental and spiritual health therapist. Isha is the co-author of *In Search of Mr McKenzie* (Woman's Press, 1991). Her work has been published in *Through the Break* (1986), *Charting the Journey* (Sheba, 1988), *Sojourner* (Methuen, 1988) and *Words of Nka Iban*, Afrikan Women Writers Group (London, 1993).

Rosemari Mealy is a freelance writer and radio host over WBAI Pacifica Network in New York. She is the author of *Lift These Shadows* (1976) and *Fidel and Malcolm – Memories of A Meeting*, (1993). A labor historian, Rosemari also teaches black literature and writing at SUNY-Empire State Corporate College Program.

Nancy Morejón was born in Havana, Cuba, in 1944 where she still resides. Her published works are numerous, including *Mutismos* (1962); *Amor, ciudad atribuida* (1964); *Richard trajo su flauta y otros argumentos* (1967); *Parajes de una epoca* (1979); *Octubre imprescindible* (1982); *Grenada Notebook* (1984), translated by Lisa Davis; *Where the Island Sleeps Like a Wing* (1985), translated by Kathleen Weaver. She has written critical works on Nicolas Guillen and on other aspects of Caribbean culture. Her work has been translated into numerous languages and anthologies and she has worked as a director of Casa de las Americas. Her work has been the subject of theses in the US, the Caribbean and Europe. She has read her poetry in universities across the world.

Sheila Mysorekar was born in 1961 in Dusseldorf, West Germany, of an Indian father and a white German mother. She spent her early childhood in India but went to school in Germany. She has undertaken studies in English language and literature, social anthropology and drama in Cologne, West Germany, and London (MA). She has been active in the Black women's movement in Britain and has worked as a radio journalist (politics/economics) and as an editor and reporter for the *Daily Gleaner* in Kingston, Jamaica. Her work as a freelance journalist in India, Argentina and other Latin American countries has made her aware of the wide communities of women of color. She is active in the Black German movement, ISD (Initiative Schwarze Deutsche), and has one stepdaughter and a new baby daughter, Maya. Her current home base is Buenos Aires.

Roseli da Cruz Nascimento was born in 1957 in São Paulo. She is a social assistant and her works have been published in *Cadernos Negros* (1986) and *Criação crioula, nu elefante branco* (1987).

Sister Netifa is a performance poet, chanter, actress, mother, revolutionary and author of several short stories. Her works have previously been published in the *Arts Revue Journal* of the University of the West Indies, Jamaica. Although she possesses a wealth of written material, Netifa has been selective in the performance of her works. She has read to audiences in Germany, France and in Britain, and has toured with the Network Rapso Riddum Band of Trinidad and Tobago and Jamaica's Mystic Revelation of Rastafari and with her own band, the rootsical-reggae all-women Determined Band. She has worked extensively with the Caribbean Focus programme organized by the Commonwealth Institute. In London, where she runs the Uprising Cultural House, she is perhaps better known for her efforts as a dedicated community worker, concert producer and craftswoman. One of the few women working within the rapso/dub tradition, she has provided supporting harmonies for various distinguished artistes both live and in studio. She is a journalist who has served as a correspondent on one of Trinidad's leading newspapers. She is the founder of the Masimba Connection, a cultural collective based in London, and conducts workshops in natural jewelry. She has two albums, *A Woman Determined* (Masimba, 1988) and *I AM A POEM* (Masimba, 1991). Poems in this collection are from *A Woman Determined*.

Lissette Norman is a jazzy kind of girl from Harlem, NY, born of parents from the Dominican Republic and the British Virgin Islands. She has a BA in English from SUNY-Binghamton and is currently working on a book of poetry and prose entitled *Searching for Drums*.

'Molara Ogundipe-Leslie, a Nigerian professor, writer and poet on the faculty of the University of Ibadan for over a decade, and later head of the Department of English at Ogun State University, Nigeria, has held teaching and visiting positions at major universities in the US, Europe and Africa. A leading scholar in women's studies, African studies and critical theory, her work as a poet has appeared in authoritative anthologies such as *The Penguin Book of Modern Poetry* (1985), *Voices from Twentieth Century Africa* (1988), *New African Writing* (1981), *Voices* (1992) and *Daughters of Africa* (1992). Her books are *Sew the Old Days and Other Poems* (1985) and *Recreating Ourselves: African Women and Critical Transformations* (1994), a selection of her critical writings over the years. She has done a great deal of work in women's organizing in Africa, being in the founding body of AAWORD (Association of African Women in Research and Development) and Women in Nigeria.

Amelia Blossom Pegram has internationally published short stories, poetry, book reviews and critical articles. Some anthologies in which her work appears include short stories in *Somehow We Survive, Unwinding Threads,* and *Raising the Blinds*; poetry in *The Dark Woods I Cross, Breaking the Silence, Say that the River Turns* and *Daughters of Africa*. Her work has also appeared in *Staffrider, The Thinker, Essence, Callaloo, Presence Africaine, Geneve-Afrique,* and *Pacific Quarterly*. Her dramatic work performed includes 'The Dance Goes On', 'Women at the Cross' and 'You've Struck a Rock – Women in Struggle'. Her collections of poetry are *Deliverance* and *Our Sun Will Rise*. She has performed her poetry in Europe, Canada, Ghana, and the US. The performances are presented with percussion accompaniment.

Marlene Nourbese Philip is a poet and writer who lives in Toronto. She has published four books of poetry: *Thorns, Salmon Courage, She Tries Her Tongue; Her Silence Softly Breaks,* and her most recent, *Looking for Livingstone; An Odyssey of Silence,* a poem in prose and poetry. Her first novel, *Harriet's Daughter* (1988), was a finalist in the 1989 Canadian Library Association Prize for Children's Literature; the Max and Greta Abel Award for Multicultural Literature, 1990 and the Toronto Book Awards, 1990. Her manuscript *She Tries Her Tongue* ... was awarded the 1988 Casa de las Americas prize for poetry. In 1990 Marlene Nourbese Philip was made a Guggenheim Fellow in poetry and in 1991 became a MacDowell Fellow. Her short stories, essays, reviews and articles have appeared in magazines and journals in Canada, the UK and the USA and her poetry and prose has been extensively anthologized. Her most recent work, *Frontiers. Essays and Writings in Racism and Culture*, was published in November 1992.

Velma Pollard is a senior lecturer in language education in the Faculty of Education of the University of the West Indies, Mona, Jamaica. Her major research interests are Creole languages of the anglophone Caribbean, the language of Caribbean literature and Caribbean women's writing. Pollard is also involved in creative writing and has published poems and short stories in regional and international journals. She has published two volumes of poetry – *Crown Point and Other Poems* (1988) and *Shame Trees Don't Grow Here* (1992) – and a volume of short fiction, *Considering Woman* (1989). Her novel *Karl*, which won the Casa de las Americas literary award (1992), has been published by Casa as a bilingual (English and Spanish) text. A novel, *Homestretch*, and a collection of short stories (including the novella *Karl*) are due to be published in 1994.

Aida Cartagena Portalatin is the most recognized woman writer in twentieth century Dominican literature. She is the author of *Del sueno al mundo* (poetry, 1944); *Vispera del sueno* and *Llamale verde* (poetry, 1945); *Mi mundo el mar* and *Una mujer esta sola* (poetry, 1956); *La voz desatada* and *La tierra escrita* (poetry, 1961); *Escalera para Electra* (novel, 1969); *Tablero* (short story, 1978); *La tarde en que murio Estefania* (novel, 1982); *Yania tierra* (poetry, 1982); *En la casa del tiempo* (poetry, 1984); *Culturas africanas: rebeldes con causa* (essays, 1985). Widely acknowledged and respected for the quality and militancy of her poetry, Portalatin's better-known works are *Una mujer esta sola*, the first openly feminist poem published in the Dominican Republic, and *La voz desetada* and *La tierra escrita*, poems of angry protest against racial discrimination and exploitation. A retired college professor, Portalatin continued to live in the Dominican Republic and engaged in literary activities until she passed away in June 1994.

Esmeralda Ribeiro was born in October 1958 in São Paulo, of working-class parents. She is a journalist and became a member of Quilombhoje in 1982. Her works have been published in *Cadernos Negros* (1982–91); *Reflexões* (1985); *Criação Crioula, nu elefante branco* (1987); and *Pau de Sebo – coletânea de poesia negra* (1988).

Astrid H. Roemer was born in Paramaribo, Surinam in 1947. She moved to Holland as a young person to study and now lives in The Hague where she makes a living from her writing and as a family therapist. She has written numerous plays for the theater and radio and has been active in creating musical and television programmes that deal with multiracialism in Holland and in the Surinam community in general. Astrid H. Roemer writes essays and columns, and gives lectures on writing courses. She is always on the road, giving readings in Holland and abroad. Her books include *Sasa* (1970) a volume of poetry, and several novels including *Nergens ergens/Nowhere, Somewhere* (1983), *Neem mijn terug, Suriname/Surinam, Take Me Back, Levenslang gedicht* (1985), *Een naam voor de liefde/A Name for Love* (1987) and *Over de Gekte van een vrouw/About a Woman's Madness* (1979).

Sonia Sanchez was born in Alabama. She is a professor and a poet who has produced several noteworthy collections, including *Homecoming* (1969); *We a BaddDDD People* (1970); *Love Poems* (1973); *A Blues Book for Blue Black Magical Women* (1974); *I've Been a Woman* (1978); *Homegirls and Handgrenades* (1984); *Generations* (1986); *Under a Soprano Sky* (1987). She has also written children's books and edited two anthologies. A stunning reader of her own poetry, Sonia Sanchez has a history of activism which originated in the black arts and political movements of the 1960s. She has taught black literature at several universities and is currently a professor at Temple University.

Mayra Santos Febres, born in Carolina, Puerto Rico, in 1966, consistently describes herself as a black Puerto Rican woman. She has a PhD in English from Cornell University and now teaches at the University of Puerto Rico. Poems here are from her collection *Anamu y Manigua* (1991).

Dorothea Smartt is a *zami* writer and performing poet with a passion for black women's literature, 'black British' cultures and 'our ties with our mothers' lands.' She has been most recently anthologized in *Black Women Talk Poetry* eds. D. Choong et al. (1987) and *Intimate Wilderness* ed. J. Barrington (Oregon, 1991) and *What Lesbians Do in Books* eds. C. White and E. Hobby (1991). She was one of the organizers of the Black Women's Café (Creative Space) at Centreprise in London.

Eintou Pearl Springer is an artiste/activist. She is well known as a poet, actress, playwright and storyteller. She has performed and lectured extensively in England and the Caribbean, and has recently concluded a successful lecture/performance tour of some American universities including Cornell, Amherst, Binghamton and Ohio State. She holds an MPhil in information sciences and is librarian in charge of the West Indian Reference Library in Port-of-Spain,

Trinidad. Her publications include *Waiting Game and Theresa* (two short stories 1980); *Out of the Shadows* (1986); *Godchild* (1988); *The Caribbean, Its Lands and Peoples* (1988); *Focussed* (1991). Eintou is the author of one of the first essays on Caribbean women, 'The Caribbean Woman as Writer,' published in *Sturdy Black Bridges* (1979). She has adapted numerous Caribbean novels for stage performance.

Chezia B. Thompson-Cager, a native St Louisian and graduate of Washington University and Carnegie Mellon University, has studied in West Africa and the Caribbean. Her work as a writer and director of research connects the lives of people of African descent throughout the diaspora. A product of the poet-dramatist tradition, her directing work included staging the full text of Jean Toomer's *Cane,* the American premiere of Trinidadian writer Earl Lovelace's *Jestina's Calypso,* and the production of the one-woman show, *An Evening with Rosalind Cash.* She currently lives in Baltimore with her family. She has published poetry and articles in many journals in and out of the US and her collections of poetry include *Jumpin Rope on the Axis* and *Giant Talk: The Presence of Things Unseen.* She is currently a faculty member at the Maryland Institute College of Art and is completing *DRAGON: An Analysis of the works of Earl Lovelace and Black Performance.*

Patricia Turnbull is St Lucian by birth, has lived in Tortola, Virgin Islands, for many years and calls the Caribbean home. She is the winner of the 1991 Cedars Prize for Contemporary Poetry. Her work has been published in literary journals and magazines including *The New Voices, The Caribbean Writer* and *The English Journal.* She is the author of *Boysie and the Genips, Now and Then* and *Let's Take a Dip,* three collections of Virgin Islands stories for young readers. Poems in this collection are from her collection *Rugged Vessels* (1992).

Lia Vieira is a teacher, artist and economist and holds a degree in tourism. Born in 1958, she comes from Rio de Janeiro. She is also a militant member of the Black Movement (Movimento Negro) and the Black Women's Movement (Movimento de Mulheres negroes). She has published poetry in Spanish, French and Italian, in addition to Portuguese. She is the author of *Eu, mulher – mural de poesias* (1990) and her work appears in the following anthologies: *Reflexos – coletánea de novos escritores* (1990); *Mural Ane no.2* (1990); *Vozes mulheres – mural de poesias* (1991) and *Cadernos Negros* (1991).

Storme Webber is an African-American, lesbian poet of Cherokee ancestry. Originally from Seattle, Washington, she has lived and performed in San Francisco and New York City and in the UK for the last three years. Her work as a poet incorporates a striking combination of blues and jazz song, dance, theater, painting and sketching. Her poetry, especially recognized for its sensuality, concerns the personal and political liberation of African people and women and lesbians. She is the author of a self-published collection of poetry and graphics entitled *Diaspora* and a cassette of her poetry/song. Her work has been featured in *Serious Pleasure* and *More Serious Pleasure* (1988 and 1990), and her poems have been anthologized in *The Popular Front of Contemporary Poetry* (1992).

Donna Weir is a third-year Mellon doctoral fellow in the Department of English at the University of California, Berkeley. She is a teacher, performance poet, dramatist, short-story writer, essayist and a budding novelist. She has performed extensively at several colleges and universities and at the Audre Lorde Cele-Conference held in Boston in 1990. Her work has appeared in *Sage: A Black Woman's Scholarly Journal*; *Brownstone*; *The Returning Women's Magazine*; *Nommo*; and *Poder* (Hunter College); *The One You Call Sister*; and *New York Woman's Magazine*. President of the Audre Lorde Women's Poetry Center at Hunter College from 1988 to 1990, Donna thanks the late Audre Lorde, Melinda Goodman, and all the positive women from that collective for supporting and inspiring her work. Lastly, and most importantly, Donna is a down-to-earth, Jamaican sistah and the mother of a fierce and beautiful son, Jedhi.

Index